THE IMPORTANCE OF JAMES BOND
& OTHER ESSAYS

by

JEF COSTELLO

EDITED BY GREG JOHNSON

Counter-Currents Publishing Ltd.
San Francisco
2017

Copyright © 2017 by Counter-Currents Publishing
All rights reserved

Cover design by
Kevin I. Slaughter

Published in the United States by
COUNTER-CURRENTS PUBLISHING LTD.
P.O. Box 22638
San Francisco, CA 94122
USA
http://www.counter-currents.com/

Hardcover ISBN: 978-1-940933-07-8
Paperback ISBN: 978-1-940933-08-5
E-book ISBN: 978-1-940933-09-2

Library of Congress Cataloging-in-Publication Data

Names: Costello, Jef, 1973- author. | Johnson, Greg, 1971- editor.
Title: The importance of James Bond & other essays / by Jef Costello ; edited by Greg Johnson.
Description: San Francisco : Counter-Currents Publishing Ltd., [2017] | Includes bibliographical references and index.
Identifiers: LCCN 2016003904 (print) | LCCN 2016005478 (ebook) | ISBN 9781940933078 (hardcover : alk. paper) | ISBN 9781940933085 (pbk. : alk. paper) | ISBN 9781940933092 (E-book)
Classification: LCC AC8 .C6655 2017 (print) | LCC AC8 (ebook) | DDC 081--dc23
LC record available at http://lccn.loc.gov/2016003904

Contents

Foreword ❖ iii

1. The Importance of James Bond ❖ 1
2. *Skyfall* ❖ 29
3. The Cat is Back! ❖ 38
4. *Fight Club* as Holy Writ ❖ 46
5. *Breaking Bad:* A Celebration ❖ 76
6. *Adieu, Breaking Bad* ❖ 83
7. *Better Call Saul!* ❖ 89
8. The Flash in the Pan: Fascism & Fascist Insignia in the Spy Spoofs of the 1960s ❖ 95
9. *The Man From U.N.C.L.E.:* A Cautionary Tale ❖ 107
10. Guy Ritchie's *The Man From U.N.C.L.E.* ❖ 128
11. Gangway for a Führer: Proto-Fascist Cinema of the Great Depression ❖ 133
12. Disingenuous Genius: A Tribute to Leni Riefenstahl ❖ 152
13. Why Tim Burton's *Dark Shadows* Sucks ❖ 159
14. *The King's Speech* is C-C-Crap ❖ 168
15. Rage Against the Machine: A Very American *Ring* Cycle ❖ 173
16. Dystopia is Now! ❖ 180
17. Tito Perdue's *Lee* ❖ 193
18. The Vermont Teddy Bear is a Giant Phallus ❖ 198
19. Bi-Coastal Adventures in Modern Art ❖ 203
20. Why I Live in the Past ❖ 209

Index ❖ 215

About the Author ❖ 224

Foreword

This volume gathers together my essays on the arts, with a focus on film and television, but also including novels, an opera production, a couple of trips to modern art galleries, and even a ridiculous TV advertisement. My perspective is openly and unapologetically "New Right."

Although the New Right is difficult to encapsulate in terms of one single idea or guiding principle, it typically involves realism about race differences and sex differences, nationalism, anti-egalitarianism, radical traditionalism (co-existing, uneasily, with "archeofuturism"), anti-feminism, anti-globalism, anti-multiculturalism, anti-capitalism (from a Right-wing socialist perspective), and sometimes neo-paganism. The common denominator of all of these is that they are "reality based." This is true even of neo-paganism, since (among Right wingers, at least) it is almost always a direct consequence of racialism and nationalism.

One of the aims of the New Right is to deconstruct Leftist hegemony in the arts and to establish our own counter-hegemony. Art is inescapably political, because it both reflects reality and changes it. This is why the Left fights so hard to control the production and interpretation of art. And this is why Counter-Currents Publishing and its webzine and print journal *North American New Right* put so much focus on art and art criticism.

Each of the "artistic products" dealt with in these essays is treated as a window into our culture. Some enable us to view the cultural rot quite vividly. This is true, among other things, of *The Man from U.N.C.L.E.*, Tim Burton's *Dark Shadows*, and a recent *Ring* cycle.

Others, however, are fascinating because they show writers and artists *reacting against* the rot and presenting us with films and television shows that are crypto-Right wing. This is certainly true of James Bond, to whom I've devoted three essays, including the essay from which this book takes its title. It is also true of *Fight Club* and *Breaking Bad*. (My essay on *Fight Club* is a piece of which I am particularly proud.)

It is fascinating that the makers of these works are almost certainly unaware of the implications of what they have produced. But it is the task of the critic to draw those implications out. The makers of *Invasion of the Body Snatchers* (a classic example *not* discussed herein) didn't realize their film was about communism. But it was. Artistic products, which always have to be situated in a cultural context, mean more than their creators intend.

These essays are intended to provide insight, but they are also supposed to be fun. (Indeed, my third essay on Bond, "The Cat is Back," is more a bit of . . . *ahem* . . . fluff than a serious commentary.) In a few cases, I've skewered things that I just hated (and had a lot of fun doing so). This is true of Burton's *Dark Shadows*, *The King's Speech*, and a few others.

Usually, however, I write about cultural products I love. I am a huge James Bond fan, and loved those films and novels long before my political "awakening." Ditto *Fight Club*, which I never tire of watching. And even though I rake *The Man from U.N.C.L.E.* TV series over the coals, as well as the old Matt Helm films, they are guilty pleasures.

It is my hope, therefore, that the reader will not just come away with a few insights from these essays—but also that he will have as much fun reading them as I had writing them.

I want to thank Greg Johnson, John Morgan, Michael Polignano, James O'Meara, and Kevin Slaughter for their work on producing this book. I also thank the readers, writers, and supporters who make Counter-Currents possible. Finally, I wish to thank Jack Donovan, Christopher Pankhurst, and James O'Meara for their promotional quotes.

This book is dedicated to the real-life superheroes and secret agents in our movement, and to the quiet young men who listen until it's time to decide to join them. I hope it is an inspiration to you all.

Jef Costello
New York City
February 19, 2017

THE IMPORTANCE OF
JAMES BOND

The James Bond films turned fifty in 2012, an event commemorated by the eagerly-anticipated release of the 23rd Eon Productions 007 epic *Skyfall*.

The Broccoli family say they will keep making these films as long as audiences still want to see them. Since the Broccolis at this point have more money than God, we can be sure that this is entirely a labor of love (as Rosa Klebb might say, running her bony fingers through our hair). To date, the Bond films have grossed $5 billion. (Bond is the second highest grossing film series of all time, after Harry Potter.) And the books have sold around 100 million copies.

What can explain why these films have endured for half a century and are bigger now than ever before? (Bond himself, of course, has been around longer than that: the first Ian Fleming Bond novel — *Casino Royale* — was published in 1953.) I'm going to try to explain this — but, as usual, the real explanation is a far cry from what most people (especially critics) think it is.

Sex, Sadism, & Snobbery?

Let's begin with the noteworthy fact that both the Bond novels and films have always pissed off the right people, and for the right reasons.

Attacks on Bond have come from both Left and Right. From the Left Bond has been accused — correctly — of sexism, racism, heterosexism (aka homophobia), classism, lookism, elitism, imperialism, and much else. This Leftist critique is still regularly trotted out. Just four years ago the BBC's online news magazine published a piece asking "Is James Bond Loathsome?" The piece quotes one professorial authority who proclaims "Ideologically, none of us should like the Bond films. They are sexist, heterosexist, xenophobic, everything that is not politically correct. Either the audiences don't notice these ideological issues or the films provide a different kind of pleasure." (A third possibility: perhaps the very political incorrectness of the Bond films is the source of that "different kind of pleasure.")

The Kremlin itself weighed in on the first Bond film, *Dr. No* (1962) condemning it as capitalist propaganda. A more mainstream Leftist critic, Cyril Connolly in *The Sunday Times*, said that Fleming's novel *You Only Live Twice* was "reactionary, sentimental, square, the Bond-image flails its way through the middle-brow masses, a relaxation to the great, a stimulus to the humble, the only common denominator between Kennedy and Oswald." (Both Kennedy and Oswald were readers of Fleming.)

In the '50s and '60s, those on the Right tended to complain mostly about Bond's amorality. They deplored the "sex" (such as it was) in the novels and films, the "hedonism," and the callous disregard for human life. They found it shocking that an assassin — a man with a "licence to kill" (!) — could be romanticized and regarded as a hero. Indeed, in retrospect this *actually is* rather shocking — but something we take completely for granted today. Bond was seen as a particularly bad influence on little boys. *The Guardian*'s reviewer remarked that the second Bond film, *From Russia With Love* (1963) was "highly immoral in every imaginable way; it is neither uplifting, instructive nor life-enhancing." (Though he admitted it was "fun.") Predictably the Vatican condemned both the books and the films. But, oh, what a difference five decades makes! Just the other day the official Vatican newspaper *L'Osservatore Romano* gave *Skyfall* two thumbs up. (This made international news.)

However, the classic conservative critique of Bond came from the pen of none other than Paul Johnson. Writing in *The New Statesmen*, he summed Bond up with the words "Sex, Sadism, and Snobbery." Johnson was actually reviewing Fleming's 1958 novel *Dr. No*. This now-famous review began with the line, "I have just finished reading what is without doubt the nastiest book I have ever read." It was actually the first time Fleming had come in for any major criticism, and Johnson opened the floodgates. For years afterwards those three words — sex, sadism, and snobbery — would be quoted again and again, as a derisive way of dismissing both Bond and his creator.

Sex? Well, yes. Of a kind. Bond does wind up bedding women quite a lot, and without any moral compunction. But Fleming doesn't treat us to the gory, bedroom details (and there is very little humping in the Bond films). What Johnson and others found offensive was really the *attitude* toward the whole thing. For example, Fleming notes that Bond has a penchant for affairs with married women, apparently because there's little chance of emotional entanglement—something about which much is made in the 2006 film of *Casino Royale*. In the novel, written 53 years earlier, Bond muses that "Women were for recreation."

And then there are all those "Bond girls" with names like Honey Rider, Mary Goodnight, and—of course—Pussy Galore. That last one still takes the breath away, even after all these years. What an audacious, salacious old bugger that Fleming was! Then there are the names invented just for the films: Sylvia Trench (I'm convinced that's a dirty one, but others may disagree), Plenty O'Toole ("Named after your father, perhaps?" quips Bond), Holly Goodhead, Octopussy, and Xenia Onatopp. In the films they're all incarnated in jutting, jiggling, Technicolor pulchritude. The novels are more conservative. Fleming described *Dr. No*'s Honey Rider as having a boy's bottom. This prompted his friend Nöel Coward (a *real* old bugger) to write to him, "I know that we are all becoming progressively more broad-minded nowadays but really, old chap, what *could* you have been thinking of?"

Sadism? Well, yes. And it's actually more interesting and more imaginative than the sex. In the very first novel, the villain strips Bond naked and repeatedly assaults his testicles with a carpet beater. (A scene lovingly recreated in the recent film version, though with a rope instead of a carpet beater.) In the second novel, *Live and Let Die* (1954), the villain arranges for the lower extremities of Bond's best friend to be nibbled away by a shark. The still-living Felix Leiter is then found with a note that reads "He disagreed with something that ate him." (This also found its way into the films, though in 1989's *Licence To Kill*.[1]) In the literary

---

[1] More sadism was borrowed from the same novel and placed in 1981's *For Your Eyes Only*: Bond and the heroine are tied together and dragged over coral reefs.

Dr. No, Honey Rider is staked out on a Caribbean island to await the arrival of flesh-eating crabs. And the list just goes on and on. In general, the novels are *far* more sadistic than the films.

Snobbery? Yes, I'm afraid so. And here things become rather ridiculous. Fleming spends pages describing Bond's taste in spirits, suits, shirts, shoes, ties, pajamas (yes, he wears PJs), shampoo, cars, and even eggs. Bond insists that his egg be boiled for precisely three minutes. And it must be a speckled brown egg laid by a French Marans hen. (I am not kidding you.) The egg must be served with two slices of whole-wheat toast, and a pat of Jersey butter accompanied by Tiptree "Little Scarlet" strawberry jelly, Cooper's Vintage Oxford Marmalade, and Norwegian Heather Honey from Fortnum's. Should the eggs be scrambled, they must be served with smoked salmon and champagne. But not just any champagne: Taittinger's.

We are supposed to be left with the impression that Bond is a man of *very* discerning tastes. The impression we are actually left with is that Bond is a pretentious middle class snob trying to put on airs. This kind of thing must have seemed very exotic to the reading public of Great Britain in the 1950s, with post-war austerity still a very vivid memory. And it must have seemed exotic and teddibly British to American readers. But nowadays any yahoo with a wireless connection can order a jar of Frank Coopers Vintage Oxford Marmalade on Amazon.com and get it delivered in two days. And he will probably think it inferior to Smucker's. (And he'll probably be right.)

The classic example, however, is the vodka martini, shaken *not* stirred. This is how the recipe for the Bond martini is stated in just about every film, but the actual Bond Martini is a little more complicated. Here's how it first appears in Chapter Seven of Fleming's *Casino Royale*:

"A dry Martini," he said. "One. In a deep champagne goblet."

"Oui, Monsieur."

"Just a moment. Three measures of Gordon's, one of vodka, half a measure of Kina Lillet. Shake it very well until it's ice cold, then add a large thin slice of lemon-peel.

Got it?"

Yes, but why shake it? And why be so particular about *not* stirring it? Does it really make a difference? Believe it or not, this issue has actually prompted a scientific study. The Department of Biochemistry at the University of Western Ontario found that a shaken martini has more antioxidants than a stirred one. So perhaps Bond is just much more health-conscious than we had originally thought. All kidding aside, he finally comes to his senses in the 2006 *Casino Royale*. Asked by a bartender if he wants his vodka martini shaken or stirred, Bond replies "Do I look like I give a damn?"

So, yes, the world of Bond is guilty as charged — of sex, sadism, and snobbery. But this just completely misses the point, because there really is something important about James Bond — very important. James Bond is a modern hero, a hero for the modern age. Actually, this claim has often been made. But I mean it in a special sense: Bond is a hero *in spite of* modernity; an anti-modern hero who manages to triumph over — and, indeed, harness — the very forces that turn most modern men into soulless, gelded appendages to their desktop PCs. *This* is why Bond is important, and this is why we've worshipped at the cinematic altar of Bond for half a century. We long to be as free as he is.

BOND'S SPIRITUAL VIRILITY

As Julius Evola might have put it, Bond is *spiritually virile*. He is a self-contained, self-actualized man who appears to be a self-indulgent hedonist, but is in fact fundamentally detached from the pleasures and distractions that obsess and enthrall most men.

Let's begin with the much-discussed sex issue. In fact, Bond does *not* chase after women; women chase after him. This is established in the very first scene in which Sean Connery is introduced as Bond in *Dr. No*. He is playing Chemin de Fer at a London club. An attractive woman asks his name from across the table: "Mr. . . . ?" Famously, Connery replies "Bond. James Bond," while lighting a cigarette and flourishing his great, caterpillar-like black eyebrows. The woman—Sylvia Trench, played by Eunice Gayson—pursues a rather disinterested Bond, acquires his business card, then breaks into his apartment and seduces him (over Bond's protestations).

Later in the same film, in a brief but iconic scene, we see a female hotel receptionist ogle Bond as he makes his way across the lobby. *Dr. No* establishes the sexual pattern for all the succeeding films (which does indeed have its basis in the novels). Women practically throw themselves at Bond, who often seems rather weary of the whole thing. (The Bond imitators—those who brought us Matt Helm, Derek Flint, and others—often failed to get this, turning their pseudo-Bonds into lascivious, salivating womanizers.) The ease with which Bond attracts women has often been noted, and chalked up to "male fantasy wish fulfillment." This is true, but what exactly is the wish? It's not just the desire for easy sex. It's also the desire—only dimly understood by most men—to be free of the tiresome indignity of having to pursue women.

At some level, men realize that there is something unmanly about Don Juan. They realize that Bond, by contrast, has "got something" that makes it possible for him to attract women without effort. But that "something" consists in the fact that he doesn't care about it as much as they do (perhaps because he's proved his masculinity in other, more significant areas). He is detached. As a result, Bond doesn't just attract a lot of babes, he attracts extraordinary women. One of the great myths about Bond—particularly as far as the films are concerned—is that Bond girls are brainless, helpless bimbos. This perception is now cynically exploited by the filmmakers, who every so often announce that "the Bond girl in the *new* film is different: she's strong, she's capable, she's Bond's equal," blah blah blah.

But this has been true from the very beginning. Honey Rider tells Bond in *Dr. No* that she murdered a man who raped her by putting a black widow spider under his mosquito net ("A female, and they're the *worst*. It took him a whole week to die.") Pussy Galore is a ball-busting lesbian and leader of her own gang of Amazons. And Octopussy is cut very much from the same cloth. Fiona in *Thunderball* is a cold-blooded assassin, and even Domino—rather bimbo-like for most of the film—winds up executing the villain herself. By my count, no fewer than ten of the cinematic Bond girls are spies or assassins. Two of the Bond girls are scientists: a geologist in *A View to a Kill* and a nuclear physicist in *The World Is Not Enough*. (Though it must be admitted that the actresses who play these parts are *not* very convincing.) Yes, there a few helpless bimbos—like Mary Goodnight in *The Man With The Golden Gun*—but actually *most* of the Bondian heroines are strong, capable women. Which is just the sort of women we would expect a spiritually virile man to attract.

And as for Bond's seemingly absurd culinary pretensions, they're not actually born of a desire to impress, nor are they an expression of hedonism. Bond explains himself rather well in Chapter Eight of Fleming's *Casino Royale*:

> "You must forgive me," he said. "I take a ridiculous amount of pleasure in what I eat or drink. It comes partly from being a bachelor, but mostly from a habit of taking a lot of trouble over details. It's very pernickety and old-maidish really, but then when I'm working I generally have to eat my meals alone and it makes them more interesting when one takes trouble."

Besides, when you're facing death on a daily basis, every meal could be your last! *Of course* Bond takes a lot of trouble over details; of course he lives life to the full. *Hagakure*, the "Book of the Samurai," states that "The Way of the Samurai is found in death. . . . If by setting one's heart right every morning and evening, one is able to live as though his body were *already dead*, he gains freedom in the Way."[2] Bond has learned to face life as if death could come at any moment. This has the effect of heightening his senses and his tastes. He notices the nuances of food and drink that most men miss, and he takes greater pleasure in them, as he takes greater pleasure in sex.

---

[2] Yamamoto Tsunetomo, *Hagakure: The Book of the Samurai*, trans. William Scott Wilson (Tokyo: Kodansha International, 1979), 23–24, emphasis added.

Bond's pleasure is greater than that of other men — but paradoxically he is free of desire in a way most men are not. His constant brushes with death have given him a unique perspective: he is keenly aware of the impermanence of things, and of what matters and what does not. Bond enjoys food, drink, and sex so much precisely *because* of their unimportance. Other men, who have never faced death, place too much importance on these things and — again, paradoxically — are less able to enjoy them.

Bond takes pleasure in the things of this world, but he is not mastered or absorbed by his appetites. This is the *real* meaning of the Bond family motto "The World is not Enough" (introduced in the novel *On Her Majesty's Secret Service*, and later its own Bond film title). This is usually taken to be an expression of rapacious desire. In fact what it says is that the things of this world, which would be too much for most men to handle, are not enough for James Bond. He is greater than they are, thus he can "use them" without being corrupted by them. It's unsurprising that book and film critics would be unable to understand any of this, and would simply see Bond as a "hedonist" and "snob."

RIDING THE TIGER

But, again, Bond's spiritual virility is achieved in a uniquely modern context. He is an "organization man" through and through. Unlike earlier heroes such as Sherlock Holmes, Bulldog Drummond, and Doc Savage, Bond works for someone else. And not just anyone. He serves the state. And not just any state. He serves the tattered remnants of that Great Satan of yesteryear, the British Empire. Furthermore, Bond is a Commander in the Royal Navy. He is relatively low-ranking on the intelligence totem pole, and accustomed to obeying orders. All of this is part of the reason audiences identify with James Bond. This is an observation that may surprise some, since Bond is normally thought of as a superman we long to be, not someone we identify with. Yet we do. Like us, Bond works for a boss — and he is a rather small speck in the scheme of things. In this modern world we are all functionaries and office flunkies. Fleming actually spends a fair amount of time discussing the tedium of Bond's office work — since he only goes on missions once or twice a year.

We long to be able to leave the office—which we loathe just as much as Bond does—and have adventures. And we note, rather enviously, that Bond has managed to be an employee, a part of a vast organization, without being spiritually reduced by it. Bond does not lie awake at night worrying about office politics. Bond does not suck up to the boss. Bond does not get ulcers. It's been made very clear to Bond that he is quite expendable—as it's made very clear to all the ordinary folks working corporate jobs!—but somehow he's found a way to ride this tiger.

Day after day, we grow more and more anxious about the extent to which work encroaches on our lives. And a huge part of the problem has to do with our much ballyhooed advances in technology. As C. S. Lewis recognized in *The Abolition of Man*, every new advance in technology is an advance in some men's ability to control others. So that now thanks to our cell phones and email the boss can always access us. Every new advance in software means more for us to learn on the job. It never ends, and we never outrun the fear that eventually we will simply not be able to catch up. This is yet one more way in which our culture puts all the emphasis on youth—for the young always know the new technologies better, the young can always adapt more swiftly to new innovations. Some of us even fear that new technologies will replace us entirely, as has actually happened to many people, both blue-collar and white-collar.

Needless to say, technology has always been a big part of James Bond. This is much truer of the films than the books, though there's a slim basis for it in the books. The films, however, go whole hog and are thoroughly "modernistic." There are gadgets galore in the Bond films; they seem to celebrate technology. But here again, things are much more complicated than they seem. If we pay careful attention to the Bond films we will realize that Bond's attitude towards technology is *disdainful*. This is the basis for the well-known comic tension between Bond and crusty old Q, the gadget master.

Q first appears in *From Russia With Love*[3] in which he provides

---

[3] A "Major Boothroyd," who is apparently supposed to be the

Bond with a clever trick attaché case and folding sniper's rifle. It's a brief scene without any comedic elements, though Bond seems a bit amused by the gadgets. It's *Goldfinger*, the next film in the series, that establishes the familiar pattern. Bond visits a humorless Q who provides him with an Aston Martin equipped with revolving license plates, machine guns, smoke screen, tire slashers, radar, oil slick, and—most famously—an ejector seat. Bond seems completely unimpressed and rolls his eyes when Q tells him that he won't take more than an hour or two of his time. When they get to the ejector seat Bond sneers and says "You must be joking!" Q responds, deadpan, "I never joke about my work, Double-Oh-Seven."

It is clear that Bond regards the real business of spying as a matter of physical stamina and mental agility. He is contemptuous of the idea that what he does could be done better by—or even *with*—machines. However, time and again Bond gets himself out of tight spot with one of Q's gadgets. And so he does make a kind of uneasy peace with technology. But again and again when the time comes for Bond to really save the day he does so with his own wits and guts. In other words, the films wind up siding with Bond and declaring that technology—and *technē*—is not the answer.

Sometimes the producers forget this, however, and when they do the films tend to go off the rails. The first time this happens is in 1965's *Thunderball*. By that point, after the major success of *Goldfinger*, the Bond gadgets had gotten a lot of publicity and the producers were careful to load up *Thunderball* with as much tech as possible. It begins in the pre-credit sequence, in which Bond escapes pursuers in a jetpack (!). The Aston Martin then reappears. And in the film's climactic underwater action sequences, Bond dons a kind of underwater jetpack that fires projectiles. The effect is ridiculous. Author John Brosnan comments that the scene makes Connery look like a "clown." And

---

same person as Q, appears in *Dr. No*. But there he is merely an "armourer," who provides Bond with his famous Walther PPK. He is also not played by Desmond Llewelyn, the actor most famously associated with Q, but by Peter Burton.

he writes of the whole film, "With *Thunderball*, James Bond tended to become depersonalised, turning into a sort of bland dummy whose only function was to manipulate the various gadgets and act as a catalyst to keep the whole show moving."[4]

The Bond films of the '60s started off as relatively realistic spy thrillers, but over time gee-whiz technology took over and dwarfed the Bond character. In their first decade, the pinnacle of this technological silliness was reached with *You Only Live Twice* (1967), which one reviewer dismissed as looking like an episode of TV's *Thunderbirds*. Everyone, including the producers, felt that something had been lost. The verdict was usually that the films had become too "outlandish." The truth, however, is that what made Bond Bond had been negated: he wasn't riding the tiger anymore; he was being dragged along behind it.

And so with 1969's *On Her Majesty's Secret Service* the producers dumped the gadgets, and cranked things back to the minimalism of *From Russia With Love*. The result was a film that many fans, myself included, regard as the best of the series. But this pattern has been repeated several times in its history. The producers again and again allow Bond to become diminished by high-tech and special effects, and again and again realize their mistake and swear never to repeat it. In truth what is happening here is that, like all of us, they are struggling with the allure—and the danger—of technology.

In later films, as actor Desmond Llewelyn aged into a lovable old codger, the Q character was softened a bit and given more to do. But early on he is as mechanical and charmless as the gadgets he dispenses. He is man become technics, who cares more about his inventions returning "intact from the field" than about Bond's body returning intact. This, indeed, becomes a running joke and Bond seems to take delight not just in belittling Q's gadgets but in demolishing them.

Bond also delights in destroying the villains' hardware as well. The classic Bond villains tended to set themselves up with ultra-modern lairs filled with impressive technological marvels. And all of it constructed out of miles and miles of gleaming,

---

[4] John Brosnan, *James Bond in the Cinema* (London: Tantivy Press, 1972), 73.

stainless steel. By contrast, Bond's own environment—M's office, Whitehall, and Bond's apartment (seen in two films)—is ultra-traditional. (Interestingly, Q's environs look just like the villains'.)

The contrast could not be clearer. The good dwells in small, warm, and human spaces surrounded by organic materials (wood and fabrics of various kinds), and decorations chosen for their charm, or because they suggest national heritage (the paintings and busts in M's office). These spaces are inhabited by individuals with distinct characters and quirks: the crusty but benign M; the stalwart, love-sick Moneypenny, etc.

The evil, by contrast, dwells in huge, cold, intimidating, depersonalized spaces made of metal, stripped of anything charming and anything that suggests national identity—or cluttered with objects suggesting a confusion of national identities (e.g., Dr. No's living room, Blofeld's various apartments, etc.). And here the space is inhabited by emotionless human automata in coveralls, or Mao jackets, who often refer to each other only as numbers. I'll have more to say about what this represents later on . . .

BOND AS MODERN MYTHOLOGY

A handsome knight, a favorite of all the ladies at court, is sent to a remote part of the kingdom to investigate the disappearance of another knight. There he learns that a terrifying wizard is responsible. The wizard lives on a mysterious island, to which many have journeyed—but from which none has ever returned. Our hero teams up with a knight from a distant kingdom that is also being plagued by the wizard's magic. Then, accompanied by a curmudgeonly but loyal dwarf, as black as the night, our hero journeys to the island. Unexpectedly, they find themselves assisted by an avatar of Venus, who suddenly rises from the ocean. Together, the trio explores the wizard's island. One night, they encounter a terrible dragon, who breathes fire on the swarthy dwarf and kills him. The dragon is in thrall to the wizard, however, and is under orders not to kill our hero and his Venus. He takes them captive and drags them down into the wizard's subterranean lair.

When they finally meet the wizard himself they find that he

is a frightening, but also rather pathetic figure. He has no hands, having sacrificed them in order to read the leaves of Satan's book and discover the secret of producing a terrible form of black magic. The wizard tries to seduce our hero with promises of magic power, but when he proves incorruptible the wizard seals him in a dungeon. The knight quickly finds, however, that it contains a tiny door that leads him into a vast labyrinth, filled with one terrifying challenge after another. The final challenge involves a fight with a giant sea monster.

The knight kills the beast and finds his way into the wizard's secret chamber, where the evil necromancer is in the midst of a black magic rite. Over the smoky, hell-like abyss from whence comes the wizard's power, the two men struggle. The knight seems doomed, but in the end the fates deal out poetic justice to the wizard. His lack of hands — the very hands he sacrificed to obtain his magic — makes him unable to cling to the altar over the abyss, and he plunges into it. Our hero then rescues Venus from certain death at the hands of the wizard's flesh-eating demons, and together they leave the island, never to return.

For the uninitiated, this is exactly the plot of *Dr. No*.[5] Bond is sent to Jamaica to investigate the disappearance of another British agent. There, he teams up with a CIA agent investigating recent radio interference with American rocket launches. They discover that the man responsible seems to be a reclusive scientist named Dr. No, who lives on an island called Crab Key. Bond sails to the island, accompanied by a local black fisherman named Quarrel. The next morning, the beautiful Honey Rider appears, rising out of the ocean. (She had come to the island looking for shells.) Earlier, Quarrel had warned Bond that the island is guarded by a dragon, and that night the three actually encounter it. But the "dragon" turns out to be a tank of sorts, fitted out with a flamethrower — which kills poor Quarrel. Men with machine guns pile out of the "dragon" and take Bond and Honey down to Dr. No's subterranean installation.

Over dinner, Dr. No reveals that he lost his hands as a result

---

[5] I have actually amalgamated elements from both the novel and the film.

of his experiments with nuclear power.⁶ He tries to recruit Bond, unsuccessfully. Dr. No places Bond in a cell, and gives him the option of staying there or traversing a labyrinth. Bond chooses the latter, but much to his discomfort. He is shocked, burned, and almost drowned. (In the novel he is also attacked by poisonous insects.) Finally (in the novel only) Bond must defeat a giant squid. In the film version, Bond then infiltrates Dr. No's reactor room. There is a final climactic battle, and Dr. No—owing to his lack of hands—is unable to stop himself from slipping into the steaming reactor pool.⁷ Things start to explode, and Bond rushes off to rescue Honey (who—again, in the novel only—is about to be eaten by flesh-eating crabs). Together, they escape the island.

That the Bond stories are "modern myths" has often been asserted, and there's quite a bit to this. John Brosnan, states that "Dr. No, Ernst Stavro Blofeld, *et al.* are the descendants not of Al Capone but of Dracula himself." And he continues:

> Seen, then, in this context the Bond books and films become twentieth-century folk epics with Bond as a latter day St. George fighting against evil incarnate. They are the same basic stories that have been passed down through the centuries but with the hero and the villain adapted to our technological age. No longer is it Satan's power that people fear but the new demons of machinery and atomic power. So the vampire has exchanged his castle for Dr. No's subterranean laboratory, his fangs for Dr. No's steel claws, and his unholy source of power for Dr. No's atomic reactor.⁸

This is actually a very insightful analysis, from one of the earliest book-length studies of the Bond films. All the traditional mythic elements are present in Bond, only they have been rather straightforwardly modernized. One might also mention the fact that Bond's gadgets are simply modernized versions of things

---

⁶ In the novel, he betrays the Tong society, who cut off his hands.
⁷ In the novel, Bond buries Dr. No under a pile of bat guano.
⁸ Brosnan, 11

like magic swords and spears, helmets of invisibility, and indestructible shields. M is actually a sort of Odin figure, whose feelings of paternal affection for his No. 1 hero don't change the fact that he controls Bond's destiny, and is willing to send Bond to his death. And I could go on.

The Bond character has often been derided by critics as an exaggerated superman. And, in truth, his exploits are often incredible, in the literal sense of the term. Slaying the giant squid is just one example. He's saved the entire world more often than anyone can remember, without so much as mussing his hair. Yet the exploits of the heroes of Celtic and Germanic mythology are just as implausible, often more so. But no one criticizes them as "unrealistic."

Bond is indeed the stuff of modern myth. And audiences have responded to him so strongly because we have a need for this sort of thing. It provides a kind of spiritual fuel. Of course, the same could be said of *Star Wars* (indeed, Lucas consciously wove mythic motifs into his films). Yet *Star Wars* has never come in for anything like the criticism Bond has received. I think that this has to do with the fact that the ethos of the Bond films is *implicitly pagan*. Whereas the ethos of the *Star Wars* saga is implicitly Christian, and therefore more in line with the liberalism of most film critics (however secular they may imagine themselves to be). But I'll have more to say about that later on . . .

In case you haven't figured this out, I have been fascinated by James Bond since a very early age — in fact, since *before* my parents allowed me to see a Bond film. I first learned about Bond from my mother, who one night told me about a secret agent who had a special car outfitted with machine guns and an ejector seat. I then acquired the classic Corgi toy version of the Bond Aston Martin (still being manufactured years after *Goldfinger* was released). But my parents decided that the films were "too adult" for me to see. Besides, I became interested in Bond during the three-year hiatus between 1974's *The Man with the Golden Gun* and 1977's *The Spy Who Loved Me*. There just was no Bond for me to see — except on television. But back then the films were all broadcast with absurd "parental advisories" which scared my parents into changing the channel.

I longed for something like Bond to appear on television. But, alas, these were the days of shows like *Kojak*, *Starsky and Hutch*, and *S.W.A.T.*, which all struck me (even as a child) as cheap, seedy, and naturalistic. I longed, although I did not realize it, to see the present *mythologized*. Science fiction and fantasy didn't appeal to me much. (I was the only kid in school who didn't see *Star Wars* a second time.) I wanted to see grand conflicts between good and evil, with extraordinary heroes doing extraordinary things, but set in the *here-and-now*.

When we think about the traditional myths, sagas, and folktales that have been passed down to us, we tend to think that the "mythic elements" include such things as powerful kings, castles with moats around them, knights in armor, imperiled princesses, poisoned blades, and court magicians. But when our traditional myths were composed these things *actually existed*. They were the *realistic* elements in the myths. What the myths and sagas did was to take the here-and-now and introduce elements of the supernatural, and superhumanly heroic.

Myths make the present extraordinary.[9] Thus, it actually seems a bit weaselly to refer to Bond as "modern myth." Kind of like calling discrimination against whites "reverse discrimination." No, it's just discrimination. And Bond is *just myth*. When the *Volsung Saga* and *Parzival* were written they were "modern myths," i.e., myths of *today*. In making the present extraordinary, myths make clear the difference between good and evil, which is often hard to discern when we are caught up in the complicated details of the moment. They show us eternal truth shining through present actuality. And they erect archetypes of heroism and virtue; they gave us something to aspire to.

This was what I wanted to see as a child: I wanted to see the world around me made mythic. And when my parents finally allowed me to see a Bond film (*The Spy Who Loved Me*, in 1977), this was exactly what I found. And I've been hooked ever since. It was for the same reasons that, in my early twenties, I responded so strongly to Ayn Rand's novels. Rand called her literary style "romantic realism." She laid her stories in the present

---

[9] This is why Bond, as myth, is actually superior to Tolkien — and why he appeals to a wider audience.

day, but her characters were larger than life and did extraordinary things. It seemed natural to her to include elements of science fiction—just like in the Bond films. And so her characters invent new technologies, and hide them in secret valleys beneath holographic projection screens (see *Atlas Shrugged*).[10] As Brosnan noted in writing of the Bond films, "modern myths" substitute science fiction for the supernatural. (There seems to be some kind of cultural or literary necessity to this.) "Romantic realism," is just the same thing as myth, properly understood.

BOND'S MORALISM

So how exactly do the Bond myths make clear the difference between good and evil? (The idea that there could be a *moral dimension* to Bond would strike many people as absurd.) I actually alluded to this earlier. To see this we have to look at who Bond is fighting, and how he fights them.

In the films, it was rarely the Soviets. When Fleming got tired of making Russians the villains, he invented S.P.E.C.T.R.E. (the SPecial Executive for Counter-intelligence Terrorism, Revenge, Extortion), a multi-national criminal organization headed by the diabolical Ernst Stavro Blofeld (Moriarty plus Mabuse).[11] S.P.E.C.T.R.E. first appears in Fleming's novel *Thunderball* (1961), but the filmmakers inserted the organization into their version of *Dr. No*, making the eponymous villain a S.P.E.C.T.R.E. agent (in the novel he's working for the Soviets). The sinister organization then appears in five of the next six films (it's even worked into *From Russia With Love*, in which the Russians only *appear* to be the baddies—it's actually Blofeld and company).

Blofeld and his white Persian cat make their first appearance in *From Russia With Love*. In an early scene he explains the *modus operandi* of the organization in terms of the fish in his office aquarium:

"Siamese fighting fish. Fascinating creatures, brave but on

---

[10] It's no surprise that Rand was gaga over *Dr. No*. But she disliked the later films, thinking that they undermined Bond's mythic heroism.

[11] Actually, he co-invented S.P.E.C.T.R.E. See "The Cat is Back."

the whole stupid. Yes, they're stupid. Except for the occasional one such as we have here, who lets the other two fight. He waits. Waits until the survivor is so exhausted that he cannot defend himself. And then, like S.P.E.C.T.R.E., he strikes."

The idea is that S.P.E.C.T.R.E. will allow the two superpowers to fight it out, then move in and pick up the pieces. Does Blofeld want merely to profit financially, or does he seek world domination? Probably a bit of both. (And is there a difference?) What is fascinating here is that the organization is, as it were, "triangulated" vis-à-vis the U.S. and U.S.S.R. In fact, what S.P.E.C.T.R.E. embodies is Heidegger's thesis of the metaphysical identity of the superpowers. S.P.E.C.T.R.E. represents the *core* of both: materialism, dehumanization, homogenization, globalism, and Heidegger's *Gestell*.

These are the real villains. These are the things we are *really* worried about. And both the U.S. and the U.S.S.R. were out to advance them, each in their own way. But suddenly now it is little England (no longer an imperial power) that is caught in the pincers. So off goes Bond to slay the dragon of homogenization, and make the world safe for British eccentricity (which, if you think about it, was exactly the premise of TV's *The Avengers*).

But there's another significant sort of villain that Bond finds himself up against: the crazy idealist. These are mainly an invention of the films—there's really only one in the Fleming novels. The villain in the literary *Moonraker* (1955), Sir Hugo Drax (really Graf Hugo von der Drache) is a Nazi who plans to destroy London with a missile as revenge for the defeat of Hitler and—I kid you not—as revenge for various forms of social humiliation inflicted on him in English boarding schools. The cinematic Drax is a much crazier idealist: he plans to destroy all life on earth using nerve gas, while creating a new master race on an orbiting space station. The villain of the previous film, *The Spy Who Loved Me*, plans to destroy the earth by provoking nuclear war between the U.S. and U.S.S.R., while creating a new master race in a city beneath the sea.

Hmm... did these two guys ever meet? Needless to say, Bond

vanquishes both of them. In the name of what? In the name of finitude and imperfection; in the name of this world, warts and all. This is surely one of the things that bothers liberal critics. Bond is not an idealist. His "world affirming" attitude extends well beyond a tolerance for marmalade.

But though Bond may not be an idealist, he certainly is a moralist. I have always been convinced that one of the reasons liberal critics tend to hate Bond is that, unlike them, he is not morally confused. Bond has no compunctions at all about passing moral judgments. And in making those judgments he is clearly not drawing on the Sermon on the Mount. No, Bond's ethos is really that of a pagan.

In the early days of Bond, much was made of the fact that he had a "licence to kill" (I'm deliberately using the British spelling of "license"). This is what the Double-0 prefix in 007 signifies. In Britain in the '60s, Bond was frequently depicted in film trailers and radio spots as "the gentleman agent with the licence to kill!" The concept of a "licence to kill" is really a legal one. What it means is that Bond is officially authorized to kill in the line of duty, and, presumably, in Britain he cannot be prosecuted or otherwise held liable for deaths he causes on the job. It does not really mean that he can kill anyone he wants to, at any time. Yet, that's sort of what "licence to kill" communicates to people and — let's be honest — it gives us a bit of a thrill.

If only I had a licence to kill. I'd probably start with some of the people I work with. Then I'd move on to . . . Well, it's pointless to sit around fantasizing, pleasant though it might be. It is odd, isn't it, that the concept of a licence to kill seems so Romantic. It makes Bond seem larger than life. Why? Because it suggests that he has been liberated from the mundane, popular moralism that constrains and confuses us.

In thinking about Blofeld and what must be done with him, Bond does not take time to ponder whether there might really be some good in everyone. ("After all, he does really seem to love that cat. He never goes anywhere without it . . .") Nor does Bond feel the necessity to Mirandize Blofeld and turn him over to the proper authorities so that he can get due process and a speedy trial. No, Bond simply *executes* Blofeld (or he tries to — repeatedly).

Bond electrocutes people, harpoons them, strangles them, feeds them to piranha fish, dumps them into pits of boiling mud, explodes them with shark gun pellets, drops them off cliffs, throws them from airplanes, sets them on fire, and sometimes just shoots them (often repeatedly: see how Bond executes Stromberg in *The Spy Who Loved Me*). Usually, after each execution, Bond utters a memorable witticism. After harpooning one man with a shark gun in *Thunderball*, Bond remarks "I think he got the point." After dumping someone in a pool of piranha in *You Only Live Twice*, Bonds wishes the little critters "Bon appétit."

He doesn't agonize over it later (though, admittedly, there's a tiny bit of that in the novels). He doesn't wonder if he did the right thing. No, one of the things that characterizes Bond is moral certainty. He knows who the bad guys are, and he knows they deserve it. And he doesn't seem to wonder what God thinks about the matter either. No, Bond relies entirely on his own judgment, and is sure in his judgment. And sure of his moral authority to punish evildoers. This is the sort of thing that drives liberals crazy.

But what is it that guides Bond's moral judgment? Though he takes it upon himself to be judge, jury, and executioner, Bond is never arrogant or capricious in his decision to take a life. Bond is no sociopath. When the assassin Scaramanga suggests in *The Man with the Golden Gun* that he and Bond are morally equivalent, Bond responds, memorably, "There's a useful four letter word. And you're full of it." Bond is beyond good and evil — but only in the sense that he's beyond Christian (or liberal) moralizing. This is typified by the title *Live and Let Die*.

The filmmakers have long employed a brilliant dramatic device that appears in most of the Bond films. At a certain point in the story, an ally of Bond (or, at least, a sympathetic character) will be killed by the villain or the villain's henchmen. This introduces a note of pathos into what are often extremely light-hearted stories, and it also allows Bond to show some emotion and reveal some vulnerability (in *On Her Majesty's Secret Service* he actually cries). But these scenes are important for yet another reason. Always up until that point in the story Bond has been pursuing his mission for Queen and Country. But the death of his friend makes the mission *personal*.

However, it would not be accurate to say that from that moment forward Bond is acting for Bond. Rather, he is acting according to his own, personal sense of justice. And it is interesting that what catalyzes this is invariably that good-old-pagan virtue of loyalty, and that good-old-pagan desire for *vengeance*. This is, in fact, the entire premise of 1989's *Licence to Kill*, which is actually an eloquent commentary on the very concept of the "licence to kill." In the story, M revokes Bond's licence. But Bond goes rogue, bent on avenging the brutalization of his friend Felix and the rape and murder of Felix's fiancée. What the title of the film means is that although Bond's legal licence to kill is revoked, the events of the story grant him a *moral licence* to kill. This is the stuff of the pagan, pre-Christian sagas.

But what would Jesus do? Who bloody cares?! I've been asking myself for years "What would James Bond do?" Bond is my moral compass.

BOND AS RACIALIST & NATIONALIST

Let's talk a bit more about Ernst Stavro Blofeld. Odd name, isn't it? It's German, except for the middle name, because Blofeld is half German, half Greek.[12] This is a pattern we often find with Bond villains: they are mutts of some kind, or something other than what they appear to be. Dr. No is German and Chinese (a frightening combination, if ever there was one!). Not being British is bad enough, but these men are double trouble. Perhaps the most chilling example is Donovan Grant, the homicidal killer in *From Russia With Love*. Fleming provides us with the details of his paternity in one lurid sentence: "Donovan Grant was the result of a midnight union between a German professional weight-lifter and a Southern Irish waitress." Poor fellow. One gets the impression that for Fleming having German ancestry must be one of the worst things that could befall a man. (Too bad for the Queen!)

Clearly, Fleming was bothered by the idea of contamination by the non-white, and the not-quite-white. And he obviously endorsed the idea that "the wogs begin at Calais." The filmmakers,

---

[12] He was born in Gdynia, Poland, when it was part of Germany.

probably without quite realizing it, have carried on this tradition. Perhaps someone will correct me, but I can't think of a single villain in the Fleming novels or the films who's genuinely English (aside from some very minor ones like Major Dexter Smythe in the "Octopussy" short story).

Even the non-whites in Fleming are of mixed parentage. I've already mentioned Dr. No. Then there's Mr. Big in *Live and Let Die*. Fleming tells us that he was born in Haiti and is "half Negro and half French." That novel, by the way, is usually cited as Fleming's most racist. The book actually alternates between a kind of naïve, unselfconscious racism and overt attempts to be racially "broadminded." When Bond is first briefed on Mr. Big he says:

> "I don't think I've ever heard of a great Negro criminal before . . . Chinamen, of course, the men behind the opium trade. There've been plenty of big-time Japs, mostly in pearls and drugs. Plenty of Negros mixed up in diamonds and gold in Africa, but always in a small way. They don't seem to take to big business."

But then Bond immediately follows this up with "Pretty law-abiding chaps, on the whole, I should have thought." Not to be out-run on this race to fantasyland, M responds: "the Negro races are just beginning to throw up geniuses in all the professions—scientists, doctors, writers. It's about time they turned out a great criminal. . . . They've got plenty of brains and ability and guts." Perhaps M had just had a snort of Bond's Benzedrine.

But Fleming wasn't fooling anybody. The title of Chapter Five in the British edition of *Live and Let Die* was "Nigger Heaven." When it was published in the U.S. a year later this was changed to "Seventh Avenue," and certain racially-charged passages were heavily censored.

Aside from the villains that are foreign mixtures of various kinds, there are the ones who are *pretending* to be British—which is almost as bad. Sir Hugo Drax in the literary *Moonraker* is actually half German, but he's passing himself off as a British war hero.

Goldfinger is perhaps the most interesting case: he's Latvian, but a naturalized British subject. The surname Goldfinger is almost always German-Jewish, which has led to some speculation as to whether the character—who is obsessed with amassing great hordes of gold—is intended to be a kind of anti-Semitic caricature.

In the novel, Bond encounters Goldfinger for the first time in his hotel in Miami (just as in the film). Goldfinger is cheating a wealthy older gentleman at gin rummy—a fellow by the name of Du Pont, who happens to be an old friend of Bond's. (Bond villains are not gentlemen: they tend to cheat at games. Goldfinger will cheat again at golf, Hugo Drax cheats at cards, Kamal Khan cheats at backgammon in *Octopussy*, and Max Zorin cheats at horse racing in *A View to a Kill*.) Bond and Mr. Du Pont actually discuss whether or not Goldfinger might be Jewish. Du Pont says "You'd think he'd be a Jew from the name, but he doesn't look it." He then volunteers that were Goldfinger Jewish he would never have been admitted to the hotel (!).

But Fleming may just have been trying to throw us off the scent. It's a well-known fact that he borrowed the name of his most famous villain from his neighbor, the architect Ernö Goldfinger. (In the novel the character's first name is Auric—a clever play on the chemical symbol for gold, Au.) Goldfinger the architect was indeed Jewish, and Fleming seems to have disliked him intensely. Goldfinger's designs represented the worst of modern, post-war architecture.

Ernö Goldfinger capitalized on post-war devastation and homelessness in Britain by creating some of the most hideous high-rise flats imaginable. His designs were completely devoid of charm, and anything suggesting Englishness. Ever the traditionalist, Fleming was horrified. And he was personally affected by it: Goldfinger had a number of cottages in Fleming's neighborhood razed in order to make way for his new, butt-ugly modernistic home. The cherry on the cake is that Goldfinger also designed the post-war headquarters of the British Communist Party.

When Fleming's novel was published, Ernö Goldfinger threatened to sue. Fleming responded by suggesting the book be re-titled *Goldprick* (a move that would have delighted Austin

Powers). However, Goldfinger was apparently pleased by the publicity the book brought him, so he dropped his case in exchange for Fleming paying his legal costs and six free copies of the book. While Fleming may have delighted in naming his villain after the odious architect, the characterization of Goldfinger is actually said to have been based on Charles W. Engelhard, Jr., an American millionaire involved in the precious metals industry, and thoroughbred horse racing (just like Auric Goldfinger). Engelhard was also Jewish.

There were also "fake Englishmen" created exclusively for Bond's cinematic exploits. Alec Trevelyan in *GoldenEye* (1995) starts off as a British agent—and friend of Bond—but turns out to be descended from Cossacks and bent on revenge against the U.K. (It's a long story . . .) Perhaps the most dramatic example in the Bond films of the "fake Englishman" is Gustav Graves in *Die Another Day* (2002; the worst of the Pierce Brosnan Bonds). Graves actually turns out to be a North Korean mastermind who has undergone "gene therapy" and physically transformed himself into an Englishman. (Possibly the most confused and implausible plot element in any Bond film.)

It's one thing to be some heavily-accented, foreign counterjumper trying to pass himself off as an English gentleman. But the case of Graves suggests that there may be people out there who are genetic fakes: English, but not really. Come to think of it, doesn't this describe Tony Blair and all the ethnomasochists of the Labour Party, who've pretty much destroyed England? And—ouch—doesn't this also describe any American of English ancestry? Perhaps "gene therapy" is the solution to the U.K.'s immigration problem. They'd still be flooded with Pakis and Arabs, but at least they'd *look* English. (And let's be quite honest with each other: to a significant degree, immigration is an *aesthetic* problem, as well as a cultural and racial one.)

It's not just their race and ethnicity that makes the Bond villains so frightening: they're usually also physically and psychologically screwed up. Dr. No has no hands. Blofeld has a syphilitic scar in the novels (and what appears to be a dueling scar in one film). Emilio Largo is missing an eye. Tee Hee in *Live and Let Die* is missing a hand. Scaramanga in *The Man with the Golden*

Gun has a third nipple. Nick Nack, in the same film, is a dwarf. Jaws in *The Spy Who Loved Me* has steel teeth, and Stromberg has webbed fingers. Max Zorin is the product of Nazi experiments. Alec Trevelyan is hideously scarred. Renard in *The World is Not Enough* is incapable of feeling pain or pleasure. And Le Chiffre in *Casino Royale* cries blood.

In short, the Bond villains are "special." In today's world these people would all get to sit in the reserved benches at the front of the bus (even Scaramanga with his nipple: remember, not all disabilities are visible). But in Fleming's world they are accorded no sympathy. In Fleming's world there's a healthy horror of physical abnormalities, and a classically Greek intuition that what's twisted on the outside is twisted on the inside. The flip side of this is the much-maligned Bondian focus on beauty. (Though what most feminist critics don't seem to get is that Bond is offered to us as a sex object as well.)

Then there are all those perversions. *From Russia With Love* is a veritable cavalcade of perverts. Rosa Klebb is a lesbian who gets off on torturing people. Donovan Grant is a serial killer who derives a sexual thrill from killing (but only when the moon is full! This didn't make it into the film). Finally, another *From Russia With Love* assassin, Krilencu, also kills for pleasure. So does Vargas in *Thunderball*. Blofeld is described as asexual. Wynt and Kidd in *Diamonds are Forever* are gay. And Scaramanga only makes love prior to killing. This just scratches the surface.

Thank god that physical deformity and sexual perversion don't exist in Fleming's England!

Actually, the most iconic Bond villain of all may be Le Chiffre in the literary *Casino Royale*. "Le Chiffre" means "the cipher." The man in question adopted this name after the war, when he was liberated from Dachau. He claimed to be suffering from total amnesia, and at first was unable to speak. He could not remember his nationality. (M's dossier, however, states that he has "large [ear]lobes, indicating some Jewish blood"!) Nor could he even remember his own name. And so he adopted the name Le Chiffre, to express his complete lack of identity. Le Chiffre is the perfect modern villain—and a perfect villain for the first Bond adventure. He embodies everything that Bond is fighting against: he is a rootless cosmopolitan, a man without a country, and without any allegiances (other than to himself).

Bond himself is the antithesis of this. Despite his Overmanish qualities, he's a patriot who sees himself as serving Queen and Country. Much has been made of the fact that Bond is a kind of wish fulfillment for the post-imperial British. He came along at a time when British power and prestige were on the wane. But Bond allows the British to pretend that they are still a world power and that it's up to them to come to the rescue. There's a lot to this analysis, actually. For one thing, isn't it significant that Bond so often has to come to the aid of the hapless Americans? This actually begins in the novels, in which Bond is always ordering around Americans like Felix Leiter, who are portrayed as classless and inept. Kingsley Amis put it best, writing in *The James Bond Dossier*:

> The point of Felix Leiter, such a nonentity as a piece of characterization, is that he, the American, takes orders from Bond, the Britisher, and that Bond is constantly doing better than he, showing himself, not braver or more devoted, but smarter, wilier, tougher, more resourceful — the incarnation of little old England with her quiet ways and shoestring budget wiping the eye of great big global-tentacled multi-billion-dollar-appropriating America.

This is all true, and I suppose that if one sees things from this perspective, Bond (and Fleming) come off seeming a trifle pathetic. But the truth is that Bond doesn't really have any illusions about British power and influence. He's just fighting for his country. Not because he thinks it's the greatest country in the world, or because he thinks it has a mission to civilize the rest of the planet. The loss of the Empire really makes no difference to him, because he doesn't need a *reason* to love England and the English. He simply loves what is his own. Would that there were more Englishmen like James Bond. . . .

PROSPECTS FOR THE FUTURE

I am writing this some days prior to *Skyfall*'s release in the U.S. Based on the advance publicity, and reviews by critics in the

U.K., I am cautiously optimistic.

During the gap between 1989's *Licence to Kill* and the first Pierce Brosnan film, *GoldenEye* (1995), I worried that when Bond returned he would be made politically correct. But the producers actually seemed to signal that that wasn't going to happen. In *GoldenEye*, the now-female M informs a bemused (and unrepentant) Bond that he's a "sexist, misogynist dinosaur."

Yes, I was bothered a little bit by the female M. (And puzzled as to why they hadn't followed Sir Humphrey Appleby's suggestion in *Yes, Minister* and changed the code name to F.) But the real head of MI6 at the time was a woman, and Judi Dench is a fine actress, so I was willing to go along with it. It also didn't bother me that there were token blacks surrounding M. So what? And Pierce Brosnan bedding down with Halle Berry didn't trouble me at all (from *Octopussy* to Octoroon, I suppose one might say). After all, Bond has been bedding non-white women since *Dr. No*. I don't think he plans to have children with any of them.

And I am also willing to overlook the fact that Bond no longer smokes. I still vividly recall an interview with Pierce Brosnan who described shooting a scene in *Tomorrow Never Dies*. Bond is sitting in the dark, lying in wait in someone's hotel room, wearing shirtsleeves, cradling his gun and drinking vodka (in short, kind of like a scene in *Dr. No*). Brosnan said the scene "just cried out for a cigarette." But he couldn't bring himself to do it. It would have been a bad influence on the kiddies. Let me get this straight: he's sitting in the dark, swigging Smirnoff, about to kill someone—but smoking a cigarette would have sent impressionable viewers the wrong message? (Meanwhile, apparently, Brosnan was shooting Lark commercials in Japan.)

Yes, I'm willing to forgive James Bond quite a lot, actually. And at this point I'm not really concerned that the producers will ruin the series with political correctness. They're too smart for that. I *am* concerned, however, that many of the things I've discussed in this essay—things that make Bond Bond—are falling by the wayside.

I was delighted with how the producers chose to "reboot" Bond in 2006's *Casino Royale*. I had been saying for years that major changes needed to made; that the series was riding on nostalgia; that it had become stale. I also think that Daniel Craig is the best Bond since Connery. Why? Because he actually manages to make Bond into a three-dimensional, believable character. Timothy Dalton did this as well, but he somehow wasn't quite the right "fit" — and Brosnan always gave me the impression of a man playing a man playing James Bond. However, one of the ways in which they've made the character more believable is to make him less self-possessed. This new Bond is unsure of himself in many ways. He seems a bit unstable, and is not fully in command of himself and his surroundings. He's not riding the tiger yet. Maybe he's learning to ride it, but I don't know.

And this new Bond has no critical distance from technology. There's something about seeing James Bond with a cell phone pressed against his ear that *really* bothers me. He's become too much like us. Too swamped by the tech. Too swamped by the organization. He seems smaller and more vulnerable. He seems *beleaguered* — as we all are today. Is the character going to continue growing and developing? Will he grow into the old James Bond, who showed us that it is possible to ride the tiger of modernity and not be trampled by it? I hope so.

Despite my misgivings, I will be first in line to see *Skyfall* when it opens. And I have already ordered my 50th anniversary Blu-ray set of all twenty-two earlier Eon Productions Bond films. I've learned a whole lot about life from James Bond, and I will continue to defend Bond and continue seeing these films from now till my dying breath . . .

. . . unless they make Bond black.[13]

Counter-Currents/*North American New Right*,
November 8, 2012

---

[13] Calm yourselves: this business about casting a black man as Bond has been around for years. It's a publicity stunt.

SKYFALL

Bond films always seem to be judged "good" or "bad" relative to other Bond films. But *Skyfall* is not only a good Bond film, it's a good film period. Daniel Craig apparently ran into Sam Mendes at a party and, on a whim, asked if he might be interested in directing a Bond film. This was a real stroke of good fortune, as Mendes's *Skyfall* is perhaps the most exciting, visually arresting, and emotionally moving film in the entire series.

In the old Sean Connery days, the Bond films were both innovative and daring. The cinematography, editing, set design, and music set new standards and were endlessly imitated. The films were also considered daring in their violence and in their rather frank and amoral approach to sexuality. But though the Bond films have made gobs of money for fifty years, they have been neither innovative nor daring since the 1960s.

Yes, they are still imitated. But it's primarily the elements of the archetypal, '60s Bond that have been the object of imitation. And, notoriously, the Bond films began imitating themselves practically as soon as the '60s came to an end. Worse yet, Bond has often been guilty of following trends set by other films. First came the Blaxploitation Bond, *Live and Let Die* (1973). Then *The Man with the Golden Gun* (1974) tried to cash in on the popularity of martial arts movies. The nadir was reached when *Moonraker* (1979) took Bond into space, chasing after the *Star Wars* audience.

But the Daniel Craig films, which "rebooted the franchise" (an expression I detest), have changed all that. These films, starting with 2006's *Casino Royale*, are fresh, original, and feature cutting-edge talent in all areas. And *Skyfall* is the best of them, by far (better than *Casino Royale*, which was excellent, and far better than the lackluster *Quantum of Solace*, which appeared in 2008). This one is going to inspire imitators, and it is destined to be thought of as one of the "classics" in a series that might well celebrate its hundredth anniversary someday.

Cinematographer Roger Deakins has filled *Skyfall* with scenes that are often extraordinarily beautiful (especially those set in

Macau—a location Bond visited in *The Man with the Golden Gun*, but with rather less spectacular results). The acting is also the best in any Bond film. Craig has managed to turn Bond into a believable, three dimensional character. He is still larger than life, but he contains depths never plumbed by any other actor. And, yes, that includes Sean Connery. Craig is the better actor, and his is the more credible Bond. I realize that this is heresy, but the same opinion was recently put forward (albeit more politely) by Roger Moore, who has never been accused of great acting. (Connery himself could not be reached for comment.) Judi Dench (as M) and Javier Bardem (as Silva, the villain) are also excellent.

Skyfall's screenplay (by Neal Purvis, Robert Wade, and John Logan) is fresh, the dialogue intelligent and snappy. There's not a line in it that made me wince. Even Bond's one-liners are excellent (leaving a Chinese thug to be devoured by a Komodo dragon, he quips, "Ah, the circle of life . . ."). The story is also thoroughly surprising and unpredictable. How many times have you been able to say that about a Bond movie? When *A View to a Kill* appeared in 1985, one critic commented, memorably, that going to see a Bond movie is like going to the zoo: you're either pleased to see the same animals again, or you're not. Gone are those days. Even Thomas Newman's music score for *Skyfall* deserves praise: it's a great improvement over David Arnold's often shameless attempts to imitate John Barry. (I honestly think it's the best non-Barry score for a Bond film.)

The plot, as everyone knows by now, concerns a former MI6 agent (Bardem) out for revenge against M, who betrayed him years earlier to the Chinese. The story takes many twists and turns, but the basic simplicity of the villain's motivations is actually a great virtue of this film. (Some Bond movies have plots so complicated they rival *film noir*.) It's not the first time there has been a Bond revenge movie: 1989's *Licence to Kill* has Bond going rogue, out for revenge against the villain, and the bad guy in 1995's *GoldenEye* is motivated by revenge.

But this film breaks with a lot of Bond plot conventions, and the major one concerns "the Bond girl." The classic Bond formula actually involves three girls. Two of them usually only appear briefly. One is often killed, and sometimes one is an enemy agent (who also gets killed). The third is often introduced well into the film (e.g., Honey Rider in *Dr. No*, Pussy Galore in *Goldfinger*), but she sticks around until the end, and is the "female lead" of the production.

Skyfall follows this formula—up to a point. There's a black female MI6 agent named Eve (played by Naomie Harris) who's introduced at the beginning of the film, then disappears for much of the rest of it.

Then Bond encounters another female, this one held in thrall to the villain (another nod to *The Man with the Golden Gun*). She is Séverine (a name lifted from Luis Buñuel's *Belle de Jour*), played by Bérénice Lim Marlohe. And she is the film's "sacrificial lamb," killed by Silva before Bond's eyes. This is a familiar plot device in the series. It's there to allow Bond to show his human side, and to make us hate the villain more. Though here, curiously, Bond reacts coldly to Séverine's death.

The curious thing, however, is that after Silva blows poor Séverine away with his dueling pistol, no beautiful babe shows up to help Craig carry the rest of the film. There is no "third girl" in *Skyfall*. This struck me as strange . . . until I realized the obvious: in this film, M is the Bond girl. (A point which has been made by a number of reviewers.)

In large measure, *Skyfall* is really about the relationship between Bond and M. It's a relationship which hasn't been explored much in the films. In Fleming's novels, it's made clear that Bond both loves and hates his boss. M is usually cold and stern with Bond—but there are occasional, brief flashes of fatherly affection. M is actually a keen psychologist, and he no doubt realizes that the best way to keep Bond on his toes is precisely through leavening his disapproval with only a small amount of warmth. Bond is, after all, an orphan who lost his father and mother at the age of eleven. Inevitably, he can't help but see M as a father figure. And M is surely not above exploiting this.

This dynamic between Bond and M was never explored on screen before the Daniel Craig era. And his films faithfully draw upon the problematic Bond-M relationship as depicted in the novels. Except, of course, that Craig's M is a woman. And if anything, this makes the situation much, much more complicated.

M is a mother figure to Bond, but she bosses him around like dear old dad might have. And though he is drawn to her and desires her approval, the truth is that no adult male ever quite gets used to taking orders from a woman. He loves M, and resents her at the same time — probably much more than he would a male M. To make matters even more complicated, M makes it abundantly clear — *especially* in *Skyfall* — that she is willing to throw Bond to the wolves if the situation demands it. Like all orphans, at some level Bond feels abandoned. He longs for the love of the mother who left him (*twice* in the Craig films he breaks into M's apartment — wanting to be near her). But the love of his mother-substitute is more than a little doubtful. After all, she is willing to have him killed!

Poor, confused Bond. The key difference, in fact, between Craig's Bond and all the others is that he's very believably screwed up. The Craig films explore all the psychological dynamics one would expect to find in the life of an orphan who becomes a cold-blooded, government assassin. And they do so very credibly, very plausibly. This extra depth makes all the difference in the world. As I've said, Bond is still larger than life, but he is no longer a kind of unapproachable cartoon superman (as Brosnan generally played him). We admire him, and we feel for him also.

Much has been said about the Craig movies making Bond "relevant to today." Indeed they do, but it has nothing to do with Bond banging black chicks (which he's been doing since *Live and Let Die*), or wearing a Bluetooth headset. What has happened is that Bond has been made relevant to today's *younger males* — mainly thirty-somethings (according to what I've read, the audience for *Skyfall* is overwhelmingly male and over the age of 25). Few male Bond fans are orphans, of course, but most feel arrested at some earlier stage of development. Arrested, for instance, by overbearing parents and a society that has never challenged them sufficiently. They . . . uh . . . *we* are all like Edward Norton's character in *Fight Club*, who calls himself "a thirty-year-old boy." Like us, Bond is screwed up. But he holds up to us the possibility of transmuting the shit of our lives into gold.

Skyfall takes the complicated dynamic of Bond's relation to M and pushes it toward a climax that is truly bizarre and dreamlike — thick with symbolism and psychological catharsis. At the risk of understatement, it is unlike anything you've ever seen in a Bond film before.

To make a long story short, Silva almost succeeds in killing M, and Bond realizes that the only way to protect her is take matters completely into his own hands and spirit her off to someplace safe. So, he essentially kidnaps M and tells her that they must go back "into the past." The first stop on the way is to pick up Bond's Aston Martin DB5 from *Goldfinger*. When the car is first seen, the audience in the theatre where I saw the film cheered and applauded (and I have read that audiences have reacted similarly all over the U.S. and Europe). In a delightful touch, Bond threatens to remove a censorious M from the car by firing the passenger ejector seat. Like a passive-aggressive Jewish mother, M grumbles "Go ahead. Eject me. See if I care."

They head north, all the way to the Scottish Highlands and to Bond's ancestral home, Skyfall (this is not mentioned in Fleming, nor is the name ever explained in the film). It's a broken down, disused old manse. One gets the impression that Bond has not seen it since he lost his parents. (Fleming tells us that after his parents died — in a climbing accident, no less — Bond was raised by his aunt Charmian in "the quaintly named hamlet of Pett Bottom near Canterbury in Kent.") A kindly old caretaker named Kincade appears, a figure from Bond's childhood, played by Albert Finney. And with the addition of this new character, a strange new dynamic is now established. M, of course, is cast in the role of Bond's mother, while Kincade now emerges as a father figure. (In one amusing scene, he even tries to teach Bond to shoot! In another amusing touch, he hears "M" as "Em" and addresses her henceforth as Emma.)

They know that Silva will eventually track them down, so Bond is keen to find out if the gun cabinet is still well-stocked. Alas, all the guns have been sold to an American collector (it just had to be an American, didn't it?). All that remains is the old hunting rifle that had belonged to Bond's father (inscribed with the initials "AB," for Andrew Bond). And a knife. "Sometimes the old ways are best," says Kincade, laying the knife on the table. Bond and Kincade then set a number of clever booby traps for the villains. A last resort for M, should the going get really rough, is a secret passage leading out of the house, built centuries earlier.

Rifles, knives, secret passages, escapes across (and under) the heath. It's all very, very "low tech." In my essay "The Importance of James Bond," I discussed Bond's equivocal relationship to technology, and I expressed the concern that Daniel Craig's Bond was becoming too tech-friendly. I'm happy to say that *Skyfall* has allayed all my concerns about this. From beginning to end, this film is strongly traditionalist, and deeply skeptical about the "blessings" of technology.

Indeed, the event that catalyzes the whole story is the theft of a hard drive that stores the identities of all British agents who have infiltrated terrorist organizations. Smart move, putting all that on somebody's hard drive. Naturally, Silva gets ahold of it. And then he hacks into MI6's network and brings it down. Oh, and then he blows up MI6's high-tech HQ! M and company are forced to relocate to a bunker used by Churchill during World War Two. All of this is importantly symbolic: the gee-whiz computer technology overused in *Quantum of Solace* is gone. Now all that can save the day is Bond's cleverness and guts.

But the "experts," armed with electrocardiograms, word association tests, and other paraphernalia pronounce Bond unfit for duty. Bugger the experts! Bond proves them all wrong, accomplishing what *technē* pronounced impossible. And he does it with precious little from the new Q, now a young computer geek. Q equips him with exactly two gadgets: a gun that only he can fire and a little radio. "Not exactly Christmas, is it?" quips Bond. But both the little radio (actually, a homer not unlike the one he used way back in *Goldfinger*) and the gun (a similar gun appears in *Licence to Kill*) save his life.

At one point we see M is testifying before a subcommittee of the House of Commons, being grilled by "experts" who think that putting actual agents in the field is rather old fashioned in this high tech world. Patiently, M—no stranger to high tech, but souring on it — explains to them why the old ways really are best. Then, in a scene that made me tear up, she quotes Tennyson's poem "Ulysses," as her men risk their lives in the streets to stop Silva:

> One equal temper of heroic hearts,
> Made weak by time and fate, but strong in will
> To strive, to seek, to find, and not to yield.

And where does it all wind up? Again, with a journey back in time. All tech is gone. Bond is reduced to loading a hunting rifle, setting booby traps, and strapping a knife to his body. And the tough, ball-busting M is reduced as well — reduced to being a woman who must be rescued by a man. But Bond himself is *not* personally reduced. He has returned to this strange, primal scene, and has been reunited with his "mother" and "father." But now he must do what he was unable to do when he was a child, but which he *can* do as a man: he must save them from death. In doing so, he exorcizes these ghosts from his past.

I won't discuss all the details of what follows. But I must correct one omission in what I've said above. The one piece of "tech" Bond makes use of is the Aston Martin. I was pleased that, unlike some of the other films in which the car has reappeared, some sensible use was actually made of it here. Bond hides in the car, then fires its front machine guns at Silva's men as they approach the house. But this use of tech delighted me — and it has important symbolic significance. Today's younger audiences tend to look down their noses at anything predating the era of the internet (I've even heard young audiences laugh out loud at rotary phones). Here the one piece of tech Bond utilizes — with deadly effect — is that old-fashioned, pre-electronic Aston Martin from that hopelessly old-fashioned film that grandpa loves.

In the end, Bond winds up killing Silva with the lowest-tech gadget imaginable: the knife seen earlier, plunged deep into Silva's back. Much to my shock, M then dies in Bond's arms, of wounds suffered during the attack on the house. And, yes, I shed a tear at this as well. But, in my defense, so does Bond! This is only the second time in the history of the series that Bond has cried. The first time, of course, was in 1969's *On Her Majesty's Secret Service*, when Blofeld murdered Bond's bride, Tracy. That was a moving scene as well, but Craig is a much better actor than George Lazenby, and this time we actually see the tears, which seem quite real (in *OHMSS* we don't actually see the tears, we just hear Bond sob). I thought of *OHMSS* as I watched this scene, as Bond cradles his "mother" here much as he does Tracy. That there is something Oedipal to this is more than obvious. The film's entire Scotland sequence plays like a long, Freudian dream.

But this is not all. The final scene of the film is extraordinary. Eve, the black MI6 agent seen earlier, returns and reveals herself to be Eve Moneypenny (who never had a first name in the books or any earlier film). At the beginning of the film she accidentally shoots and almost kills Bond. (Memo to the screenwriters: there's a reason that there aren't any black female sharpshooters in real life.) Now she has decided to take a new job: as M's receptionist. Sometimes the old ways are best . . .

And what of M himself? The new M is Mallory, a character seen earlier, played by Ralph Fiennes. But the most extraordinary thing of all is that his office is a recreation of the one seen in the old Bernard Lee days, complete with the padded leather door. Gone are the female M's high-tech digs from the past six films. And M has gone back to being a man! Yes, it bears repeating, sometimes the old ways really are best. And this film returns us to them. It is an unabashed celebration of tradition, and a clear reaction against the "modernizing" of Bond that has taken place since *GoldenEye*. It is, in fact, a reaction against much of modernity itself. And — if I do say so — as a confirmation of the thesis I advanced in "The Importance of James Bond" it is everything I could have wished for. "James Bond is back!" the ads always proclaim. Indeed he is.

I'm such a big Bond fan I once had a nightmare that I had gone to see "the new Bond film" and found it to be an unimaginably lame and pathetic failure (sort of how Indiana Jones fans must have felt when they went to see *Kingdom of the Crystal Skull*). But *Skyfall* feels like I went to sleep and dreamed of that Bond film than which no greater can be conceived. One that not only delivers in terms of action, thrills, and all the traditional Bondian elements—but which also contains philosophical and psychological depth of a kind I never expected to find in this series.

I cannot praise *Skyfall* enough. Do yourself a favor and see it today. Even if you don't think you like Bond films, see it anyway. This one will convert you.

Counter-Currents/*North American New Right*,
November 13, 2012

THE CAT IS BACK!
THE SPECTRE BEHIND S.P.E.C.T.R.E.

This essay is dedicated to Savitri Devi.

James Bond overheard pouring his heart out to a bartender, while downing his sixth vodka martini: "Aside from the torture devices, the explosions, the mindless, soulless, robotic minions, and the miles and miles of stainless steel, there's one thing that still haunts me about Blofeld's hellish world, one thing I can't get out of my bloody nostrils: *that godawful litter box smell!*"

Yes, ladies and gentlemen, the cat is back! And Blofeld's got him. I need not alert you to spoilers ahead, as by now everyone has heard that *Spectre*, the new Bond film starring the incomparable Daniel Craig, features the return of Ernst Stavro Blofeld. Though I found much of this film to be rather disappointing (an inevitable letdown after the superb *Skyfall*), I am delighted that the old man is back again. And I'm happy that Blofeld is back as well.

Let's start with a little bit of history. Blofeld and the organization known as S.P.E.C.T.R.E. came about through the collaboration of Ian Fleming, Kevin McClory, and Jack Whittingham on a never-filmed screenplay titled *James Bond of the Secret Service*. The work began, I believe, in 1958, and it was apparently McClory who was the primary creator of Blofeld and his organization. Fleming liked the idea, as he was tired of using the Russians as villains. When nothing came of the project, Fleming adapted the script into his novel *Thunderball*, published in 1961.

The trouble is that Fleming . . . uh . . . forgot that the story was the result of a collaboration. McClory and Whittingham, understandably, filed suit — and won. The outcome was that Fleming's health was ruined (he died a year after the court case concluded), and McClory was declared legal owner of S.P.E.C.T.R.E. and Blofeld. This created a difficult situation for everyone concerned. Fleming had already used Blofeld in two other novels: *On Her Majesty's Secret Service* (1963) and *You Only Live Twice* (1964).

Furthermore, producers Albert R. Broccoli and Harry Saltzman had added the S.P.E.C.T.R.E. organization to their film of *Dr. No* (1962; it did not figure in the novel), and both the organization and Blofeld were written into *From Russia, With Love* (1963; again, neither is in the novel). This meant that after the 1963 court decision, McClory could have sued Eon Productions for the use of his creations in its first two films. This problem was solved when Eon offered McClory a substantial amount of money to "lease" S.P.E.C.T.R.E. and Blofeld from him for a period of ten years, understood as beginning in 1962.

Since Broccoli and Saltzman had already bought the rights to *Thunderball* from Fleming, this presented an arguably more complicated matter — one that was solved by Eon co-producing the film version with McClory (who also, by the court's decision, won the film rights to the story). This worked out to be a nice arrangement for Mr. McClory, since *Thunderball* was an absolute blockbuster. In today's dollars it made approximately a billion.

But rather than get on with his life and perhaps create a dense and radiant muffin of his own design, the odious Mr. McClory spent the rest of his days trying to capitalize on the success of Eon's Bond films by launching a competing Bond series of his own. This process began almost immediately after Eon's "lease" on Blofeld expired in 1972. The evil genius was last seen in an Eon Bond film in 1971's *Diamonds Are Forever*. By the mid-'70s, reports were circulating that McClory was planning a film titled variously *James Bond of the Secret Service*, or *Warhead*. McClory quickly got Sean Connery involved, as actor, producer, and collaborator on the screenplay. And these two then brought the redoubtable Len Deighton on board.

Eon Productions fought back with an endless series of injunctions against McClory. And while the first *Warhead* script appears to have been completed in 1976, it would not be filmed until 1983, by which point the title had become *Never Say Never Again*. This would be McClory's one and only victory. After this film, he had planned to make other Bond adventures, all somehow or other based on the original *Thunderball* screenplays to which he owned the rights, and presumably starring Connery. But Eon successfully defeated this in court.

Like the cinematic monster that just will not die, McClory kept on fighting. As late as 1999 Sony Pictures announced that, in collaboration with McClory, they would be making their own competing series of Bond films. When this was quashed, McClory then filed a suit against Eon claiming he was owed money (above and beyond the amount of his original lease) for all the Eon films featuring S.P.E.C.T.R.E. This too was quashed — and by now everyone could see that Mr. McClory was one of those people Ayn Rand called moochers and looters.

McClory died in 2006, whereupon Eon Productions (now headed by Barbara Broccoli and her half-brother Michael G. Wilson) quietly made a deal with his estate. For an undisclosed sum, they bought the rights to Blofeld and S.P.E.C.T.R.E. Partly, this was done to end — once and for all — attempts on anyone's part to try to launch a competing Bond series through the back door of the complicated *Thunderball* rights. But Eon also wanted to bring back Bond's most celebrated nemesis.

Actually, they had long wanted to. Originally, the villain in 1977's *The Spy Who Loved Me* was to have been Blofeld. But when McClory refused to negotiate the rights, and announced plans for *Warhead*, the villain's name was changed to "Stromberg," and he was given a new motive for his dastardly scheme: not extortion but idealism. Everything else remained the same — including the Mao jacket and the bit about dunking betrayers into a shark tank. (And the actor cast as Stromberg, Curt Jurgens, would arguably have made the all-time best Blofeld.) In 1981, in what has rightfully been interpreted as a giant middle finger held up to McClory, Eon featured a Blofeld-like villain in the opening sequence of *For Your Eyes Only*. The character — who is never named — is dispatched by Bond, but not before pleading "We can do a deal! I'll build you a delicatessen in stainless steel!" (A line reportedly contributed by Cubby Broccoli.)

So, what is it that made this unnamed villain recognizable as Blofeld? I'm glad you asked. First, he is bald — as Donald Pleasance was in *You Only Live Twice* (arguably the most physically memorable Blofeld). Second, he wears a Mao jacket. And third, he lavishes affection on a luxurious white Persian cat wearing a diamond collar. Without question, this is the feature of the

Blofeld persona that everyone remembers. It has been copied and parodied countless times. One of my favorite instances of an outright copy is in the Bruce Lee film *Enter the Dragon* (1973), where the villain appears wearing a Blofeld-like jacket and carrying a white Persian cat. (I'm guessing it was not the same cat.) I love this one because it's not camp, it's naïve. Apparently somebody in Hong Kong just thought that white Persian cats are an indispensable accessory for the super-villain. And then, of course, there is the Persian-rendered-bald in the Austin Powers movies, about which the less said the better.

Now, I knew that S.P.E.C.T.R.E. was making a comeback in *Spectre*. Indeed, the film is called *Spectre,* which was definitely a clue. But I was unsure that Blofeld would be resurrected. After all, I kept hearing that the film's villain (played by Christoph Waltz) was called "Oberhauser." Imagine my delight when, near the end of this overlong movie, "Oberhauser" announces that he has assumed a new name: Ernst Stavro Blofeld.

Admittedly, there are problems. First, S.P.E.C.T.R.E. is now Spectre; the acronym (SPecial Executive for Counterintelligence, Terrorism, Revenge, Extortion) is gone. I heard they thought it seemed corny now. But still more problematic is why this Blofeld is Blofeld. The film reveals that the guy's name really is Oberhauser. He decides to change it after, decades earlier, murdering his own father after he agreed to become legal guardian to the young James Bond. Yes, rather than share his toys with James, the psychotic young Oberhauser kills his father. And this is why he hates Bond, and why all that has happened in the previous three Bond films has been orchestrated by Oberhauser. Or something like that. If this seems pat, overcomplicated, unnecessary, and implausible it is because it is simultaneously *all* of these things.

Oh, I forgot: after committing patricide Oberhauser changes his name to Ernst Stavro Blofeld. The explanation: "Mother's bloodline," he says to Bond. Okay, so his mother's maiden name was Blofeld. But from whom did he lift the Greek middle name? Things were a lot less complicated in Fleming: he's named Ernst Stavro Blofeld because his father is German and his mother is Greek.

But setting this aside—saints preserve us he's wearing a Nehru jacket (or a janker; it depends on your perspective)! And they use an adaptation of the old Spectre ghost/octopus emblem (first seen in *From Russia, With Love*). Oh, and by the way: Blofeld wears his Nehru jacket with slippers and no socks. I'm still trying to figure that one out (see the film—I'm not making it up). This is revealed in the *Spectre*'s rather grim torture sequence in which—yes!—*the cat appears*.

At first I thought I must be dreaming. A number of critics have commented on the fact that in this film, Eon has tried to give us more of the "old Bond" that many have missed in the Craig entries. And this definitely appears to be true. I'm not surprised we got Blofeld back, but the filmmakers deserve real credit for not restraining themselves on the cat issue. So what if it's now camp? After the highway of despair that was the last three Craig movies (they're good, mind you—but grim) we deserve a little camp.

As you must have gathered from the foregoing, I think that *Spectre* is a mixed bag of a movie. But almost anything was bound to disappoint us after *Skyfall*. Here I wish only to celebrate the return of the cat. Let us now take a trip down memory lane and recall the highlights of this evil cat's nine lives:

1. The cat is introduced in *From Russia, With Love* (1963). Blofeld wears a regular suit in this one—looks black, or very dark blue. Every time I watch the scenes where he's holding the cat I think about the fur problem. And I imagine Hans, the huge, blond superman thug from *You Only Live Twice* whisking him with one of those sticky lint rollers. Blofeld's face is not seen. His body is played by Anthony Dawson, who was Professor Dent in *Dr. No*, and he is voiced by Eric Pohlmann. We watch as Siamese fighting fish go at it in Blofeld's fish tank. Then Blofeld feeds one of them to the cat. This is about all the cat has to do, I'm afraid. Poor pussy. But he was only getting started.

2. *Thunderball* (1965). The cat's next appearance is two years later. Blofeld's face is again unseen, and he is played by the same two actors for body and voice. This is the famous S.P.E.C.T.R.E. board room sequence. Blofeld realizes one of his underlings has betrayed him. At a command from the cat in his lap he presses a

switch and electrocutes the reckless fool. The best part is when the chair sinks into the floor, then rises again without the body. Actually, I am kidding: the cat doesn't tell Blofeld to do it. But there is really no way to know what Blofeld is thinking, is there?

3. *You Only Live Twice* (1967). In this one, Blofeld's face is finally revealed. The producers originally cast Czech actor Jan Werick to play him. But after five days of filming, he was deemed unsuitable. ("He looked like Father Christmas," said director Lewis Gilbert.) Werick was replaced by Donald Pleasance, who is suitably pervy and creepy. I should note here that Christoph Waltz plays Blofeld in similar creepy fashion. And — Spoiler alert! — he winds up near the end of the film with a scar just like the one they gave Pleasance.

Two notable scenes in *You Only Live Twice*: Watch carefully the scene near the end of the film in Blofeld's control room. As the ninjas attack and bombs start going off the cat looks REALLY scared, and is clawing the hell out of Pleasance's Mao jacket. This is the first time Blofeld is seen in this getup, by the way. Later: when Blofeld is escaping, as he goes to flip the self-destruct switch in his gigantic volcano lair, he is still carrying the cat. Is the cat there to soften Blofeld's image? Curious.

4. *On Her Majesty's Secret Service* (1969). Here Blofeld become Telly Savalas. Not an inspired piece of casting in this, the best of all Bond movies. The producers thought Pleasance unsuited to the film, due to the fact that this Blofeld is more vigorous (he skies, for instance). The cat makes an all-too-brief an appearance, first being stroked by Savalas in his lap (Savalas wearing a janker), then being tossed out of Savalas's lap when he learns that Bond has escaped his mountaintop lair.

5. *Diamonds Are Forever* (1971). About the cat being there to "soften" Blofeld's image: in this one we actually see the cat sitting on Blofeld's desk eating Tender Vittles out of (what else?) a stainless steel bowl. This is the scene that makes me think about the litter box. Where is it? Under Blofeld's gigantic desk? In the ornate bathroom that Bond breaks into when first arriving in Blofeld's penthouse lair? What kind of litter does Blofeld use? Clumping? Scented? Well, in this film he would have to use that Arm and Hammer multi-cat litter because here we get *two* cats!

Yes, Blofeld has a double. And, appropriately, his cat has a double as well. Confronted with the two Blofelds, Bond thinks he knows which is real. So he savagely kicks one of the kitties, sending it sailing, claws ablaze, into the chest of one of the Blofelds. Then he pulls out a concealed bolt-gun and kills the man with a shot to the head. Alas, it is the double, not the real thing. "Right idea, Mr. Bond," purrs Blofeld. "But wrong pussy," Bond replies.

In this film Blofeld is played by Charles Gray, in some scenes wearing a lovely pearl-grey Mao jacket. Gray's Blofeld is very, very, very gay. And, as a result, for the first time we notice just how froo froo an accessory this cat really is.

Later on, Bond girl Tiffany Case (Jill St. John) sees an old woman heading for a chauffeured limousine and carrying a Persian cat. Somebody must have tipped Tiffany off about Blofeld being a cat lover, because she is instantly suspicious. And, yes, it turns out that the old woman is Blofeld *in drag*! Poor Tiffany is captured and shoved into Blofeld's limo. "Well, well," he says. "Look what the cat dragged in." Later, in conversation with Bond, millionaire Willard Whyte (Jimmy Dean) refers to Blofeld as "your friend with the cat." It becomes official with this film: it doesn't matter who plays Blofeld or what he looks like. The cat is the thing. Is "Blofeld" just there to mind the cat? And what is this cat's name? Macavity?

By the way: just how do Tiffany and Whyte know that Blofeld has a cat? The only possible answer is that Bond talks about it. A lot.

To Tiffany, lying next to her in bed smoking: ". . . That's not the worst thing. That's not what's bothering me. It's that cat that he has. Arrogant little bastard! I can't get its eyes out of my head, or . . ." (picking fur out from under his lip) ". . . or its hair out of my mouth. The bloody hair is everywhere." Tiffany: "James, it's okay. It happens to every man now and then."

To Willard Whyte: "You still don't get it, do you! That laser is a gigantic cat toy. . . . Don't look at me like that. Have you ever seen a cat chasing a spot projected by a laser? This thing is so powerful it can project a spot on the moon—or burn through solid metal. In the hands of that cat, we're all mice down here!"

6. As discussed earlier, Blofeld and pussy disappear from the Eon films after *Diamonds are Forever*. Well, except for *For Your Eyes Only* (1981). This is the one where the character who "looks like" Blofeld makes an appearance. Fun cat fact: When Bond's helicopter lifts "Blofeld's" wheelchair (see the film), the cat immediately abandons him. This means either (a) the cat does not like Blofeld, or (b) the cat is a cat.

7. *Never Say Never Again* (1983). In the odious Mr. McClory's not-bad Bond movie, Max von Sydow plays Blofeld. Here he wears a standard suit, as he did in the McClory-produced *Thunderball*. The cat features prominently in one shot, when von Sydow picks him up. Otherwise, it has nothing to do — except gaze at the camera at one point, in an exquisite close up.

Which brings us to . . .

8. *Spectre*: All I can add to what I have said before is that here — for the first time in Bond history — the cat jumps into Bond's lap. "Hello pussy," he says. Now, *this* would have given Blofeld a much more plausible motive for revenge. I know people like this, who can't stand it when their pets show affection to others.

Will the cat return in the next Bond movie? Because there almost certainly will be a next. *Spectre* is nowhere near as good a movie as *Skyfall*, but it's still raking in the money. At the end of this film Blofeld is captured — and we know what that means: someone will spring him. He will be back. And where there is Blofeld, the cat cannot be far behind. The cat, after all, is clearly the brains of the outfit.

Counter-Currents/*North American New Right*,
November 9, 2015

FIGHT CLUB AS HOLY WRIT

1. I AM JACK'S MOST DEVOTED SPACE MONKEY

I have hesitated to write an essay on *Fight Club* for some time, as it would mean breaking the first two rules of Fight Club. But I can no longer remain silent.

Fight Club has now displaced *Network* (1977) as my favorite film—not because it's a better piece of cinema, or "the greatest film of all time." The reason is that *Fight Club* speaks to me in a way that no other film does. I have watched it countless times with countless people under all sorts of conditions (it seems to go particularly well with Jägermeister). This film addresses my problems and the problems of the age; it speaks to my own deepest dissatisfactions and darkest desires; and proposes (or at least *seems* to propose) many of the right solutions to what ails us. (Though, as I shall explain, there is one major lacuna in the film's ideology.)

Fight Club has the capacity to inspire me like no other film. If I am feeling down, depressed and discouraged by "things today" or by my own inability to put the chicken shit of my daily life into perspective, one late-night viewing of *Fight Club* is enough to get me back on track and restore my sense of "mission." In a certain way, I have to admit that I feel slightly awkward about this. After all, *Fight Club* is (I think) a film intended for a much younger audience. In many ways its aesthetic belongs very much to the present. And let's not lose sight of the fact that as great as this film is, it is a Hollywood product. I am a highly-educated man. I've read every major work in the Western canon. How can a recent Hollywood movie (with Brad Pitt for Christ's sake!) be so important to me? And yet it is. And I make no apologies for it.

I'm also far from being alone. This film has struck a chord with countless young and youngish men. It has probably been responsible for recruiting more young guys to mixed martial arts academies than any pay per view broadcast of the UFC. (One of my best friends tried to interest me in Brazilian jiu-jitsu—in which he is now a black belt—by telling me "it's like Fight Club!") Note that

I've referred so far only to men, because if ever there was a "guy flick," *Fight Club* is it. *Fight Club* has now surpassed the Three Stooges as the most effective way to drive women out of the living room. In terms of our struggle against the modern world *Fight Club* is the most important artwork of the last fifty years — and the only artwork to be directed exclusively at men. But in order to change the world one must always appeal, primarily, to men.

You will have noticed in all of the above that I have been referring solely to the film of *Fight Club*, not to the novel. There are two reasons for this. First, *Fight Club* belongs to a group of cinematic adaptations of novels that have almost completely eclipsed their original source. If I mention *Gone With the Wind*, do you think of the film or of the novel? Ditto *The Wizard of Oz*. And consider James Bond: nobody reads Fleming anymore. So, in writing of *Fight Club* for readers of Counter-Currents it is the film, primarily, that I must speak of.

Second, the film improves upon the book in a number of significant ways. None of this is meant to disparage either the novel or its author, Chuck Palahniuk. In fact, one can really speak of the film and novel *together* because although the film does depart from the novel in some ways, for the most part it follows it very closely. (A huge amount of Edward Norton's voiceover narration in the film is taken directly from the text.) Without Palahniuk, there would be no cinematic *Fight Club*, and so we must all bow to his genius. However, as I will discuss later on, his genius is of a very peculiar and problematic kind.

And this leads me to a very important point, which I must state up front: I am not the slightest bit interested in what Palahniuk has said *about* his novel, or its film version. The reasons for this have to do with that peculiar and problematic genius I will (I promise) elaborate on later. For now, I will simply invoke Roland Barthes's infamous "death of the author" thesis: texts mean more than their authors think that they do, and an author's intentions or personal understanding of his work is not the be-all-and-end-all of interpretation. I am also not the slightest bit interested in what director David Fincher or screenwriter Jim Uhls think of their film. (I will tell *them* what it means, thank you.)

2. I AM JACK'S *THUMOS*

No lengthy plot summary is necessary. I'll wager virtually everyone reading this has seen *Fight Club*. The central character in both the novel (which is told in the first person) and the film is not named initially. And to keep matters straight we can't begin by calling him by the name we later learn is actually his own. The screenplay refers to him as "Jack," in reference to a series of brief anatomy primers that he discovers, bearing titles like "I Am Jack's Colon." (In the novel, it is "Joe.")

Our friend Jack is the Last Man. He works as a recall coordinator for a major, unnamed car company and he is living "the American dream." When not working, he spends his time stocking his climate-controlled, concrete-lined condo (in Wilmington, Delaware—though the film only hints at this) with IKEA furniture, duvets, and dust ruffles. He has it all: CK shirts, DKNY shoes, AX ties. And absolutely nothing else. Had this film been made (or the novel written) more recently no doubt a large portion of Jack's evenings, and days off, would be spent looking at porn online and masturbating.

Jack says "I would flip through catalogues and wonder, 'What kind of dining set defines me as a person?'" My God, I've done the exact same thing. I've spent many an afternoon winding my way through IKEA looking at their displays thinking "Is this the sort of couch a person like me would have?" Or, worse yet, "What do I want to say about myself by buying that bedspread?"

Fight Club does a marvelous job of conveying the utter barrenness of this modern life—especially the way it tries to cover its stench with the sickly-sweet perfume of moral superiority. Jack buys "Rislampa wire lamps of environmentally-friendly unbleached paper," and "glass dishes with tiny bubbles and imperfections. Proof they were crafted by the honest, simple, hardworking indigenous peoples of . . . wherever." And, of course, there are the awful, smarmy support groups where everything is referred to in euphemisms, everyone who suffers is "heroic," and every death is a "tragedy."

And everywhere there is the oppressive vulgarity of a processed, homogenized, corporate world: "When deep space exploration ramps up it will be the corporations that name everything.

The IBM Stellar Sphere. The Microsoft Galaxy. Planet Starbucks." (Of course, it seems now that the dream of deep space exploration has just been quietly dropped. Perhaps it's a good thing that this planet is the only one we will trash.) *Fight Club* not only captures the ugliness and emptiness of today, it captures its inhumanity as well. The automated phone lines with their menus within menus, the corporations that knowingly put our lives at risk with shoddy products, the bosses who think your life belongs to them, and the complete and total lack of any sense of community, any sense of caring for others. This plush little Rislampa lit paradise we've created is hard and cold, filled with harried, angry people.

It's the men who are angriest of all. The women, true enough, are awful: brittle, desiccated career harpies; emotionally stunted and even physically damaged by their religious commitment to infertility. And this is, in many ways, very much a woman's world. It is soccer-mom safe. Oriented around material comfort, security, and the suppression of *thumos*. As I said in my essay "Dystopia is Now!":

> *Thumos* is "spiritedness." According to Plato (in *The Republic*) it's that aspect of us that responds to a challenge against our values. *Thumos* is what makes us want to beat up those TSA screeners who pat us down and put us through that machine that allows them to view our naughty bits. It's an affront to our dignity, and makes us want to fight. Anyone who does not feel affronted in this situation is not really a human being. This is because it is really *thumos* that makes us human; that separates us from the beasts. (It's not just that we're smarter than them; our possession of *thumos* makes us different in kind from other animals.) *Thumos* is the thing in us that responds to ideals: it motivates us to fight for principles, and to strive to be more than we are.

Now, what is important to understand is that although *thumos* is a human possession, it is pre-eminently a *male* possession. Actually, it's even more complicated than that. It's possible to be a male, a grown-up male, and not be a man (or as we sometimes say "a *real* man"). All men intuitively understand this, even drag queens. (Want to get slugged by a drag queen? Just impugn her manhood.) Becoming a man has everything to do with the expression and management of *thumos*.

Young men often think they will impress older men through an unbridled expression of thumotic rage. They quickly learn that this is greeted with disapproval. A real man doesn't fight unnecessarily, and he sure as hell doesn't fight in order to "prove something" (beyond a certain age, the desire to "prove you're a man" is a sign of stunted emotional growth and narcissism).

But a real man will fight (physically or verbally) when something important is at stake—including his dignity and honor, or the dignity and honor of his family, or his people. Whereas the inability or unwillingness to fight when the situation calls for it—especially when this is due to fear—marks a man as unmanly, and exposes him to the contempt of other, manlier men.

How *thumos* gets expressed, and what counts as a situation calling for its expression, differs from culture to culture. For example, the phenomenon of "honor killings" fills us Westerners with horror—and indeed the dumber the humans, the dumber will be their expressions of *thumos*. But the *Untermenschen* at least have some *thumos*, whereas ours seems to have been sliced off some time ago.

Yes, it's with emasculation that *Fight Club* begins. Literally. (And literal emasculation is a thread that runs through the entire film.) The world of *Fight Club*—our world—is a world where all healthy, male expressions of masculinity have been pathologized and suppressed. And the story of *Fight Club* starts when Jack, an emotionally repressed insomniac looking for some kind of catharsis, visits a support group for men with testicular cancer: "Remaining Men Together." Some of these men have literally been emasculated. One of them, Bob, has developed "bitch tits" because testosterone therapy caused his body to up his estrogen level.

How did Bob get in this predicament? We are told that he was a "champion bodybuilder." And like all champion bodybuilders he was a roid head. (Bob gives us a litany of the drugs he used to use, saying of one of them "They use that on racehorses for Christ's sake!"). It is implied that Bob's steroid abuse led to his testicular cancer. How ironic. Here's a guy who pumped himself full of synthetic man hormones and built enormous man muscles—why? Well, to be manly for gosh sakes. And it led to his manhood being removed.

Punishment from the gods, if you ask me. Like Jack and so many other men today, he felt a sense of masculine inferiority. And like so many men today he addressed it through the external, through the cosmetic. So he built big muscles (which, of course, any fairy can do in a gym in Chelsea). Others allow a quarter inch or so of stubble to accumulate on their faces, and carefully trim it every few days. Others buy snazzy cars.

Still others respond to those "penis enlargement" spam emails. Why is penis size such a big issue these days? Why are there countless websites and pills promising to give a guy three inches in three weeks? Why do guys in gyms now wear their underwear into the shower? (Something which would have been considered really weird in my father's day, when guys swam naked at the Y without shame, and without anybody thinking it was "gay.") Is it just because we're exposed to more porn now than ever before, and have a distorted image of what's "normal"? No, it's because *all the traditional ways in which men have proved their masculinity are now closed to us.* And so masculinity becomes purely a matter of externals, of looks and size: height, size of muscles, size of penis, size of bank account, size of house, etc.

Fight Club is about reclaiming lost masculine rites of passage and pathways to male self-actualization. It's about reclaiming masculinity itself. Note that I did not say "reinventing" or (choke) "reimagining" masculinity. That's what the phony "men's movement" is all about: creating a new, feminist-approved masculinity. Sitting in sweat lodges, banging drums, and weeping about how the "traditional masculine gender role" has been "hurtful" to them. Palahniuk is, partly, parodying this with Remaining Men Together. But don't misunderstand me, there's nothing wrong with men crying—so long as they don't cry too often, too easily, and over too trivial a matter. Read *The Iliad*. Those guys cried more than Republican hopefuls in an election year.

When Bob embraces Jack at Remaining Men Together, after a

moment's hesitation Jack begins weeping freely. (When he releases Bob and we see the tear stains on Bob's grey shirt it looks kind of like the image on the Shroud of Turin. This always gets big laughs from audiences, for some reason.) Why does Jack cry—or, better put, what is he crying over? He's crying over the shrieking nothingness he lives the rest of the day (to borrow some words from Paddy Chayefsky's *Network*). He has every reason to cry—and so do we. There's nothing wrong with feeling sorry for yourself so long as you've really got something to be sorry over. We're Last Men living at the End of History, in the wreckage of the Great Society, drowning in the brown tide. And to add insult to injury we've had our balls handed to us. "Go ahead, Cornelius. You can cry."

But Tyler Durden put it best:

> I see in Fight Club the strongest and smartest men who have ever lived—an entire generation pumping gas and waiting tables; or they're slaves with white collars. Advertisements have them chasing cars and clothes, working jobs they hate so they can buy shit they don't need. We are the middle children of history, with no purpose or place. We have no great war, or great depression. Our great war is a spiritual war. Our great depression is our lives. We were raised by television to believe that we'd be millionaires and movie gods and rock stars—but we won't. And we're learning that fact. And we're very, very pissed-off.

Then, in the screenplay (but not in the finished film), Tyler says: "We are the quiet young men who listen until it's time to decide." A very significant line, as we shall see . . .

3. I Am Jack's Dialectic

I said earlier that expressions of male *thumos* differ from culture to culture. But what remains constant in masculine identity is this central role of *thumos*, however expressed. For women, femininity is a state of being. For men, masculinity is an ideal to be achieved and maintained. As Derek Hawthorne has put it,

"Women *are*, but men must *become*."[1]

Femininity has to do primarily with a woman's attractiveness to a man. But a man whose "masculinity" was pinned principally on his attractiveness to women would be regarded by other men—real men—with contempt. (This was what so disgusted American men about Rudolph Valentino in the 1920s.)

Males have an innate drive to become men, and this means to strive, to compete, to fight, to risk, or die trying. He who doesn't, isn't. (Isn't a man, that is.) Again, to quote Derek Hawthorne:

> If men did not feel driven to make their mark on the world and prove themselves worthy of being called men, there would be no science, no philosophy, no art, no music, no technology, no exploration. "There would also be no war, no conflict, no competition!" feminists and male geldings will shriek in response. They're right: there would be none of these things. And the world would be colorless and un-utterably boring.[2]

But, as I have said, our modern world makes it virtually impossible for men to become men, and beats them down with avalanches of drivel about "sensitivity."

In truth, *Fight Club* really begins not with Jack's visit to Remaining Men Together. (This is simply the moment when he meets men who express physically and externally what he feels spiritually and internally.) Fight Club begins when Jack meets Tyler Durden. There's no need for me to cry "Spoiler Alert!" at this point, for everybody in the world by now knows that Jack eventually discovers that Tyler is his alter ego, and that he suffers from what shrinks now call "dissociative identity disorder." So, when Jack meets Tyler Durden, it's really Tyler Durden meeting Tyler Durden.

The Tyler he meets (played by Brad Pitt) is the Tyler that Jack (i.e., Tyler) has the potential to be, but has not yet consciously become: absolutely self-confident, strong, charismatic, and free in

---

[1] http://www.counter-currents.com/2010/10/jack-malebranches-androphilia-a-manifesto/

[2] *Ibid.*

every possible sense of the word. Free of materialism, free of the desire for the approval of others, free of the desire for comfort, free of the desire for security, and free of desire as such (he is an awakened one, a Buddha, and the novel and film actually make a number of references to Buddhism).

In the film, Jack meets Tyler on a plane. (In the novel, oddly enough, they meet on a nude beach.) But the crucial moment comes after Jack's condo has been blown to smithereens, and after Jack and Tyler have had three pitchers of beer and are standing outside Lou's Tavern. That's when Tyler asks Jack to hit him. "I don't want to die without any scars," Tyler says. "How much can you really know about yourself if you've never been in a fight?" (How true. Most men today have never been in a fight, and somewhere, at the back of their minds, Tyler's question nags all of them.) And so Jack and Tyler begin to fight; or rather, Jack/Tyler begins to fight *himself*. Fight himself for what?

What is absolutely brilliant here is that both novel and film initially present this conflict as man vs. man, and then later present the same conflict as man vs. himself. But in *both* cases, two personalities are struggling for dominance. To understand all this, we will have to go three rounds with Hegel.

Just about the only part of Hegel's *Phenomenology of Spirit* that anybody can understand is what scholars have dubbed "the master-slave dialectic." Hegel posits a primal scene, the Beginning of History, in fact, where two adversaries confront each other and battle it out, risking death. But at a certain point, one yields to the other. The one who will not yield, who is truly willing to die rather than give in, is the Master. The one who yields has placed love of life over honor. He is the Slave. It is the Master who is truly human, for he places an ideal (his honor) over mere life. (Animals place nothing above survival; they cannot conceive of ideals like honor.)

On that fateful night behind Lou's Tavern, Jack and Tyler, like two infants learning to fight, take the first baby steps towards a recovered manhood. The initial point, as any viewer of the scene will realize, is for their benumbed modern Bonobo bodies to actually *feel something* again. Note the way they linger over their sensations. Note the wonder in Jack's voice when he says "Wow, that really hurt . . ." But soon it moves from a gleeful "Now you hit me again . . ." to the two just pounding each other. Now they're fighting. They're one step closer to that primal scene where the object is to see who will be Master and who will be Slave. But, in this first fight, neither seems to emerge as Master. They fight and finish as equals.

Of course, what is *really* happening is that the two sides of Jack/Tyler's soul are fighting each other. And in the interior of his psyche, there really is a struggle for dominance going on. Jack has lived all this time as a Slave—a slave to the corporation, "a slave to the IKEA Nesting instinct." "Tyler" (Brad Pitt) is his Masterful alter ego, the man he *could* be. The man who has realized that "the things you own, end up owning you" (perhaps the film's most memorable line). And behind Lou's Tavern the ordinary, everyday slavish Jack is taking his first steps towards submission to his higher self. But in this particular submission, there is no shame: he is yielding to the better, stronger side of himself. In reality, two individuals do not struggle: one individual struggles to become an *Übermensch*.

Tyler Durden is an *Übermensch* who aims to destroy our Last Mannish utopia, squatting fat and happy at the End of History. How? By *restarting history*. By recreating that primal scene at the Beginning of History where manhood first flowered; where men struggled against each other using only their own strength and will, some becoming Masters, others Slaves.

Jack's submission to the Tyler persona is a complicated issue in *Fight Club*. As everyone knows, in the end, when he realizes that Tyler (Pitt) is his alter ego, he seems to rebel against Tyler, to attempt to thwart Tyler's plans, and, ultimately, to kill the Tyler in himself. Some interpreted this as Jack's "emphatic rejection" of the "amateur fascism" fomented by Tyler (that's what the British Board of Film Classification claimed, at any rate). I'm not so sure. Not at all. But I'll have more to say about this later on . . .

4. I AM JACK'S UNORGANIZED GRABASTIC PIECE OF AMPHIBIAN SHIT

Now let's be honest: the countless young (and, in my case, youngish) men who have responded so strongly to this film all want to be Tyler Durden. I'm actually torn between wanting to be Tyler Durden and wanting to be Tyler Durden's best friend. (After all, if I were Tyler I'd be awfully lonely. My Space Monkeys would keep me company, but let's face it, there's nothing like the comradeship of equals.) You can actually find sites online that will sell you replicas of Brad Pitt's red leather jacket, pimp sunglasses, and "Sock It To Me" tee shirt. So sad. For some becoming Tyler Durden means dressing like him. But everything gets commodified in our culture, even an icon of anti-commodification.

So, how do you become Tyler Durden? Well, this is obviously where lots of young guys can go radically wrong, and the film and novel have actually inspired real-life (and very silly) acts of violence and vandalism. Obviously, guys wanting to prove they're Tyler. In *Fight Club*, however, the path to becoming Tyler Durden requires a Master. This comes out, of course, in the Jack-Tyler relationship (where, in effect, a higher part of the psyche is mentoring a lower). When I saw the film for the first time, the "plot twist" really bothered me: I wanted Tyler to be real. But later I came to understand why this was necessary, and appreciated Palahniuk's brilliance. We are all Jack, and "Tyler" is not "somebody else." He is the higher part of ourselves. We must become that. We must become who we are.

Nevertheless, in accomplishing this it is useful to have a spiritual Master. This really comes into play once Jack and Tyler form Fight Club—and especially once Fight Club morphs into Project Mayhem. The cult Tyler forms is made up of equal parts military boot camp, Zen, and skinhead zaniness. "Applicants" must wait outside the door of the house on Paper Street for three days and three nights, enduring constant, brutal discouragement from Jack and Tyler before they are allowed to enter and begin their "training." This is a Zen thing, in case you didn't know. But what does the training consist in?

Well, of course part of what's going on here is that Tyler is building a revolutionary army, and his "Space Monkeys" are being trained to do mischief. But the real training is in becoming a man, and it is modeled closely on boot camp. The Space Monkeys buzz off all of their hair (except for Angel Face, who for some reason is allowed to keep his). They abandon all their possessions except for two black shirts, two black trousers, two black socks, one black coat, and "three hundred dollars of personal burial money." The discipline and denial is martial. The resulting aesthetic is pure *Romper Stomper*.

Once inside the house, shorn of hair and dressed in basic black, the Space Monkeys will find themselves part of what can accurately be called the anti-support group. The novel and film draw numerous sly parallels between Remaining Men Together and Fight Club. In one meeting of Remaining Men Together, the leader says "I look around this room and I see a lot of courage..." Tyler opens one meeting of Fight Club with the words "I look around..." The screenplay refers to all the support group leaders simply as "The Leader." In the film Jack says in one voice over commentary during a Fight Club meeting (referring to Tyler), "The leader walked around in the crowd, out in the darkness."

But in *Fight Club* all the New Agey support group garbage is tossed out: opening the heart chakra, power animals, inner childs. (The only yoga Tyler teaches is a kind of *karma yoga*, but that's a tale for another time.) The Space Monkeys are *not* supported. They are torn down. "You are not a beautiful and unique snowflake," Tyler tells them. "You are the same decaying organic matter as everything else. We are all part of the same compost heap." In classic boot camp fashion, they are broken down and then built back up again; given a new identity that centers on their membership in a warrior band, serving a common purpose. In this case, the purpose is the destruction of the modern world (my purpose, in fact). Fight Club and Operation Mayhem are a re-creation of the classical Germanic *Männerbund*—living on the fringes of society; a volatile force that can be used for good or ill.

The way *Fight Club* approaches this process of male self-transformation is often disturbingly (and unnecessarily) nihilistic. (This is especially true of the novel.) Tyler tells us (as worded in the original screenplay): "Self-improvement is masturbation. Self-destruction is the answer." After Tyler gives Jack the chemical burn kiss (a *Männerbund* rite of passage if there ever was one), he tells him "Congratulations. You're one step closer to hitting bottom."

All of this can be very easily misunderstood. I've known guys like Jack who drank or drugged themselves into oblivion over despair at life in the modern world. They were truly engaged in self-destruction, with no higher purpose. This is pure nihilism. What Tyler is actually doing, however, is breaking down that portion of Jack's (and the Space Monkeys') self-image that is built on conformity to the norms of modern, consumerist society. Fighting, drinking, theft, vandalism, self-mutilation, living in filth (the whole skinhead lifestyle, actually) — these are all "hitting bottom" by the standards of our Brave New World. But for Tyler and his followers these are means to self-realization. And these men do become awakened, transformed beings.

Death (like castration) is everywhere in this film. There are the dying people Jack meets at his support groups (like the unforgettable Chloe: "I have pornographic movies in my apartment and lubricants and amyl nitrate . . ."). Jack's job as recall coordinator puts him in constant contact with death. ("Here's where the infant went through the windshield. Three points.") And it is primarily through brushes with death that Jack and these other men are learning to recover their lost manhood. Tyler's terrorizing the convenience store worker, Raymond K. Hessel, is an effort to shock this man out of his complacency and give him a second birth ("Tomorrow will be the most beautiful day of Raymond K. Hessel's life. His breakfast will taste better than any meal you or I have ever eaten"). The major example of this, of course, is the car accident Tyler deliberately causes and that almost claims his (and Jack's) life and that of their two Space Monkey passengers. "We just had a near-life experience," Tyler says afterwards. It's a very significant line.

Most people don't set out to *make* such experiences happen in their lives. And all things considered that's a very good thing. (How'd you like to be in the lane opposite Tyler's?) Instead, this is simply the sort of thing that fate hands people from time to time, and it has the beneficial effect of putting the garbage of life into perspective and making you a stronger person. The trouble is that the modern world greatly minimizes the possibility of brushes with death, of "near-life experiences." Everything has to be made "safe," so that mom doesn't have to worry about you. Risk-taking in young men is frowned upon and often punished institutionally with a kind of inhuman rigidity, as if being a boy itself were a crime. So Tyler has to break the rules and bring us close to death so that we can truly learn to live. The effect on those around him is dramatic.

Jack tells us that "After Fight Club, everything else in your life got the volume turned down. You could deal with anything." Jack says this (in voice over) at work, while dealing with his idiot boss. And in a line that does not appear in the finished film, he adds "The people who had power over you had less and less." Like Jack, most of the men in Fight Club lead double lives, with one foot in the modern and the other in the primal masculine world of Tyler Durden. "Even if I could tell someone they had a good fight, I wouldn't be talking to the same man. Who you were in Fight Club is not who you were in the rest of the world. You weren't alive anywhere like you were there. But Fight Club only exists in the hours between when Fight Club starts and when Fight Club ends."

Tyler makes soap, but his main enterprise is making men. And men are made by challenges to the spirit, not by means of free weights and machines. "I felt sorry for all the guys packed into gyms, trying to look like what Calvin Klein and Tommy Hilfiger said they should." Standing on the bus, Jack and Tyler spot a fashion ad featuring one of those hairless muscle twinks. "Is that what a man looks like?" Jack says to Tyler, derisively. At just that moment a long-haired lard ass rudely pushes past Jack and moves to the rear of the bus. This is a very deliberate inclusion on the part of the filmmakers. Why doesn't Jack react? Why doesn't he challenge this S.O.B.? Why doesn't he get into a fight with him? Answer: he no longer has anything to prove. He's no longer a "thirty-year-old boy." He's a man now.

5. I AM JACK'S BURNING BUSH

Membership in the Fight Club *Männerbund* confers meaning on even the most mundane aspects of their lives. Jacks says, "Fight Club became the reason to cut your hair short and trim your fingernails." Even soap takes on a spiritual significance: "The first soap was made from the ashes of heroes. Like the first monkeys shot into space." Their lives have been given a purpose, and that purpose contextualizes everything else and gives it significance: everything becomes meaningful simply by being something one does as a means to the end of . . .

Well, what exactly is the end? Fight Club seems to form itself—seemingly without Jack/Tyler and any of the other men involved being aware of its having any special or higher purpose. It was a response to a need these men all dimly felt. "It was right in everyone's face. Tyler and I just made it visible. It was on the tip of everyone's tongue. Tyler and I just gave it a name." But Fight Club has a logic all its own, that no one owns and no one (it turns out) can control. Because whether these men realized it or not, the formation of Fight Club was the rejection of the modern world.

They recovered their manhood and the next thought was, "Now what?" You cannot achieve that kind of psychic transformation and keep it confined to a basement forever. And so Fight Club had to come out of the basement: it had to achieve something in this world (namely, this world's destruction; the resuscitation of history). "Fight club was the beginning," Tyler says. "Now it's out of the basement and there's a name for it—Project Mayhem."

Tyler says, "Our great war is a spiritual war." He means, of course, that theirs is a war to reclaim their souls from modern corruption. But things in *Fight Club* are "spiritual" in another sense, however. There is undeniably a religious dimension to these proceedings. On the surface, however, there is a rejection of religion, a rejection of God. Tyler tells Jack:

> Our fathers were our models for God. If our fathers bailed, what does that tell you about God? Listen to me. You have to consider the possibility that God doesn't like you, he never wanted you. In all probability, he hates you. This is not the worst thing that can happen. We don't need him. Fuck damnation. Fuck redemption. We are God's unwanted children.

Superficially, one has to say that *Fight Club* is atheistic, and even nihilistic (or at least pessimistic, in a Schopenhaurean way).

Remember, you are "the same decaying organic matter as everything else"; and we are "all part of the same compost heap." In short, we're just meat; nothing special. No souls; no cosmic significance. But, of course, if we take a step back from this rhetoric and look at Tyler and the men he creates we can easily see that these words are simply false.

In recovering their *thumos*, in fighting for an ideal we become more than mere "organic matter." We set ourselves apart from the animals and actualize in ourselves a little piece of something that the gods also have. This is why virtually all philosophers from Aristotle to Hegel to Nietzsche have seen humans as super-natural beings, part beast and part god. And this is why, in Germanic mythology—our sacred scriptures, folks—human beings are created from the ash and the elm when the brothers Odin, Vili, and Ve confer on them, respectively, *odhr* (equivalent to *thumos*), will, and openness to transcendence (i.e., what is now often called "spirituality").

Tyler's words should not be taken at face value as *Fight Club*'s metaphysics: an existentialist metaphysics of cosmic meaninglessness. He directs these statements at Jack and at the Space Monkeys as part of their "training"; part of breaking them down and building them back up again. Building them back up again involves, as I have said before, actualizing their *thumos*. But *thumos* is always directed toward some ideal or other. In this case, the ideal is really their own manhood. The objective of Project Mayhem is the destruction of the modern world—but what sets the Space Monkeys on that course is the (correct) perception that the modern world stunts and denigrates their manhood.

Make no mistake: there is a religious dimension to *Fight Club*. What Tyler and the Space Monkeys are worshipping is manhood itself. I know this may seem peculiar and even, to guys who smoke Newports, suspiciously "gay." So let me explain. Minimally, religion always involves orientation toward some ideal that always remains just out of reach; that pulls us on and causes us to strive and do more and be more. But that's what manhood is to men. As I said earlier, for women femininity is a state of being. For men, manhood is an ideal to be achieved and maintained.

Even the men most confident in their manliness always seek

new challenges, new ways to express their manliness, and avoid anything that would diminish their manliness in the eyes of themselves or others (like wearing anything made by that Bonobos company). Men admire manliness in others, and it inspires them. When Jack asks Tyler who he would most like to fight (alive or dead) he says "Hemingway." Why? Because Hemingway is an icon of rugged, straight-talking, two-fisted, hard-drinking, terse-prosed manliness. If you can beat Hemingway, well...

Men are always striving to climb upwards. Femininity is horizontal: radiating out warmth and nurturing toward surrounding others, and producing new others to warm and nurture. Masculinity is vertical. It's aiming upwards, towards an ideal to be achieved in a man's self. And women are always screaming at us to get down off the damned ladder before we break our necks. (It has to be this way. Always has been and always will be.)

All religions have been "created" by men, and I have a pet theory that all religions are just covert ways in which men worship themselves. I don't mean that Tom, Dick, and Harry are worshiping Tom, Dick, and Harry. I mean that they're worshiping what they *could be* and calling that God. There's a reason why God is He and Him and His. And Our Father (or All Father). And it's the same reason why "virtue" comes from "*vir-*", an Indo-European root that means "manly" (we get "virile" from this too). And have you ever seen a *lingam*? God, Allah, Shiva, Buddha, Mithras, whatever, are not just guys, they're *guyness*. Tyler is being more honest with his men when he says "You are the all-singing, all-dancing crap of the world." (Jesus was a guy too, but Tyler could beat the shit out of him.)

There are a great many religious allusions in *Fight Club*, and matters are cast in religious terms both in the dialogue and in the screenwriter's descriptions. (As for the novel, it's been so long since I read it that I can't remember.) In one of Jack's voice overs during an evening at Fight Club he says, "Their hysterical shouting was in tongues, like at a Pentecostal church. Afterwards, we all felt saved." When Jack encounters Bob again after a long separation and Bob tells him he's joined Fight Club, the screenwriter says "An intense look of born-again fervor comes over Bob's face." Later, after Jack and Bob exit Fight Club one evening, the script says "They both grin with religious serenity."

Bob, of course, becomes Fight Club's first martyr, and a religious ritual grows up around him, with Fight Club members throughout the country huddled together in secrecy chanting "His name is Robert Paulson. His name is Robert Paulson. His name is Robert Paulson..."

6. I AM JACK'S GAY PANIC

And now we come to the part that bothers a lot of guys who love *Fight Club*. Chuck Palahniuk is gay.

The interesting thing, however, is that in contrast to gay authors who basically have made careers out of being gay, Palahniuk really doesn't seem to want people to know it. Sort of. He allowed a 1999 newspaper profile to state that he had a wife and "was not planning on having kids." In fact, he was and is living with a male partner. In 2003 Palahniuk granted an interview to *Entertainment Weekly*, then got wind of the fact that their report intended to "out" him. Palahniuk went on the war path. He later stated, admirably, "Of all the things we'd talked about, now it boiled down to, 'where do you put your dick?' I felt so pissed that I couldn't be a human being, that the only thing interesting about me was this one aspect of my persona." (Shades of Jack Donovan denouncing gay as "sexuality as ethnicity" and asking "Why should I identify more closely with a lesbian folk singer than with [straight] men my age who share my interests?")[3]

The quote above from Palahniuk comes from a 2008 interview he gave to *The Advocate* (yech!). Interestingly, however, after meeting with their reporter Palahniuk abruptly cancelled their photo shoot and refused to cooperate further with the magazine. It seems pretty obvious that he isn't entirely comfortable with people knowing that he's gay. He states part of the reason in the *Advocate* interview: "I know people who have spun their nationality or their sexuality or their race, but after a few books it's really limiting... They find themselves pigeonholed, documenting the same small aspect of self over and over."

But I think that there is another, unstated reason why Palahniuk initially hid his sexuality. He feared that if his young, male

---

[3] *Ibid.*

fans found out about his sexuality, some of them would take another look at *Fight Club*, his masterpiece, do a spit take with a mouthful of Bud, and bellow "Dude, it's gay!"

And let's face it. If you're really trying to look for something "gay" in *Fight Club* you're going to find it. Plenty of it. All the shirtlessness, particularly that of Brad Pitt (hey, why is it a "rule" of Fight Club that you have to be shirtless?). All the "male bonding." And—egads!—there's that scene where Jack watches Tyler take a bath and Tyler says, "We're a generation raised by women. I'm wondering if another woman is really the answer we need." Holy hell! *Fight Club* is trying to punk us all out!

Calm yourself, for this is all a product of your fevered imagination. When Tyler says "We're a generation raised by women" he's alluding to the fact that so many young men today either grow up without fathers, or with fathers who are ineffectual or AWOL much of the time. (Remember: "Our fathers were our models for God. If our fathers bailed, what does that tell you about God?") And so they were raised, and dominated by women. As I have alluded to already, this modern world is really, to a great extent, a world dominated by woman's preferences, in which men are asked to "redefine" their masculinity to suit women's desires. The "thirty-year-old boys" of this world, like Jack, grow up wayward, callow, and spiritually empty, enduring schools that must drug them to make them sit still, so that they can find jobs that take the best years of their lives and offer them nothing in return save the means to procure status symbols.

What's the answer to this? Well, quite naturally a lot of these guys think it's cohabiting with a woman. At least they'll get regular sex and companionship and—who knows?—maybe love. But this is a trap. We all need love, but this won't address the contempt we feel for ourselves. Latching himself onto another woman and seeking to meet her needs won't turn that thirty-year-old boy into a man. And this is why Tyler wonders if "another woman is really the answer we need." (Anybody who seriously thinks this means "let's have gay sex" is really too stupid to deserve *Fight Club*.)

As for the rampant shirtlessness, Fight Club specifies no shirts (and no shoes) for basically the same reason we see this in boxing and MMA. If there's something "gay" about Fight Club, then there's something "gay" about the UFC.

Of course, there are plenty of "clever" people who *would* say there's something gay about the UFC. Those are the same gender-bending P.C. morons, pumped full of the Freudian-Lacanian-Frankfurt Schoolian hermeneutic of suspicion, who announced a few years ago that Abe Lincoln was gay because for a while he was so poor he had to share a bed with another guy. These people see *Fight Club* as "homoerotic," or latently gay. They want to ruin it for us men, precisely because *Fight Club* has such tremendous potential to awaken us.

These are the people who saddled us with the "man hug." They've worked to destroy every male-dominated institution or activity. They've introduced women into the Citadel and sued clubs for men only. What they couldn't wreck through infiltration and litigation they've wrecked by sowing the seeds of suspicion and insecurity. ("Is it gay?" "Was that gay?" "Is he gay?" "Am I gay?")

Male bonding involves, at various times, competition, horsing around, boasting, showing off, working together, suffering together, innocent physical closeness, and innocent affection. By contaminating all these things with the terror of "latent" gayness, *they* (you know who *they* are) have virtually destroyed male bonding in the West. And that's a tragedy of epic proportions, since the formation of *Männerbünde* (of various kinds) is absolutely necessary not just to the survival of a nation, but to its excellence. It is the male bands that protect the future, biological survival of the race, the women and children. And it is in male bands — chiefly — that the sublime virtues of courage and loyalty manifest themselves and make us *worthy* of survival.

Is there something "homoerotic" about male bonding, and about *Fight Club*? Well, things only seem "erotic" to those who find them erotic. Male bonding, and *Fight Club*, are homoerotic, but only to homos. Notoriously, male bonding — in all-male bands and all-male environments (boy's schools, prisons, ships, etc.) — sometimes leads to sexual activity among men. The Army used to have what it called a "queen for a day policy," which recognized that sometimes guys with overactive hormones will, well, you know . . . and shouldn't necessarily be punished for it, because it's almost always a one shot deal. And, of course, ancient cultures like those of the Spartans or Samurai had no moral problem with men forming sexual bonds, and even in some ways encouraged it. But it wasn't "gay." There's a big difference between the Spartan Three Hundred and the Radical Faeries.

The "gay lifestyle" is a modern invention, not a timeless category. Palahniuk wants very little to do with that "lifestyle," and least of all to be defined by it. But the important thing for fans of *Fight Club* to understand is that while Palahniuk may have embraced the loathsome self-descriptive term "gay," and though he may have made the mistake of talking to the loathsome *Advocate*, he is nevertheless not a "gay writer." And there is nothing "gay" about *Fight Club*. It's a book for every man.

7. I AM JACK'S ANIMA

Of course, one important reason for thinking *Fight Club* isn't "gay" is the central importance of a character I have thus far not even mentioned: Marla Singer.

The acting in *Fight Club* is actually quite good. Brad Pitt—an underrated actor—is perfect as Tyler. (After you've seen the film, can you imagine anyone else in the role?) And Edward Norton is really fine as well.

But I'm torn: I actually think the best performance comes from Helena Bonham Carter as Marla. First of all, Bonham Carter makes the character *far* more interesting than she is in the novel. The Marla of the film is not only fascinatingly quirky, and genuinely funny, you also feel for her. My heart goes out to poor Marla in a way it doesn't go out to Jack (with whom I identify, somewhat) or to Tyler (who's admirable, but inspires no sympathy).

In the first scene of the film, Jack (in voice over) says he suddenly realizes that everything that is now happening to him (Tyler's "controlled demolition," etc.) has "something to do with a girl named Marla Singer." The language is much stronger in the original script, and in the novel: "Somehow, I realize all of this . . . is really about Marla Singer." *About* her?

As I have argued, *Fight Club* is all about the recovery (or revivification) of manhood. And I have argued that manhood is achieved through orientation towards some ideal that we strive to actualize, preserve, or protect. But we can't lose sight of the fact that man is one half of a dyad, and that part of being a man is defined in relation to a woman. To be very frank, since it's just us guys here, there is something undeniably misogynistic about the ideal of manhood. The feminists are just a little bit right. In part, we define manhood as *not* being like a woman. The degree to which a man is "womanish" is the degree to which he has failed to be a man, the degree to which he is contemptible.

Not every man thinks this way, just 99.9% of them. And perhaps they *shouldn't* think this way; but it's never going to change. Feminists imagine they're making some progress in re-educating men. In fact, men just pretend to think the way feminists want them to for the same reason men have pretended to go along with all the other shit women have ever come out with: they want to get along with them and receive regular meals and regular sex.

But though men consciously define themselves in opposition to women and the feminine, being a man involves achieving some positive relationship to these as well. Putting it mildly, this requires a delicate balance. Women are most strongly attracted to actualized, masculine men who are not totally absorbed by them and who want to achieve something in the world. In part, it's because they see such "alpha males" as capable of protecting them and their offspring. Of course, once a woman has snared a man like that she usually works overtime trying to stop him from taking risks. More often than not, he goes along with this—and dies a straw death, resenting her, and dreaming about what might have been. And she winds up feeling contempt for him, because he failed to say no to her (though she is *never* consciously aware of this).

For his part, the man wants a woman he thinks will be faithful to him. Quite simply, he wants some assurance that the children he raises will be his own. The primary sign of faithfulness he looks for is devotion: he wants a woman who truly believes in him before all others; who believes in him, in his mission, and in his ability to accomplish it. He wants, in a way, to be worshipped. If a man is able to find a woman like this and pursue his mission in life, he becomes the happiest and most self-actualized of men.

This is because the twin, and sometimes antagonistic, impulses of his nature have—through alliance with the ideal women—achieved harmony: his impulse to fight for or achieve an ideal, and his impulse to mate and reproduce himself. Such a man has found a way to produce a family *and* pursue his ideals, by aligning himself with a woman whose devotion actually *fuels* his quest for his ideal.

As Derek Hawthorne puts it in his essay on the film *Storm over Mont Blanc*:

> Without a woman a man lacks a sense of being grounded. Men tend to be so focused upon *doing* that they miss out on *being*. Their quest to achieve their purpose in life becomes something cold and barren. Ultimately, without a home and hearth and woman to return to for sustenance, they burn themselves out along the path. They feel a sense of emptiness, and drift into despair.[4]

The *Männerbund* exists in a state of tension with society. It has the potential to protect and preserve the society from which it emerges, but it is also something wild, volatile, and transgressive. Ultimately, its members, to be truly fulfilled as men, must strike a balance between their devotion to each other, and their desire for a wife and family. These two things *can* co-exist. But in order for a man to make it work, he has to overcome the influence of his comrades, who will always pull him off to some adventure rather than see him "pussy whipped." And he must resist the influence of the woman, who will (unless she is truly exceptional) always try and sabotage his relationship with his comrades. He must learn how to say "no" to both, but saying "no" to the woman will be more difficult.

Jack's relationship to Marla dramatizes this whole dynamic. But who is Marla?

She is a disaffected wanderer, like Jack. She is Palahniuk's portrait of the female half of the broken modern person. As such, she is very different from Jack. Jack responds to modern emasculation

---

[4] http://www.counter-currents.com/2011/08/storm-over-mont-blanc-part-4/

by *doing something*. He splits his personality in two, hypostatizing his higher potential for masculine self-actualization as "Tyler Durden." And then he and that higher self create Fight Club, which then morphs into a nationwide revolutionary movement.

Marla's response to modern emasculation is quite different. Having nothing to emasculate, she cannot, of course, respond to our modern predicament quite the way that Jack does. She is, for lack of a better word, "unfulfilled." And this is primarily because of the emasculation of the men around her. As I said earlier, when women get men to stop taking risks and play it safe, they get what they want—but they wind up feeling contempt for their men, and feeling that something is missing from their lives.

That household you may have grown up in where Dad gave up his dreams to make Mom happy, played by her rules, and painted plastic soldiers in his man cave—that was the microcosmic model for what is now the macrocosm. We live in a woman's world, where the Man has said a great, World-Historical "Yes, dear" to Woman. And now Woman is Marla: angry, drifting, addictive, self-destructive, slutty, weepy, and *waiting*. Waiting for some thing or some one to deliver her, like a wasted, slatternly princess locked in a tower. Only in this world she's locked herself in, and denounced the key as an "oppressor."

Jack is a pessimist. Not a nihilist. His despair leads him to try to change the world. Marla, on the other hand, is the real nihilist. She never graduates past being a tourist at support groups. She is simply waiting to die. Her whole life is one giant "cry for help," typified by her overdosing on Xanax.

It's that overdose that really brings Jack and Marla together. In his "Tyler" persona, he screws Marla repeatedly and is, by her own admission, extremely good at it. She apparently needs this rather badly, but what she really wants and really finds fulfilling is simply *being with* Jack, for whom she begins to genuinely care. (Women are not good at casual sex. They want to bond with their sexual partners. This is why women are the real victims of the sexual revolution.) Real pathos is introduced into the story, of course, by the fact that Jack keeps reverting to Jack, and kicking poor Marla out of the house. This is *Fight Club*'s "love angle."

And it makes us care about the story and the characters a lot more. Why? Well, we don't want to see poor Marla hurt. But we also want to see Jack "get together" with her. When you watch the film for the first time and don't know that Jack is Tyler, you think that Jack is secretly in love with Marla (and perhaps Marla with him) and you're waiting for Jack to come to his senses and claim Marla from the callous Tyler. When you see the film again, knowing the twist, a different sort of suspense takes over: you're waiting for Jack to realize he's Tyler and that he's been screwing Marla all along, and you want him to come to his senses before he loses Marla entirely.

Again, why? Because you know that Jack, as a man, can't be satisfied with Fight Club alone. He needs Marla. But for a man's having a woman to mean anything (and for being had to mean anything to her), a man must win the woman through his manly qualities. Fight Club becomes a means to win Marla. It's Tyler she's attracted to, but Tyler is simply Jack's manly, self-confident alter ego. Marla is initially drawn to Jack at the support group meetings because she sees that they are both lost souls. But it's only when he becomes Tyler Durden that she feels truly bound to him.

In becoming Tyler Durden, Jack becomes Man, and attracts and repairs and redeems broken Woman. Or so it seems in the end when Jack and Marla hold hands as the buildings explode and collapse around them.

In the end, Jack doesn't kill Tyler Durden. That's a misinterpretation. "Tyler Durden" just ceases to exist as a separate persona. Jack becomes Tyler. Note what happens in the film after Jack shoots himself and "kills" Tyler. Note how authoritatively he issues commands to the Space Monkeys. He's no longer screaming at them, treating them like he thinks they're insane, treating them as adversaries. Note how calmly he watches the buildings come down. The lower, "Jack" part of his psyche had not wanted this. Now it's happened. And to paraphrase Nietzsche, he must become a god, simply to be worthy of the deed. He must own everything that "Tyler" has said and done.

8. I AM JACK'S IMPLICIT WHITENESS

Since the film was released in 1999, people have debated the question of whether the film, or at least the organization depicted in it, is "fascist." Is *Fight Club* fascist?

Yes.

Fight Club and Fight Club are both fascist. Meaning: the film and the organization it depicts (later, Project Mayhem) are both implicitly fascist. Now, to repeat: I don't care what Chuck Palahniuk or anyone connected with the film has said about it. The organization in the film is clearly fascist, and the film, whatever its makers' intentions might have been, is as convincing and inspiring a cinematic argument for fascism as I have ever seen. (It's more effective than *Triumph of the Will*, which merely shows us how happy and smartly dressed everyone will be after fascism is installed — but gives the uninformed no sense as to why its installation is necessary.)

In the most essential terms, fascism is the idea that the *Männerbund* should rule. Fight Club is the formation of the *Männerbund*. Project Mayhem is the inescapable conclusion drawn by the men of the *Bund* once they are awakened: that it is they who should rule. In real-life fascism, those men have been moved by the desire to use their *thumos* to protect their people, their land, and their culture.

The problem with *Fight Club*'s fascism is that it's not at all clear that the Space Monkeys will channel their *thumos* in this direction. And the reason for my doubt about this has to do with the one major thing that those of our ilk find distasteful about *Fight Club*, those who otherwise love the film: Fight Club/Project Mayhem is depicted as "racially diverse." I can't remember if this is how it is depicted in the novel or not. (Please don't clobber me on this, guys: I just haven't had the time to re-read it.)

The fascism of *Fight Club* is clearly not racialist or National Socialist (though the soap made from human fat seems to be a rather grisly reference to one of the myths about the Nazis). *Fight Club*'s fascism is basically Traditionalist and vaguely anarcho-primitivist. Project Mayhem essentially aims to do three things.

The first is to destroy symbols of American capitalism and cultural degeneracy: blowing up corporate art, trashing a franchise coffee bar, feeding laxatives to pigeons to make them crap on a lot full of luxury cars, etc.

Second, they are out to destroy the means by which Americans distract and anesthetize themselves: blowing up computers, erasing videotapes, smashing satellite dishes, etc.

Third, and most important, they are out to destroy the financial structure of the U.S. (of the world, really) by destroying the headquarters of the credit card companies, and similar targets.

There are also, in addition to these, some rather senseless acts of mischief, like "befouling fountains," and building an "excrement catapult."

To what end? Well, Tyler gives us a very clear picture of the future he's hoping to build, in one of *Fight Club*'s most famous scenes:

> In the world I see—you're stalking elk through the damp canyon forests around the ruins of Rockefeller Center. You will wear leather clothes that last you the rest of your life. You will climb the wrist-thick kudzu vines that wrap the Sears Tower. You will see tiny figures pounding corn and laying-strips of venison on the empty car pool lane of the ruins of a superhighway.

Again, Tyler's aim is to re-start history: to destroy capitalism, globalism, technology, consumer culture, class divisions based upon wealth, etc. Is he aware that once we've returned to the semi-primitive state he dreams of, divisions will again be drawn along racial and ethnic lines and felt more keenly than ever before? Tyler may be aware of this, but Palahniuk and the filmmakers are almost certainly not.

Yes, Fight Club and Project Mayhem are racially mixed. However, one thing that I don't think viewers recognize is that they actually get *whiter* as the film goes along. What I am referring to, specifically, is the racial makeup of the Space Monkeys living in the Paper Street house.

Several things annoy me about *Fight Club*. One is that animated penguin. But the biggest thing is that long-haired, queer-looking Asian in some of the *Fight Club* basement scenes who's constantly posturing and trying to act "macho." I avert my eyes when he's on screen (just like I avert my eyes in the scene where Jack disfigures poor Angel Face). There are also some blacks in the Fight Club scenes, one of whom has a brief speaking role. When we get to the house, however, it is overwhelmingly white. It's one thing to meet a racial variety of guys once or twice a week in somebody's basement. It's quite another thing to *live* with them.

We're all more comfortable with our own kind. And so what we find in the house is almost entirely a bunch of beefy, white, buzz cut Space Monkeys. A black is glimpsed briefly in a couple scenes. He has no lines and if you blink you'll miss him. Also on screen for a millisecond is what appears to be that Asian, now with hair shorn. (It might be a different Asian—but hell, I can't tell the difference.) All the key scenes in the house—especially the scene where Bob's lifeless body is hauled in—are dominated by white actors. It's as if the filmmakers realized dimly and subconsciously that a true racial mixture in that house would simply not be plausible. The Paper Street Soap Company is implicitly white.

There's much in the film that seems to speak directly to whites. When Tyler tells Fight Club that they are "an entire generation pumping gas and waiting tables; or they're slaves with white collars," I think of white guys.

I think of all those working class guys out there who can't find decent jobs because the good jobs have been sent overseas and given to non-white wage slaves. Or, worse yet, all those guys who can't find jobs because right here at home they're being given to aliens—invaders whose "rights" are being defended by the same people who feel free to crack jokes about guys with Confederate flags in their pickup trucks. I think about all those middle class, college-educated white guys who've lost a job or a promotion to somebody who says "aks." And I think about all those smart, eighteen-year-old white guys who've been denied admission to Harvard or MIT because some other guy's great great grandparents owned slaves. We are "the middle children of history," and "we're very, very pissed off."

But remember: we are also "the quiet young men who listen until it's time to decide."

9. I Am Jack's Conclusion

Some time ago, Greg Johnson pointed out to me (correctly) that one way in which the film improves on the novel is that the film is far less nihilistic. In the novel, Tyler is planning to blow up a museum, not the credit card companies. What's the point of that? Why destroy a building full of the *good* things our culture has produced? Twice in the novel, Jack says he wants to "wipe [his] ass with the Mona Lisa." "Burn the Louvre," one character says. "This way at least God would know our names." But this reminds me of the infamous Herostratus, who burned the Temple of Diana at Ephesus in 356 B.C. so that his name would go down in history. His name went down in history, all right, as one of the most pathetic, narcissistic monsters of all time.

Some of this stuff creeps into the film. I understand the point of destroying satellite dishes and trashing corporate coffee bars. But what's the point of pissing in people's soup and splicing single frames of porn into children's films? (I understand that Tyler is very, very pissed off. But let's agree to be pissed off *productively*, and to direct our rage at the right targets.)

This is what bothers me about Palahniuk, and why my allegiance is mostly to the film of *Fight Club*, not to the novel. The stuff Palahniuk has produced since *Fight Club* is of very uneven quality and opens itself, again, to the charge of nihilism. (He seems committed to producing a novel a year, each of which he writes very quickly. This is a good strategy if you are Yukio Mishima. But Palahniuk is no Mishima. Not yet, anyway.) One critic has said that Palahniuk's books "traffic in the half-baked nihilism of a stoned high school student who has just discovered Nietzsche and Nine Inch Nails." Foolishly, Palahniuk dashed off an angry riposte to this. (The Great-Souled Man would have greeted it with silence.)

Perhaps Palahniuk's most infamous work since *Fight Club* is a short story called "Guts," which deals with grisly masturbation accidents. Palahniuk has read the story numerous times to audiences over the years, causing, as of May 2007, a grand total of 73 people to faint (I'm not kidding). Another critic has said of him "it seems like Palahniuk is just double-daring himself to top each new vile degradation with something worse." One wonders if this man really has anything to say at all, or if he's just a kind of two-bit nihilist out to titillate our jaded sensibilities with ever more dark and "daring" penetrations of the cultural rectum.

So, at this point—if indeed you've come all this way—you might be wondering whether I have just "read a lot into" *Fight Club*. A fair question. First, a disclaimer: I did warn you that I'm writing almost exclusively about the film, not the novel. However, while the film improves upon the novel, it *does* follow the novel closely. Much of what is good about the film is there in Palahniuk's text. And all the "messages" that I have found latent in the film are also latent in the text. It's just as if the film has drawn them out and made them more explicit.

The simple truth is that *Fight Club* is bigger than Chuck Palahniuk, David Fincher, or Jim Uhls. It means a hell of a lot more than they think it does. *Fight Club* means *what it means to us*. It is almost as if this novel and film have been gifted to us by the gods, and that Palahniuk, et al., were merely vehicles for its expression. This story is so powerful *to us;* says so much *to us* about our world and our generation. It moves us so much that it is a thing that belongs to the age and *to us*, not to any man or any film studio.

It is an extraordinarily rich text, and I have merely scratched the surface of all that it has to say to our time and to our predicament.

Counter-Currents/*North American New Right*,
January 9, 2012

Breaking Bad:
A Celebration

1. Yo biyotch, this show is the bomb!
Breaking Bad is the greatest television series ever made.

I continue to be surprised by how many like-minded friends have never seen it. (Then again there are a lot of TV shows out there.) But *Breaking Bad* is quite simply the best series I've ever seen, and I'm ashamed to admit that I've seen an *awful* lot of TV. (I am a radical traditionalist who can't sing any folk songs, but who knows by heart the lyrics to the themes from *The Beverly Hillbillies, Gilligan's Island,* and the *Brady Bunch.*)

Breaking Bad is the story of Walter White, a middle-aged high school chemistry teacher in Albuquerque, New Mexico. Walter is a failure. He has a Ph.D., but couldn't find a job at a university. He has watched while friends have gotten rich off work he himself had a hand in developing. He does have a wonderful wife, Skylar, but their only child—and his namesake—has cerebral palsy. To make ends meet Walter must work part time at a car wash, where he is regularly humiliated by a vulgar foreign manager with enormous eyebrows. Skylar has a sister named Marie who is married to Hank, a DEA agent. Hank is a little fireplug of a guy with a comically macho, alpha male attitude. He's fond of Walt, but loses no opportunity to remind him that he's a milquetoast.

As if things aren't bad enough, Walt discovers that he is in the advanced stages of lung cancer. At first, he decides to refuse treatment, as he is apparently not that anxious to hang on to life (who would be, in his shoes?). Under pressure from his family, however, he agrees to undergo chemotherapy. Predictably, his insurance won't pay for everything, and Walt is left not only with the prospect of death, but of leaving his family destitute.

Then, one day, Hank invites Walt to witness a DEA raid on a meth lab. While waiting in the safety of Hank's SUV, Walt watches as one of the meth cooks successfully escapes right under the noses of the cops. To his shock, Walt realizes it's a former student of his, Jesse Pinkman. Jesse was not exactly a star pupil. In fact, Walt regarded him, correctly, as a drugged-out loser.

Now, Mr. White is Mr. WASP (the surname kind of makes this emphatic, doesn't it?), and a total square complete with pocket protector. Jesse, on the other hand, is the lowest sort of whigger. His every sentence begins with "yo" and tends to end with "bitch" (my section title above is an homage to him). He's bad, but in a dopey, inept sort of way. His car actually sports a vanity plate that reads THE CAP'N—a rather imprudent reference to his street alias, "Captain Cook." Worst of all, he can't keep his hands off what he cooks.

Desperate to leave his family with a small legacy, Walt has a brilliant idea. All right, well, he has a *terrible* idea: he teams up with Jesse, and the two of them cook crystal meth. Thanks to Walt's chemical genius, it turns out to be the best meth ever to hit the streets.

2. "I AM AWAKE"

But there's a lot more going on here with Walt than a noble desire to make money for his family. And this is pretty obvious from the beginning. Over and over again in the series, Walt insists that he's doing it all for his family, that whatever he does he does for Skylar and Walter Junior (and, later, his infant daughter, who is born in the show's second season). But we're not buying it.

I'm reminded of the veteran UFC fighter I saw interviewed several years ago (I honestly forget who it was), who said that he was continuing to fight simply in order to provide for his family.

Sure.

Early in the first season, just after Walt and Jesse have teamed up, Jesse asks him just why he's getting mixed up in cooking meth. It's one of the most memorable—and significant—scenes in the entire series. Jesse confronts him: "Some straight like you, giant stick up his ass. All of a sudden, at age . . . like what? 60? He's just going to break bad?"

Oddly, Walt (who is 50) doesn't mention his family at all when he answers Jesse. He pauses a moment, looking off into the distance, then simply says "I am awake."

Facing death has awakened Walt, as it does many. But to what? To the realization not just that he has never really lived, but that he has never really lived *as a man*. What this show is actually all about is Walter White becoming a man.

Walt has always been a responsible, careful, attentive and devoted husband and father. But Walt has never taken a risk in his entire life, and he knows this. He has always played it safe. Now, facing death, he realizes he has nothing to lose.

Well wait, that can't be right. He could lose his family. His wife could leave him if she learns the truth — or the people he runs afoul of could kill his family for revenge (this comes close to happening in season four). This is the real reason why Walt's claim that he's doing it all for his family just doesn't ring true. The reality is that something is actually *overriding* Walt's concern for his family.

I would love to write a long commentary on this series, detailing how Walt's character develops over time. But there are two problems with that. First, I don't want to spoil the series for all of my readers who haven't seen it yet. Honestly, this is the most riveting, suspenseful, unpredictable program I've ever seen. Some episodes are so tense and suspenseful they are almost unbearable, and their 47 minute length passes *very* quickly. (Much too quickly, actually.) I would hate to ruin this experience for others. The second problem is that the series isn't over yet. I can't really do a decent job of talking about what *Breaking Bad* means until its fifth and final season has come and gone. Just like I can't offer an analysis of a novel I've only read four fifths of. When the series is over perhaps I'll devote a longer essay to it.

But I can't resist commenting a bit further, and in the process I promise I'll only give away a few things.

3. Amoral Virtues

This is a superbly-written series, and character development is one its great strengths. We sense from the beginning that Walt's character is going to undergo a metamorphosis; that he's going to transform from a milquetoast into . . . into what? Well, pinning this down is a bit of a problem — due in the main to the series' much-discussed "moral ambiguity."

No judgment is ever made about Walt or any of the other characters. We sympathize with Walt from the beginning, initially taken in by his claim that he is cooking meth to provide for his family. In spite of how obnoxious and amoral he seems at first, we do grow to sympathize with Jesse Pinkman and to care about what happens to him. By season four the series even makes us care about Gus Fring, the ruthless drug lord for whom Walt and Jesse wind up working. This is part of the magic of *Breaking Bad* — that it manages to create characters whose actions are often objectively evil, but who we can't help but care for. (In this respect, the series has often been compared to *The Sopranos*.)

I won't be revealing too much if I tell you that by the end of season four Walt has gone from being Mr. Clean to being a ruthless, scheming bastard. And a cold-blooded killer. Yet we still care for him — and, more importantly, we admire him. Why? Well, to draw on a distinction Jack Donovan makes in *The Way of Men*, Walt had always been a "good man," but he wasn't so good "at being a man." However, as his character develops he begins to display all those "amoral" masculine virtues Donovan writes about.

The new Walt is tough, strong, courageous, and masterful. It doesn't really matter that these virtues are deployed toward unlawful and often destructive ends. We admire these qualities in Walt nonetheless. And frankly it's hard for me to get too exercised over the unlawfulness of Walt's actions. It's hard for me to be too disapproving of anything that undermines the stability of modern American society. The men of Walt's world are killers and kingpins and assassins — but at least they are still men. One of the larger philosophical issues raised by this series — too large for me to explore here — is the tension that sometimes exists between masculinity and law and order; or: between primal masculine virtue and the virtues necessary to sustain civilization.

Walt takes obvious pleasure in his own transformation. To be sure, he is deeply ambivalent about what he has become. We see him frequently struggling with guilt over the things he has done (one of which results indirectly in the downing of a jumbo jet!).

But we also see him taking pride in his toughness and ruthlessness—pride in being the new badass in town with the badass (though amusing) alias "Heisenberg." For all his moral qualms, he is enjoying what he has become. He enjoys feeling like a man for once in his life.

One of the interesting ironies to the series is the way in which it sets up and develops the contrast between Walt and Hank, the DEA agent brother-in-law. As mentioned earlier, Hank is a sort of swaggering alpha male type who makes Walt feel rather small in his presence. Despite this, Walt has great affection for his brother-in-law (the closeness of the family is one of the more endearing aspects of the series). As the storyline develops, however, the paths of the two men sharply diverge.

Walt is faced continually with situations that require courage, boldness, and guts—and again and again he acquits himself rather well. Even when he is required to kill—and (in one stomach-churning sequence) dispose of a body. Things go very differently, however, for tough guy Hank. Given the opportunity to join a major drug task force, Hank is put in a harrowing combat situation—and basically has a nervous breakdown. Deep down, Walt the geek has got what it takes. Hank—the man who postures at being a man—simply doesn't. (Though later in the series he manages to redeem himself and win everyone's admiration.)

Jesse represents a different case of transformation. It was hard—no, it was impossible—for me to like Jesse at first. He represents so much in this culture for which I have a visceral dislike. In addition to all the objectionable qualities mentioned earlier, he is weak, cowardly, unstable, unreliable, and disloyal. But as the series develops, Jesse grows up. In season four we see him displaying true courage, loyalty, and a sense of honor.

The dynamic between Walt and Jesse is really one of the highlights of *Breaking Bad*. Series creator Vince Gilligan originally intended to kill Jesse off at the end of the first season, an event that would plunge Walt into an orgy of guilt. After he had a chance to see the chemistry between these characters on screen, Gilligan wisely changed his mind. Walt and Jesse grow to care about each other, and unavoidably (given the age difference between them) the relationship becomes like that of father and son—though neither of them would ever admit that such a dynamic is present. *Breaking Bad* is the kind of "buddy picture" they haven't made since the 1970s.

Walt loves Walter Junior, but the sad truth is that at some level he must feel dissatisfied that his only son, who bears his name, is not and never will be physically sound. Walter Junior's disabled body is like a physical externalization of the state of Walt's stunted soul at the beginning of *Breaking Bad*. Despite his many faults, Jesse becomes a kind of surrogate son to Walt. And he can be the kind of son Walter Junior can never be: tough, resourceful, and physically daring.

Walt is "awake." He has seen the world as it really is, and found in himself the qualities that really matter in a man. Walter Junior and Skylar (at least, for part of the series' run) are stuck in the realm of the shadows. There are elements to *Breaking Bad* that remind me of David Lynch, especially *Blue Velvet*.

4. Conclusion, Unfortunately

There isn't a single aspect of *Breaking Bad* that doesn't deserve praise: the writing, the cinematography, the editing, even the set decoration (check out Marie's over-the-top purple interiors). What I haven't said anything about so far is the one thing that has received the most praise from critics (who are almost unanimously gaga over this series): the acting. Bryan Cranston (who? you may well ask) is absolutely remarkable as Walt. And Aaron Paul is also outstanding as Jesse. Honestly, there's not a weak link anywhere here.

All good things must come to an end, sadly, and *Breaking Bad*'s fifth season is slated to be its last. In fact, not only is this necessary — it's actually quite good. *Breaking Bad* is a continuing story, and all stories must reach a conclusion. And I can also think of many series that went on too long, eventually running out of steam and making us forget why we had originally loved them. But there will never be another series like this one.

So what's going to happen to Walt and Jesse? I really don't even want to speculate. And it's dangerous to do so: the writers of this series are so good at being unpredictable. I know one thing: I don't want Walt to get caught. Or, put it this way: if he gets caught I don't want him going to jail. I identify much too strongly with Walt. Somehow I find it very easy to put myself in Walt's shoes, and when I watch the things he does I think to myself, "I would have done that too . . ." I don't want anything bad to happen to Walt.

One wonders, though, what thought processes the writers will go through in reaching their conclusion. If Walt gets away with it, the series seems to sanction his actions. If he doesn't, most of the viewers—and I'm certain of this—will be terribly disappointed. Of course, one plot element the writers seem to forget about from time to time is that Walt has cancer. It's now in remission—but it could come back. Perhaps this is how Walt will cheat the hangman.

Believe me, this essay has barely touched on what a rich and complex series this is. Do yourself a favor and buy it, rent it, stream it—*whatever*—as soon as you finish reading this essay.

Counter-Currents/*North American New Right*,
April 3, 2012

Adieu, Breaking Bad

This past Sunday, AMC aired the final episode of *Breaking Bad*. I wasn't expecting to feel this way, but it's as if a chapter in my life has come to an end.

I first discovered this show on an airplane flying back from Germany (sorry to disappoint you, but it was a business trip connected with my "cover identity"). I never watch TV on flights. Instead I read and occasionally glance at what people around me are watching. So I happened to look up and see—without any audio, of course—an ad for this show on AMC that I'd never heard of (which isn't unusual, since I almost never watch television anymore). The ad was so compelling I picked up the book I was reading and scrawled *Breaking Bad* in the back of it.

I had missed an entire season, so I got all the discs from Netflix and began watching the show from the beginning. I've already written an essay for Counter-Currents about my impressions of *Breaking Bad*, and I urge you to read it. I wrote that essay a year and a half ago. It was my attempt to express what the series means, and where I thought it was going. I said near the beginning that I was surprised at how many of my friends had never heard of the show. That has since changed dramatically. Now it seems like everybody in all the circles I move in has heard of *Breaking Bad*—the Manosphere, White Nationalism, Asatru, etc. It has truly struck a chord with a lot of decent folk.

Partly, of course, it's a guy thing. As I said in my 2012 essay, *Breaking Bad* is really the story of Walter White becoming a man. I drew on Jack Donovan's ideas in *The Way of Men*, and argued that while Walt was a *good man* (caring and responsible husband and father, blah blah blah) he wasn't that good at *being a man*. But as the series develops, Walt begins to display all the "amoral" manly virtues Donovan writes about in his book. Walt becomes ruthless, brave, and strong. Most of all, he becomes masterful. By the end of the series he has morphed into a criminal kingpin, the top drug lord in his neck of the woods. ("All hail the king!" trumpeted the ads for Season Five.)

Curiously, it doesn't seem to matter to any of us that Walt displays all these manly virtues in the cause of crime. And this is, indeed, rather odd. Because if you asked me what I think of meth I would tell you that I think it's horrible stuff that probably deserves to be illegal, and that it not only attracts the lowest scum on the planet but seems to have the power to turn decent people into scum. And I would also tell you that I think people who deal in meth should be prosecuted and punished to the full extent of the law.

And yet for five seasons I cheered everything Walt did (well, except for poisoning that cute little beaner). And I wanted him to get away with it. I suppose there are two reasons for this — two things that explain my apparent inconsistency. The first is that I admire those manly virtues. I'd rather see them displayed than not displayed, even if they are displayed for the sake of crime. I admired Walt for finally choosing to take risks in his life. There is something noble about this man simply seizing on something — anything — as a way to be alive. I guess it just doesn't fundamentally matter to me that that something was cooking crystal meth.

As to the second reason, I stated it in my 2012 essay on the series:

> Frankly it's hard for me to get too exercised over the unlawfulness of Walt's actions. It's hard for me to be too disapproving of anything that undermines the stability of modern American society. The men of Walt's world are killers and kingpins and assassins — but at least they are still men. One of the larger philosophical issues raised by this series — too large for me to explore here — is the tension that sometimes exists between masculinity and law and order; or: between primal masculine virtue and the virtues necessary to sustain civilization.

I would make only one change to the above: there is a *particular* tension between primal masculine virtue and the virtues necessary to sustain *modern* civilization. In fact, there's a downright incompatibility. So for me, this makes things very simple.

As a man, I regard those primal masculine virtues as what I must strive to achieve in my own life. For me, they are the good. Without them, I am nothing; I cannot respect myself. And if that striving is thwarted in modern civilization, if life in our world makes it well-nigh impossible to be a man, then modern civilization must be destroyed. You see, I told you it was simple.

Now, the truth is that Walter White knows what *Breaking Bad* is all about. Never underestimate Walt. He knows that this is about being a man. Yes, yes: he tells us over and over again that he's doing it all for his family. But he knows that it isn't true — that, at best, it's only a partial truth. Early in the first season, Jesse asks Walt why he's suddenly decided to "break bad." It's one of the greatest scenes in the series. Walt simply answers, "I am awake."

In the final episode, Walt and Skyler meet for the last time. It's a scene that brought tears to my eyes. Skyler clearly still loves Walt. But when, standing in their kitchen, it seems that Walt is once more going to claim that he did it all "for the family," Skyler almost loses it. Before she can say anything, Walt interrupts her. "I did it for me," he says. "I did it because I liked it. I was good at it. I felt alive." Finally, he admits the truth that we had known all along. (Frankly, the episode could have ended there and I would have been satisfied.)

The odd thing is that one would expect Skyler to be furious at this admission. She knew the truth too, of course, but to hear it expressed so frankly . . . And yet there is a kind of peace that follows this exchange — in the scene, I mean. Like the calm after a storm. Skyler still loves Walt, and one gets the distinct impression (here and in earlier episodes) that Skyler *respects* Walt more than she ever did before. She doesn't approve of what he's done, but she respects him for doing it — or, perhaps, for the way he did it. She loved the old Walt — the Walt who couldn't find an academic position, whose friends stole his ideas and got rich off them, who had to work a demeaning part-time job at a carwash, etc. She loved that guy and would have *claimed* that she respected him. But the reality is that she respects Drug Lord Walt a hell of a lot more.

The hard truth is that men cannot be satisfied — not *completely*, at least—by being good husbands and fathers. To be satisfied as men they have to *struggle*—in some way or other—to *achieve* something or other, and they have to *win* something or other. (Notice how inclusive I'm being; there are different paths.)

I'll offer a couple of priceless D. H. Lawrence quotes I've picked up from Derek Hawthorne:

> It is the desire of the human male to build a world: not "to build a world for you, dear"; but to build up out of his own self and his own belief and his own effort something wonderful. Not merely something useful. Something wonderful. (*Fantasia of the Unconscious*, 18)

And:

> Primarily and supremely man is always the pioneer of life, adventuring onward into the unknown, alone with his own temerarious, dauntless soul. Woman for him exists only in the twilight, by the camp fire, when day has departed. Evening and the night are hers. (*Ibid.*, 109)

Like *Fight Club*, *Breaking Bad* is really about the re-constitution of primal, human conflict—and through it primal, human virtue. Both are set in a kind of state of nature—a condition of lawlessness and barbarism, in which all modern masks are stripped away. Words no longer count, only actions. And one can't "fake" one's way through things. You either rise to the occasion and show that you are tough enough or daring enough—or you lose. And you lose big, because the stakes are big. It's not just primal masculine virtue that gets reconstituted here, folks. Because Skyler rises to the occasion too. She stands by her man, as the song says. And exhibits a good deal of toughness as well (like any good Nordic woman). (I am not as big a sexist as the chicks who read me think that I am.)

So, what did I think of the finale of *Breaking Bad*? When it was over, I felt dissatisfied. But only because the series was over. In terms of the story, I was quite satisfied with how they wrapped it up. In fact, I can't think of any other way it could have been done. Everything that happened in the finale had the quality of *dramatic inevitability*. I don't often call TV writers "brilliant," but in this case the compliment is deserved.

Walt figures out a brilliant way to get money to his family — and simultaneously stick it to the odious Schwartzes. I didn't see that one coming. The final scene between Walt and Skyler — discussed earlier — was a knockout. But the scheme Walt hatches to kill Uncle Frank and his gang (a few of whom showed up, I believe, at the recent Stella Natura festival) was a bit contrived. That machinegun attached to the garage door opener thingee worked just a bit *too* well, and the set up was just a bit too easy for Walt. But satisfying it was, nonetheless. Walt saves Jesse one last time, and Walt gets to kill psycho Todd (who looks like a Mormon missionary). There are few words in the last scene between Walt and Jesse, but one feels the strong bond between them. Words aren't really that necessary. Oh, and I cackled maniacally over the poisoned Stevia. Almost forgot that one.

In the end, of course, Walt dies, which is what I figured would happen. My prediction in 2012 was that Walt would die of cancer. By the finale it does appear that the cancer is close to killing him. But what actually takes his life is a stray gunshot to the abdomen. We're left with the suggestion that Walt bleeds to death. I wasn't happy to see Walt die, of course. But how else could the series have ended? With Walt getting caught and getting his comeuppance? If that had happened, I'm sure somebody would've hired the two best hit men west of the Mississippi to kill Vince Gilligan. (I can think of only one ending that would have been worse than this: Walt wakes up in bed next to Skyler and cries "Oh, what a terrible dream!")

No, I couldn't have come up with a better ending than what we were offered the other night. But the finale was kind of a blow, actually. Only when I saw the closing credits did it finally hit me: it's over. For good. And it was then that I realized just how important this series had become to me. They would make a few episodes and I would watch them and rave over them, then go back to my other activities and forget about *Breaking Bad* for a while. But for the last several years it was always in the background. I would think, "Well, I've got new episodes of

Breaking Bad to look forward to." Not anymore. Where will I find another "awakened" primal masculine hero through whom I can vicariously feel alive? Maybe it's time to get in touch with my inner Walt (or, better yet, my inner Tyler).

Yes, I know that they're going to do a spinoff series called *Better Call Saul*. But I don't like Saul Goodman. He's good for a few laughs, but unlike Walt there's nothing admirable about him at all. Who needs a show about that guy? But I'll probably wind up watching it nonetheless, hoping for something or other.

Adieu, Breaking Bad. I wish I could say *auf Wiedersehen*.

Counter-Currents/*North American New Right*,
October 3, 2013

Better Call Saul!

My readers are aware of my great love for *Breaking Bad*. Just about every like-minded man I know who saw the series found the story of Walter White, high school chemistry teacher turned drug king pin, to be as inspirational as I did. Weirdly inspirational, of course. But these are weird times. Walt's story was not intended to be a glorification of crime (though, well, it does kind of turn out to be). It's the story of a man becoming a man; becoming what he is. It's the televisual, inspirational equivalent of *Fight Club*.

But when I heard that the producers were planning a spin off based around the odious but amusing crooked lawyer Saul Goodman (played by Bob Odenkirk), I was dubious. Again, I found the character amusing. But I didn't like him at all, and I didn't see how he could carry an entire series. Plus, no Walt. The spin off covers the life of Saul Goodman prior to his meeting Walter White (and also gives us a glimpse of Saul's life after Walt).

By the time I actually thought of taking a look at the episodes, I wasn't even sure if the series had been cancelled. I was halfway expecting it to lay an egg, and I'd heard no buzz about it at all. (But then again, I practically live in a cave.)

Well, it turns out I really should have had more faith in Vince Gilligan, the genius who gave us *Breaking Bad*. For having now watched all ten episodes of season one of *Better Call Saul*, I am pleased to report to my readers that it is not only a worthy successor to *Breaking Bad*, but a fine series in its own right (which could be understood and enjoyed by someone who had never seen *Breaking Bad*—though it helps in a major way to have seen the first series, as I'll come to in a moment).

I wasn't terribly impressed with the first episode, however. It was, I believe, by episode three that I realized I was engrossed. (Though I think some of my initial resistance was due to my lingering skepticism, and if I went back and watched the first two episodes again I might feel differently.)

Let me explain the premise. The series is set several years before *Breaking Bad*. We knew from the earlier series that Saul's real name is Jimmy McGill, and that he chose the name "Saul Goodman" in order to sound like a slick Jewish lawyer (something that still gives me a good laugh).

Our Jimmy, we are told, started out as "Slippin' Jimmy," a con artist and all-around loser from Chicago. He lives in the shadow of his older brother, Chuck, an extremely successful lawyer with the firm of Hamlin, Hamlin, and McGill (HHM) based in Albuquerque, New Mexico. After his brother gets him out of a major problem with the law (which could have sent him to prison for some years), Jimmy relocates to Albuquerque and accepts a position in the mail room of HHM. His brush with incarceration changes Jimmy, and he decides to go straight. But he has no desire to remain in the mail room. Secretly, he puts himself through an off-shore, mail-order law school (an accredited one, nevertheless), and passes the bar on his third attempt. (Nothing to be ashamed of, say my lawyer friends.)

Jimmy expects that his brother Chuck and his preening alpha male asshole partner Howard Hamlin will hire him. No such luck. In their eyes he will always be Slippin' Jimmy — though it takes a while for Jimmy to figure out that his brother sees him this way. So, with nowhere else to turn, Jimmy sets up his own law office in a tiny back room behind a Vietnamese nail salon. The office also doubles as Jimmy's apartment, where he sleeps on the sofa bed and drinks a good deal of cheap booze.

Chuck is played by Michael McKean, in a brilliant performance. (McKean was the odious Lenny of the odious pair "Lenny and Squiggy" from the odious '70s shitcom *Laverne and Shirley*.) By the time the series opens, Chuck has been absent from his firm for several years. For reasons never made entirely clear, Chuck has descended into an extreme obsessive-compulsive disorder, with a dash of paranoid schizophrenia. He is terrified of electricity (to which he claims to be "allergic") and of electronic signals. He is almost completely incapable of leaving the house, and spends hours wrapped in a foil "space blanket," which is supposed to protect him from electromagnetic contamination. He destroyed his home's electrical connections, and lives by lantern light, storing food in a big cooler filled with ice. Contrary to what you may have concluded, Chuck is not bat-shit crazy. He is generally calm and capable of carrying on intelligent conversations. And it is clear that the man has a brilliant mind — now going to waste.

Jimmy loves his brother, and spends a good deal of time taking care of him (partly, no doubt, because Chuck's big house is a lot more comfortable than Jimmy's room in the nail salon). In the evenings, Jimmy brings him food and fuel and ice and newspapers. By day, Jimmy ekes out a tiny living as a public defender (paid a mere $700 for each case he takes). He checks his messages every day hoping that some clients will come along. They don't.

(Spoiler alert: If you have not seen the series, you may want to stop here.)

Jimmy begins to get fed up, and considers returning to a life of crime. He tries to scam a married couple who have stolen more than $1 million from the state into taking him as their lawyer. (These are the Kettlemans — a hilarious portrait of affluent "American exceptionalism.") But when his scheme goes awry and puts him in the crosshairs of the psychotic Tuco Salamanca (Raymond Cruz), who we met in the early days of *Breaking Bad*, Slippin' Jimmy is scared straight yet again. Now he throws himself into being a public defender and something amazing happens: he turns into a pretty good lawyer, and realizes it. And, something still more amazing: he turns into a pretty decent guy. A guy who, for example, returns the $1 million stolen by the Kettlemans (long story — watch the show) because it's "the right thing to do."

Can this be *our* Saul Goodman?

And this is why, dear reader, it really helps to have seen *Breaking Bad* before watching this show — despite the fact that the uninitiated could still enjoy *Better Call Saul* on its own. We, the initiated, know what's going to happen to Jimmy. He's going to turn into the odious but amusing, crooked Saul Goodman. *Better Call Saul* puts us in suspense: *how* is he going to get there? How do you turn a good man into Saul Goodman? What happens to a soul to make it Saul?

Well, in truth, our Jimmy starts out as a crooked loser. But he's got a heart, and a sense of decency that kicks in now and then. He's lovable. And he is loved — in the series by his sorta girlfriend Kim Wexler (Rhea Seehorn), a lawyer at HHM and a very appealing and likeable character.

Attentive viewers will notice in the first episode many parallels to *Breaking Bad*'s set up. A good deal of time is spent making clear to us how much Jimmy's life really sucks, and how dissatisfied he is. Like Walt, he is placed in humiliating positions. Like Walt, he has to stand by and watch as former associates thrive. And, like Walt, he feels he's been cheated. Walt was effectively cheated out of his share in the company Gray Matter, and Jimmy feels like he's been screwed by HHM. In the first several episodes it is made clear that Jimmy is eaten up by resentment against Howard Hamlin. To the point that, when he at last acquires a bit of cash, he spends some of it buying a tailor-made replica of one of Hamlin's suits, then has himself photographed in it for a billboard advertising "The Law Offices of James M. McGill," even ripping off HHM's logo. Oh, and then he has the billboard placed on the route Howard takes to work.

Jimmy reminds me of Mr. Mundy in *The Fountainhead*, who asks Howard Roark to build him a replica of "the Randolph place": the mansion of some upper crust snobs Mundy was in awe of when he was a poor boy in Georgia. Roark tries to dissuade him patiently, but a bit too honestly:

> "Don't you see?" Roark was saying. "It's a monument you want to build, but not to yourself. Not to your own life or your own achievement. To other people. To their supremacy over you. You're not challenging that supremacy. You're immortalizing it. You haven't thrown it off — you're putting it up forever. Will you be happy if you seal yourself for the rest of your life in that borrowed shape? Or if you strike free, for once, and build a new house, your own? You don't want the Randolph place. You want what it stood for. But what it stood for is what you've fought all your life."

Our Jimmy exhibits some seriously weak character, folks. Weak and infantile in a big way. And though Jimmy is likeable and, as I've said, sometimes actually decent, he is not a strong man. Ultimately, he cannot resist the darker nature within himself. Ultimately, he becomes not Slippin' Jimmy, but something much more extreme, Saul Goodman: the Alberich of Albuquerque.

When he thinks he has another shot at getting a job with HHM, Jimmy finds out that his own brother has blackballed him. When Jimmy confronts Chuck, the latter is finally frank with him: "You're not a real lawyer! You're Slippin' Jimmy. The law is sacred. With you it's like handing a machine gun to a chimp. *People don't change.*" It's a devastating scene (one that actually gave me a nightmare the evening after I saw it). My immediate reaction was to side with Jimmy and to resent Chuck for his injustice. Until I realized the next day that *Chuck is right*. People—*most* people—don't change. They are too weak to change. And we know already from *Breaking Bad* that Jimmy *doesn't* change (or, if he changes, it is for the worse). Certainly, it can be argued that Chuck's lack of faith drives Jimmy to become Saul. But the obvious answer to this is that a strong man would say "fuck you" and prove him wrong.

Instead, Jimmy's "fuck you" is, once more, of the Alberich variety. His "I'll show you! I'll show you all!" moment consists in becoming not just what Howard and Chuck see him as, but rather an astonishingly worse version of it: a buffoonish, tasteless caricature of a crooked, ambulance-chasing shyster. And a Jew. (Again, just like Alberich!)

By the final episode of season one, it seems Jimmy is just on the verge of becoming Saul. And I will admit to being somewhat disappointed with the rapidity of this transformation. I kind of like Jimmy. I don't know if I can like Saul. But I'll reserve judgement until season two.

The major difference from *Breaking Bad* should now be obvious. The earlier series gave us an imperfect character with whom we could identify, and who inspired us. This series gives us a *very* imperfect character with whom we can sympathize (up to a point), but with whom we can identify only in so far as all of us, from time to time, have been weak. But I can't be inspired by Jimmy, and the Saul of *Breaking Bad* never inspired me. If *Better*

Call Saul is going to become a great show, it probably won't be because it's inspirational. The saga of Saul will, I predict, provide us with suspense, and frequently make us cringe. But it may turn out to be nothing more than what *Breaking Bad* isn't, but what a square and a prig might take it to be: a *cautionary tale*.

Nevertheless, these ten episodes are *compelling*. And I highly recommend them. Stylistically, they are very much like *Breaking Bad*. If you enjoyed the wry humor, visual style, solid acting, and solid storytelling of *Breaking Bad*, you will like this show a lot. And I have said nothing about one of the series' major assets: it also tells the story of Mike Ehrmantraut (Jonathan Banks), my favorite character from *Breaking Bad*, after Walt. Mike is everything Jimmy/Saul isn't, and it may be his character who provides the inspiration here. Indeed, he may just steal the show.

And now for something completely predictable: You better watch Saul.

Counter-Currents/*North American New Right*,
June 18, 2015

"THE FLASH IN THE PAN"
FASCISM & FASCIST INSIGNIA IN THE SPY SPOOFS OF THE 1960S

One of my guiltier pleasures is the "Matt Helm" films of the 1960s. There were four of these, all produced by Irving Allen and starring Dean Martin as secret agent Matt Helm. The first (*The Silencers*) appeared in 1966. The story behind these films is an interesting one. In the 1950s Irving Allen was partnered with Albert R. ("Cubby") Broccoli. Things came to an end, however, when Broccoli announced that he was interested in purchasing the film rights to the James Bond novels by Ian Fleming. Allen thought this a terrible idea, and according to legend told Fleming over lunch that he didn't think his novels were good enough even for television(!). Broccoli and Allen went their separate ways, the former partnering with Harry Saltzman. Their first film together was 1962's *Dr. No*, starring Sean Connery.

The result left Mr. Allen with a considerable amount of egg on his face. Not to be deterred—and apparently burdened by neither a sense of irony nor of shame—he purchased the rights to Donald Hamilton's series of Matt Helm spy novels. These books were actually the antithesis of Fleming's: Helm was a cold-blooded, no-nonsense American assassin, a character as devoid of charm as Hamilton's realistic plots were devoid of Bondian fantasy. Irving launched a phony, "world-wide" search for an actor with balls enough to play Helm—but in reality Dean Martin apparently had the part all along.

With a vocal style uncomfortably close to that of Bing Crosby, Martin had carefully cultivated the image of a boozy, lovable playboy. (In reality, he was by all accounts a serious, introverted man whose on-stage glasses of "whisky" were actually iced tea.) He was an odd choice for an American James Bond. But the Matt Helm films were consciously aimed at an unsophisticated, lower-middle-class American audience. The people who thought Bond was just a wee bit too toffee-nosed and foreign. The cinematic Matt Helm was Bond if Bond had been from Long

Island. Helm was a boozing, womanizing wastrel. Incorrigibly lazy, he is depicted in three of the four films as unable to get out of bed to answer a call from the head of I.C.E. (Intelligence Counter-Espionage). But somehow he is always the only man who can save the world.

The Helm films borrow shamelessly from Bond but exaggerate all the Bondian elements. Instead of Maurice Binder's tasteful nude silhouettes, the credits sequence of the first Helm film features a strip show (the title "The Silencers" appears over the boobs of one of the girls, when she flings off her top). Unlike the spiritually virile Bond, who attracts women by actually seeming to be rather indifferent to them, Helm is a leering, eye-popping adolescent sex maniac. Instead of an Aston Martin complete with lethal accessories, Helm drives a 1965 Mercury Parklane station wagon complete with a bar and a bed (convenient for roadside quickies). The Helm films also frequently push the limit in sexual innuendo and double entendres. (The poster for the first film features Martin astride the barrel of a huge gun, under the words "Matt Helm Shoots the Works!") Perhaps the most amusing of these is the name of the evil organization Helm confronts in three of the four films: B.I.G.O.

Pronounced "Big Oh," the letters stand for Bureau of International Government and Order. Evil organizations with acronyms for names were a staple of the Bond-inspired films and television shows of the 1960s. The granddaddy of all of these was Fleming's S.P.E.C.T.R.E.: The Special Executive for Counter-Intelligence, Terrorism, Revenge, and Extortion. S.P.E.C.T.R.E. had been introduced in Fleming's 1961 novel *Thunderball*, which he had actually based (without attribution) on a screenplay written with Kevin McClory and Jack Whittingham.

S.P.E.C.T.R.E. was conceived by Messrs. Fleming, McClory, and Whittingham as a relatively small organization made up of the greatest criminal brains of the world. Headed by the sinister, asexual German-Greek Ernst Stavro Blofeld (Fleming's villains were often foreign mongrels) the organization was apolitical, and aimed simply at making a profit. It is never depicted as motivated by any sort of political ideology. (For example, in *Thun-*

derball S.P.E.C.T.R.E. steals two nuclear bombs with the intention of extorting £100 million from the United States and Great Britain.)

In the Bond films, which eventually completely eclipsed the novels in the popular imagination, S.P.E.C.T.R.E. became a vast organization equipped with its own secret island (*From Russia with Love*), steel-lined Paris headquarters (*Thunderball*), and steel-framed rocket base concealed inside an inactive volcano (*You Only Live Twice*). Blofeld really loved steel. In *For Your Eyes Only* (1981), Bond disposes of a Blofeld-like character who begs for his life, promising to build Bond "a delicatessen in stainless steel" (I am not kidding—watch it and see for yourself). And in the films S.P.E.C.T.R.E. has its own insignia: a stylized amalgam of a ghost and an octopus.

B.I.G.O. uniform patch from THE SILENCERS (1966)
(The circle is blue; the flash is red; the background is white.)

When S.P.E.C.T.R.E. became B.I.G.O. in the Matt Helm films, however, a curious thing happened. B.I.G.O. was not merely a vast criminal organization—it was a vast Right-wing conspiracy. The aim of the Bureau of International Government and Order was world domination: the creation of one world, fascist-style government. And, of course, it had to have its own insignia, just like S.P.E.C.T.R.E., and this is where things get really interesting: B.I.G.O.'s emblem was a lightning bolt through a circle (an "O"), uncannily similar to the official symbol of Sir Oswald Mosley's British Union of Fascists (even the red, white, and blue color scheme is the same).

Derisively referred to by critics of the B.U.F. as "the flash in the pan" (I have to admit that this is witty), the "Flash and Circle" was adopted by the organization in the summer of 1935, replacing the fasces. It was supposed to represent "the flash of action within a circle of unity" and was designed by Eric Hamilton Percy, Commander of the Fascist Defence Force.[1] A similar insignia was adopted by the Canadian Union of Fascists (a lightning bolt over a maple leaf), and in 1948 Mosley revived the flash and circle as the emblem of his new party, the Union Movement.

The "Flash and Circle" of the British Union of Fascists
(The disk is blue; the flash and circle are white; the background is red.)

The B.I.G.O. "flash and circle" was introduced in *The Silencers*, but it features even more prominently near the beginning of the second Helm film *Murderers' Row* (also 1966). In this film, the head of the organization is played to hammy perfection by Karl Malden, who is seen wearing a flash and circle ring (like the S.P.E.C.T.R.E. octopus rings prominently featured in *Thunderball*) and seated in a kind of throne festooned with flashes and circles.

As a fascist superpower, B.I.G.O. was by no means unique

---

[1] See John Millican, *Mosley's Men in Black: Uniforms, Flags and Insignia of the British Union of Fascists 1932–1940 and Union Movement* (London: Brockingday Publications, 2004), 16.

among the '60s spy spoofs. Indeed, one of the interesting features of that cinematic phenomenon—the vast scope of which (from about 1964 to 1969) is largely forgotten today—is that the villains in the American films and television shows were almost always in the B.I.G.O. mold: quasi-fascist secret organizations out to "take over the world." On the other hand, the British and Continental spy films of the period usually feature villains moved by pure profit, not ideology—or by some strangely personal motivation. (For example, the 1966 Dino de Laurentiis-produced *Se Tutte le Donne del Mondo*—released in the U.S. as *Kiss the Girls and Make Them Die*—features a villain who plans to kill off the human race and repopulate the planet by inseminating a bevy of beautiful women kept in a state of suspended animation.)

The reason for this difference between the American and European spy extravaganzas is not hard to discern. Americans had been sold on entering the Second World War with the claim that the fascists were out to "take over the world." (While we allied ourselves with Stalin, who really did aim at world domination.)

This ridiculous fabrication is still believed almost universally by Americans. Thus, villains assimilated to this "fascist" model were very easy for Americans to understand, and so Blofeld was transmuted into a plethora of little Hitlers and Mussolinis and Mosleys, armed this time with all the "secret weapons" we were frightened that the fascists might be developing in hollowed-out mountain lairs: death rays and flying saucers and doomsday devices of all kinds.

I started watching the '60s spy spoofs as a child, when local TV stations would run them in the afternoons. Bond was always a big TV event back then. He was only shown around my bedtime, and always with parental warnings (which seem absurd today). As a consequence, I was exposed to the Bond spoofs prior to ever being exposed to Bond. I thrilled to the adventures of Matt Helm, Derek Flint, *The Man From U.N.C.L.E.*, *Mission: Impossible*, and *The Avengers*. The odd thing was that I usually found the villains more attractive than the heroes. The villains, for one thing, had those terrific, steel-lined underground lairs.

They had snazzy uniforms (with thrilling lightning-bolt insignia). They were ruthless and efficient. They were serious and disciplined. They seemed bent on doing something important. The heroes, on the other hand, were usually wise-cracking hedonists—the most extreme example, of course, being Matt Helm.

Was this childhood attraction to B.I.G.O. and Thrush and Galaxy (we'll come to the latter two organizations in a moment) a sign of my incipient fascism? Probably. But much more interesting is what these American spy spoofs reveal about the modern American soul. Let's focus just on Matt Helm for the moment, as paradigmatic of the genre. It's discipline, order, duty, and iron will (the villains) . . . against hedonism, debauchery, and selfish abandon (the hero). (I didn't mention this earlier but Matt Helm always has to be talked into taking a break from chasing tail so that he can save the world.)

The conflict between America and fascism in World War II was presented as the conflict between freedom and slavery. In Matt Helm, however, the truth is laid bare and the conflict revealed for what it really was. The freedom of Matt Helm is mere license. He's out to make the world safe not for democracy and individual rights, but for boozing and boinking and sleeping till noon. That's the American Dream, and he is living it. And so when those handsome, uniformed, lock-step, lightning-bolted troops in their spotless lairs are blown to kingdom come we can all cheer. Who did they think they were, anyway?

Flint is another interesting case, almost forgotten today. He was played by James Coburn in two films: *Our Man Flint* (1966) and *In Like Flint* (1967). These are actually among the most significant '60s spy films, simply because they had some of the biggest budgets (still not as high as the Bond films—but getting there). Derek Flint is a kind of absurdly exaggerated amalgamation of James Bond and Doc Savage. He is a scientist, a surgeon, an expert in several martial arts, an accomplished ballet dancer (and teacher!), a war hero, a marine biologist, and a linguist. He is able to stop his heart to feign death. Most memorable of all is his specially-designed cigarette lighter with its 82 functions ("83 if you wish to light a cigar").

Flint is what my mother would call "higher class" than Matt

Helm (whom my mother would dismiss as "ethnic"). Nevertheless there are significant parallels—and very interesting ones, given the above analysis of the Americanization of the Bond genre. Just like Helm, Flint is a hedonist. He lives in a swanky, high tech apartment (like Helm's, only in better taste), located on Central Park West (unlike Helm, who parks his station wagon in the burbs—I kid you not). Flint is part Hugh Hefner, living with four beautiful girls ("there were five at one time, but that got to be a little much," he explains).

Just like Helm, Flint has to be convinced to set aside his personal projects to save the world. (Although Helm technically works for I.C.E., Flint is a completely free agent.) In both films, in fact, Flint ultimately agrees to go on his mission only after something happens which affects him personally. In the first film, he only really gets serious when the villains kidnap his girlfriends. Apparently saving the world from their infernal weather machine was not enough of a motivating factor for him.

In *Our Man Flint*, the villains—the ones with the weather machine—work for "Galaxy" (apparently not an acronym). Of course, they have their own insignia. Not a lightning bolt this time (that would be too perfect) but a G on a circle with Saturn-like rings encircling it (the exact same insignia, it is interesting to note, was used on the TV series *Land of the Giants*, also produced by Twentieth-Century Fox). Again, however, they are ideologically-motivated and vaguely fascist.

Galaxy is a bit different from B.I.G.O., however. They are headed by three white-coated, idealistic scientists who aim to pacify the world and create a conflict-free utopia. Ideologically, this actually puts them further to the Left, but there are strongly authoritarian overtones to Galaxy (nifty uniforms, a *"Führer-Prinzip"* of absolute loyalty to the three leaders, etc.). At the climax of the film, as Flint is poised to destroy the weather machine, one of the mad scientists pleads with him to desist: "Ours would be a perfect world!" he cries. "Not my kind of world," Flint responds, as he proceeds to demolish their handiwork.

Again, everything here is on personal terms. Our hero goes on his mission because *his* life is adversely affected; he foils the villains' scheme because their vision is not *his*. No conception of duty is at work in Flint, and no high-minded ideals. He is just looking out for number one. (It is noteworthy that on its release, *Our Man Flint* received a positive review in Ayn Rand's journal *The Objectivist*.²)

Galaxy uniform patch from OUR MAN FLINT (1966)

Flint is consciously and deliberately presented in the films as an American hero—and an American answer to Bond (in the first film, he beats up a Connery lookalike dubbed "Triple-O-Eight"). Flint infiltrates Galaxy's secret island but is captured when an eagle swoops down and attacks him. One of the guards explains that the eagle is trained to spot and attack Americans. Flint smiles ruefully and says, "The anti-American eagle. Diabolical!" Here we Americans are supposed to recognize that although the villains of this film are not the Soviets, it's still about Us vs. Them. Us vs. them foreign interllectuals with their books and their high-minded ideals. (The villains in the Helm films are always foreign and often—interestingly—aristocratic. What a delight it is to see the noble and the dignified toppled by the hometown boy!)

At least Bond still works for Queen and Country. For all his high living, it is clear that he still has a strong sense of duty. The American versions of Bond jettison all that is noble about the character and turn him into a grinning lothario, a self-involved

---

² Barbara Branden, Review of *Our Man Flint*, *The Objectivist*, 5, no. 2 (February 1966), in *The Objectivist*, Volumes 5–10 (1966–1971) (Palo Alto, Cal.: Palo Alto Book Service, 1982), 30–31.

hedonist, a perpetual adolescent, a vulgar operator always on the make. And please keep squarely in mind that this was done so that American audiences would have a character they could more easily identify with and root for. The American soul is rotten to the core.

Perhaps the most interesting of all the quasi-fascist spy villains is the one that figures in virtually all 105 episodes of *The Man From U.N.C.L.E.*: Thrush. U.N.C.L.E. creator Sam Rolfe invented Thrush actually as a fall-back villain. Recognizing that it would be difficult to invent new villains every week, with new motivations, Rolfe thought Thrush would be a convenient, regular foil for the do-gooding U.N.C.L.E. organization (that's the United Network Command for Law and Enforcement). Thrush was initially supposed to be mysterious. We were not even supposed to know what the name "Thrush" meant: it could be the name of the organization, or the code-name of the organization's leader (in one 1964 episode, "The Double Affair," Thrush is actually referred to as "him").

As the series progressed, however, the writers came up with more definite ideas about Thrush. First, the name became fixed as the name of the organization (though why it was called that was never explained in the series). Rolfe decided that Thrush was a "supra-nation" spread all over the earth. (In the pilot episode, one of the villains says "Thrush is my country.") Its center was "The City of Thrush," though this was always referred to in the series as "Thrush Central": a mobile headquarters always shifting from place to place. Thrush's agents had cover roles within their communities.

Borrowing a term from the ancient Persians, Rolfe referred to the individual, local outposts of Thrush as "satraps," each of which would be disguised in some ordinary way: as a shop, an office block, a school, a mortuary, a garage, a winery, etc. This concept, of course, was equivalent to that of the "communist cell." And Thrush, in fact, is a unique amalgam of elements of the Left and Right—but, as always with these spy baddies—the accent is on the Right.

Thrush's stated purpose is taking over the world and imposing a fascist-style state. "Thrush believes in the two-party system: the masters and the slaves," our hero Napoleon Solo intones in an early episode. "Very nicely put," concurs his Thrush captor. Like B.I.G.O. and Galaxy and all the other fascistic spy villains, Thrush is depicted as highly disciplined and regimented (the "Thrush Uniform Code of Procedure" is mentioned in two episodes written by Peter Allan Fields, the man principally responsible for much of the detail about Thrush introduced in the series; many of Rolfe's original ideas were never used). Thrush agents, again, wear snazzy uniforms (complete with black berets). They carry specially-designed guns equipped with bizarre-looking night scopes. And Thrush is always coming up with some doomsday device: an earthquake machine, a "volcanic activator," a deadly hiccup-inducing gas, a death ray, another death ray, and still another death ray.

David McDaniel, author of several of the U.N.C.L.E. paperback novels (published by Ace Books), eventually decided that Thrush was an acronym standing for Technological Hierarchy for the Removal of Undesirables and the Subjugation of Humanity. Though this is often mentioned in retrospectives on U.N.C.LE., in fact it was never used in the series and is not considered "canonical." Still, McDaniel did a nice job here in highlighting the "fascistic" nature of Thrush (at least insofar as fascism is popularly conceived).

The heroes of U.N.C.L.E.—Napoleon Solo and Illya Kuryakin—are a cut above Helm and Flint. Rolfe conceived U.N.C.L.E. as an FBI-like organization, utilizing only educated men of high moral character. And though Solo is a bit of a womanizer, both he and Kuryakin are depicted chiefly as stalwart, straight-arrow types. Still, the motives and *raison d'être* of U.N.C.L.E. are more than a bit vague. In the narration that opens the first several episodes of the series we are told that U.N.C.L.E. is involved in "maintaining political and legal order anywhere in the world." But what does this mean?

The answer seems to be that U.N.C.L.E. is out to maintain the *status quo* in our post-historical world of Last Men. U.N.C.L.E.'s only ideological commitment is opposition to Thrush, who are the quasi-fascistic Nietzschean Overmen bent on re-starting history. In other words, the good guys.

Thrush insignia from THE MAN FROM U.N.C.L.E.

Thrush's symbol was an angry, stylized bird inside a kind of shield. However, when U.N.C.L.E. was revived in the shockingly lame 1983 TV movie *The Return of The Man From U.N.C.L.E.: The Fifteen Years Later Affair*, the producers (who were not involved with the original series) forgot about this insignia. And when their designer was asked to come up with a symbol for Thrush, guess what he produced. That's right: a lightning bolt!

The American producers of the Bond-inspired spy spoofs made their villains fascists for the simple reason that Americans have been so well trained to see fascists as the bad guys. There was no need to provide any elaborate explanation for why these villains were bad — we all know these sorts of guys are bad, don't we? And yet they possess an enduring fascination and allure, with their sleek black uniforms, their arresting insignia, their discipline, their ruthlessness, their unity, and, yes, their great underground steel lairs.

Another part of the appeal is that they have rejected all of the equality and democracy bullshit — the bullshit all Americans pay lip service to (terrified of each other, as Tocqueville pointed out), but only the most craven actually believe in. The dirty little secret is that B.I.G.O. and Galaxy and Thrush are a kind of fantasy wish fulfillment for us. Fear not: at the end of the film, our oversexed playboy hero (with whom we guiltily identify) will vanquish the morally superior bad guys, and we can all give three cheers for the American way. But we all know whose way is *really* superior—and that that lightning bolt in fact strikes at the worst within us, the worst which, in our modern world, reigns ascendant.

Give me the lightning bolt and pass me the black coveralls, I want to join Thrush!

Counter-Currents/*North American New Right*,
May 11, 2011

THE MAN FROM U.N.C.L.E.:
A CAUTIONARY TALE

TEASER

On August 14th, 2015, Warner Bros. will release its big-screen adaptation of a television series most moviegoers under the age of 60 have never even heard of: *The Man From U.N.C.L.E.* (NBC, 1964-1968). The present article is devoted to the original series, which is a gold mine for New Right pop cultural commentary. Simultaneously crypto-Marxist, crypto-anti-Marxist, and crypto-anti-Semitic, this quintessential '60s cultural artifact is also ultra-cool, ultra-bad, and (as the foregoing trio of antis implies) just ultra-confused.

ACT ONE: "THE BASTARD SPAWN OF IAN FLEMING"

Hard to believe so few remember it now, because in its day *U.N.C.L.E.* was a big thing. The first TV show, in fact, to develop a cult following while it was still on the air, *U.N.C.L.E.* spawned eight feature films (released 1964-1968) which made more money than the Bond films in some parts of the world, a spin-off (the ludicrous *Girl From U.N.C.L.E.*, 1966-1967), 24 paperback novels, comic books, a magazine, a clothing line, several record albums, and so many toys a book had to be published a few years ago to catalog them all.

Public appearances by series co-star David McCallum caused literal riots. The most memorable of these occurred on February 5, 1966 when 15,000 teenaged girls showed up to see McCallum make an appearance at New York's Macy's on 34th Street. When employees panicked and abruptly cancelled the event, the ensuing melee sent several to the hospital. One dejected 13-year-old told the *Times*, "I'm going to Gimbels from now on."

When the Beatles arrived in Los Angeles in the summer of 1966 (to make one of their final live concert appearances) their first request was to meet series star Robert Vaughn—since *U.N.C.L.E.* was their favorite TV show. (It was even bigger in the U.K., where the first few *U.N.C.L.E.* feature films set box office records.) *U.N.C.L.E.* was also the favorite show of William S. Burroughs.

The story of *U.N.C.L.E.*'s success, and of how it came about at all, is arguably more entertaining than the series itself. If you know anything at all about the series, you will have heard that it was supposed to be "James Bond on television" (not quite accurate, as we shall see), and a major part of the '60s "spy craze." But *U.N.C.L.E.* was the only Bond knock-off in which Bond creator Ian Fleming actually had a hand.

After the success of his first one or two novels in the 1950s, Fleming very soon began thinking about bringing Bond either to the big screen or the small screen. He was involved in various efforts to do so throughout the decade. In 1954, the year *Casino Royale* (the first Bond novel) was published in the U.S., a TV adaptation appeared on a CBS anthology series. Barry Nelson played an Americanized "Jimmy" Bond. It was quickly forgotten (and should remain so). Two years later Fleming sold the film rights to the same novel for a mere $6,000 (these rights changed hands a few times and eventually led to the 1967 *Casino Royale*, a lavish, misfired "spoof," and then finally to Daniel Craig's first outing as Bond, the smashing 2006 *Casino Royale*).

In 1959, Fleming collaborated with producer Kevin McClory and playwright Jack Whittingham on several treatments and screenplays under the tentative title *James Bond of the Secret Service*. The result is an oft-told tale for Bond fans (and the subject of a recent book, *The Battle for Bond*; for more details, see "The Cat is Back" above). When nothing came of the project, Fleming adapted the story into the novel *Thunderball* (published in 1961). Unfortunately, he forgot to give any credit (or money) to McClory and Whittingham, even though much of the story was their invention. (Devising plots was not Fleming's forte, a point to which I will return later.) McClory and Whittingham promptly filed suit—and Fleming promptly had his first heart attack. (The second—in 1964—would kill him.)

In any case, given all the frustration Fleming had suffered as a result of his desire to involve himself with Hollywood, it's surprising that he agreed to meet with TV producer Norman Felton in October 1962, to discuss collaborating on a weekly series. At the time, Felton was a big wheel in Hollywood. He was head of both MGM-TV and of his own company, Arena Productions, which launched the hit series *Dr. Kildare* in September 1961. Interestingly, Felton's immediate predecessor as head of MGM-TV was Richard Maibaum, best known as the screenwriter for 13 of the Bond films. (In another odd coincidence, both Felton and Maibaum had attended the University of Iowa, where both studied in the Speech and Dramatic Arts Department—though not at the same time.)

Felton did not know Fleming's work, though of course he had heard of it. (It was actually Felton's agent who persuaded him to meet with Fleming, thinking something big could result.) For readers today "James Bond" equals the James Bond *films*. But in 1962 Bond was still very much a literary phenomenon. When Fleming and Felton met in New York City to begin what would be a series of largely aimless discussions, the cinematic James Bond was only twenty-four days old: *Dr. No* had premiered on October 5th in London (Fleming and Felton met on October 29th). And the film would not be seen in the U.S. until May 8, 1963.

Thus, it's important to keep in mind two things. First, it was the *literary* Bond that led to this meeting. And, second, the aim of the meeting was to produce a *new* "Fleming creation"—not to rip off Bond. What would become *The Man From U.N.C.L.E.* was—as we shall see—created before *Dr. No* was ever seen in the U.S. And the pilot episode was scripted prior to the premiere of *From Russia, With Love* (the second Bond film), and filmed prior to its U.S. release. The breezy, "tongue in cheek" quality of *U.N.C.L.E.* is best compared to 1964's *Goldfinger* (the third Bond film), which was not even released in the U.S. until December 1964, when *U.N.C.L.E.* had been airing for three months.

Thus, like the British series *The Avengers* and *Danger Man*, *U.N.C.L.E.* actually predates the cinematic Bond phenomenon, and it is inaccurate to label any of these series as imitating or "cashing in on" the cinematic Bond. Indeed, I would argue (though this is not the place to do it) that the '60s "spy craze" should be understood on analogy with the "Western craze" of the 1950s, which lasted into the '60s. In 1959 there were *twenty-*

six Westerns airing in primetime in the U.S. market. Now, arguably without the success of *Gunsmoke* (which began airing in 1955) none of these shows would have been on, and it can also be said that *Gunsmoke* (and cinematic Westerns, of course) inspired the creation of some of these shows. But the differences between *Gunsmoke* and series like *Rawhide*, *Bonanza*, *Maverick*, and *Have Gun – Will Travel* were very, very great. *The Avengers* and *U.N.C.L.E.* have about as much in common with Bond as *The Big Valley* has with *Stagecoach*. "Spy-fi," as it has come to be called, is a genre in which there are many variations, just like the Western.

When Norman Felton met Ian Fleming, Bond's creator was a very tired man. As noted earlier, he had already suffered one heart attack, and had also become weary of James Bond, and of the legal mess he had created for himself. According to Felton, they spent a couple days together walking around New York City shooting the breeze. Felton's attempts to direct the conversation back to the television project were usually unsuccessful. On the evening of October 30th, after a dinner party held in Fleming's honor, Felton typed up some notes on a "spy" character—very general stuff about a man of mystery involved in international intrigue.

The next morning, he showed the notes to Fleming, who liked them, and then suggested out of the blue that the character be called "Napoleon Solo." Felton was not entirely thrilled by this and tactfully asked why. "Well, Solo is a good name," Fleming replied, "and Napoleon just sounds good with it." This was coming, of course, from the creator of characters with names like Julius No, Honey Rider, Auric Goldfinger, Pussy Galore, Guntram Shatterhand, Ernst Stavro Blofeld, Tiffany Case, and Francisco Scaramanga. He had a knack for names. And "Napoleon Solo" undeniably has the "Fleming touch": cool, weird, and knowing it. What he failed to tell Felton, however, was that "Mr. Solo" (without "Napoleon") was the name of a minor character, a hood who gets bumped off, in *Goldfinger*. This would be the source of future trouble.

Then, dramatically, Fleming produced a stack of eleven Western Union telegram blanks on which he had written notes about Napoleon Solo, the night before. (Fleming explained that he could find no stationery in his hotel room.) His notes also contained very general allusions to international intrigue, but also some *very* specific indications about Solo. Fleming was famous for his detailed descriptions of Bond's taste in all manner of things, right down to the type of cotton his shirts were made from and the brand of marmalade he favored. Among other things, Fleming's Solo collected gold coins and bandannas. He had a pet bird he talked to regularly, which Fleming envisioned as "useful for getting over plot problems." One imagines something like the following—coming, say, after a cliffhanger at the end of Act Three:

ACT FOUR

FADE IN:
INT. SOLO'S APARTMENT—THE FOLLOWING MORNING

Solo is standing by the bird cage, wearing the same clothes we saw him in last night.

SOLO
(talking to bird)
I guess you're wondering how I got all this marmalade on me, Tweety...
(he drops a few seeds into the cage)
... Well, things looked pretty dicey when I was caught in the embrace of that giant squid. But thankfully out of the corner of my eye I spotted Dr. Lobo's breakfast tray...

And so on.

Felton had already suggested to Fleming that their main character might be Canadian, rather than American (a point I will return to shortly). Fleming worked that in, specifying that Solo had served in a Canadian Highland regiment. Solo would also have a mysterious boss, referred to only as "He." And He had a secretary, with whom Solo (of course) would flirt. Her name was April Dancer. In fact, the names "Napoleon Solo" and "April

Dancer" were the only elements from Fleming's notes that found their way into what became *The Man From U.N.C.L.E.*

April Dancer became *The Girl From U.N.C.L.E.* (not the secretary to "He"), though she had to wait until 1966. There were also a few Bondian elements in Fleming's notes (Solo wears blue suits with a white shirt and black tie—no mention of whether the tie is knitted, however—and drives a vintage car). But the general impression is that Fleming was trying to create a character distinctively different from Bond. That few of his original ideas were retained for *U.N.C.L.E.* is not exactly a lost opportunity: the ideas weren't that good.

Felton knew he didn't have that much when he parted company with Fleming on October 31st. But he also knew that without Fleming's name there would be no series—and he was anxious to produce an escapist program, having had enough of drama for the moment. Less than a month later he synthesized his own notes with Fleming's, producing a short document titled "Basic Material Pertinent to a New One Hour Television Series [entitled] *SOLO*. Assembled by: Ian Fleming and Norman Felton." And then the negotiations began between Felton's agents and MGM-TV, with the idea of bringing *Solo* to NBC, with sponsorship by the Ford Motor Co. This dragged on until March 1963, when NBC agreed that it would buy the *Solo* series without a pilot—a rarity—based upon Fleming's promised participation.

ACT TWO: "HAVE MODIFIED-P-38-WITH-ATTACHMENTS— WILL TRAVEL"

Then the pressure was really on, as Felton's experience in New York had taught him that he couldn't rely on Fleming. The enthusiasm and commitment simply weren't there. Faced with the necessity of producing a more detailed outline for *Solo*, Felton turned to Sam Rolfe, who was at that time producer of Felton's series *The Eleventh Hour*, which concerned a psychiatrist. (Intended as the psychiatric equivalent to *Dr. Kildare*, *The Eleventh Hour* was not nearly as successful, lasting only two seasons on NBC, from 1962 to 1964.)

Rolfe was co-creator of the highly-successful Western series *Have Gun—Will Travel*, which ran on CBS from 1957 to 1963. It concerned the adventures of a freelance "knight without armor," Palladin (played by Richard Boone), who was conceived as a debonair, stylish, larger-than-life hero. The series had a whimsical tone, but involved Palladin in credible adventures. (It also had a racist tone — by today's standards — with two recurring Asian characters named Hey Boy and Hey Girl, who played a kind of slanty-eyed Stepin Fetchit function for Boone's Palladin.)

Four years before *Have Gun – Will Travel*, Rolfe had scored an Oscar nomination for his first screenplay, written for *The Naked Spur*, a Western starring James Stewart. An interesting footnote: Rolfe co-wrote *The Naked Spur* with Harold Jack Bloom, who would later contribute a script to *U.N.C.L.E.*, and be credited with "additional story material" for the 1967 Bond film *You Only Live Twice*, making him the only writer — aside from Ian Fleming — to have been involved with both Bond and *U.N.C.L.E.*

Felton gave Rolfe his twelve-page sketch of *Solo* and essentially left him free to develop it as he saw fit. Now, only a couple of years earlier Rolfe had penned an unproduced pilot script for a proposed series titled *The Dragons and St. George*. A kind of modernized Arthurian romance, the hero was one Mark St. George, a freelance troubleshooter not unlike Simon Templar (The Saint) — and more than a little like Rolfe's Palladin. He was assisted by his German shepherd, Merlin, and by a mysterious blond man named Lance Mordred. Mordred had been mangled in an accident some years earlier, and his body rebuilt from various donors. Mysteriously, from each of these he had acquired a special skill (e.g., because a Parisian chef had donated a metatarsal arch, Lance was an expert in the preparation of *haute cuisine* — no kidding!). The "dragons" of the title were the various villains St. George encountered each week.

Quite a lot of this went into Rolfe's revision of *Solo*. He tossed out almost every bit of characterization Fleming and Felton had given Napoleon Solo, and essentially gave Mark St. George a name change. Lance Mordred became Illya Kuryakin, Solo's sometime partner — though the ridiculous business about his being made of spare parts was jettisoned. The dog was also dropped, but Rolfe retained another item in St. George's arsenal: a modified Walther P-38 which could fire full auto, and accept various attachments such as a shoulder stock and telescopic sight. Finally, "the dragons" were to become an evil organization that Solo would fight on a regular basis—but more about them shortly.

The biggest change Rolfe made to his original conception was to give Solo a regular employer. This was U.N.C.L.E.—an acronym, of course, but originally the letters stood for nothing. (Rolfe wanted to keep it mysterious.) U.N.C.L.E. was conceived as an international spy organization, with agents of all nationalities working for the welfare of the entire world. Sort of like if the U.N. had its own spy agency, with cool gadgets. And Rolfe intended the "U.N." in "U.N.C.L.E." to invite speculation that the two were connected. In Rolfe's lengthy "prospectus" for what would become *The Man From U.N.C.L.E.*, he gives a detailed description of the organization and its headquarters.

Rolfe envisioned U.N.C.L.E. HQ as located a few blocks from the U.N. building in New York, somewhere in the East 40s. It occupied one entire city block, and was concealed behind a row of brownstones. At one end of the block was a newer, whitestone building which actually housed an office plainly marked as belonging to U.N.C.L.E. Here some nobody sat behind a desk, ready to inform inquirers of U.N.C.L.E.'s mission, making it out to seem like something along the lines of UNICEF. Rolfe seemed to be taking inspiration here from Fleming's description in Thunderball of the "cover office" for S.P.E.C.T.R.E.: F.I.R.C.O., the Fraternité International de la Résistance Contre l'Oppression, an organization that claims to assist resistance movements around the world. U.N.C.L.E. is not, therefore, a secret organization—but its real activities are most definitely secret. Hence what lies behind the brownstones.

At the middle of the block is Del Floria's Tailor Shop (originally called Giovanni's in Rolfe's notes). This is the "agent's entrance" to U.N.C.L.E. HQ. If the elderly tailor recognizes you as an agent, you are escorted into a fitting booth. He flips a concealed switch beside his pressing machine, you twist the coat hook in the fitting booth and the back wall of the booth opens to reveal the admissions room of U.N.C.L.E. HQ. There, depending upon your security clearance, you will receive either a white, yellow, green, or red badge. But the receptionist (always a pretty girl) must attach it to your lapel herself. A chemical on her fingers reacts with a chemical on the badge, without which reaction the badge would set off every alarm in the place as soon as you walked through the first sliding, mechanical steel door.

And so on. Rolfe poured a huge amount of imagination and detail into these notes, almost as much as Gene Roddenberry famously did for *Star Trek*, or Patrick McGoohan did for *The Prisoner*. He provided a complete layout of U.N.C.L.E.'s HQ (yes there's more: such as the underground grotto with channel to the East River, never depicted in the series). He even created an organizational chart:

Section I: Policy and Operations
Section II: Operations and Enforcement
Section III: Enforcement and Intelligence
Section IV: Intelligence and Communications
Section V: Communication and Security
Section VI: Security and Personnel
Section VII: Propaganda and Finance
Section VIII: Camouflage and Deception

Napoleon Solo is Number One, Section Two (or "Chief Enforcement Agent") of the New York branch. (There are five major U.N.C.L.E. branches—in New York, Caracas, Nairobi, New Delhi, and Berlin—and innumerable smaller ones.) His second in command and frequent partner is Illya Kurakin, whose home country is the U.S.S.R. Number One, Section One, Chief of the New York branch, is Alexander Waverly. Leo G. Carroll was cast as Waverly in the series—essentially playing the same part he had played in Hitchcock's *North by Northwest* (1959; a strong cinematic influence on *U.N.C.L.E.*, as was Hitchcock's 1946 film *Notorious*). (In the pilot the character was called "Mr. Allison" and was played by Will Kuluva.)

As mentioned earlier, Rolfe imagined Solo as fitted out with a modified Walther P-38. Thus was created the famous "U.N.C.L.E. Special" with multiple attachments. Several of these were built by prop men for the series (after an earlier attempt with a Mauser proved unusable—the Mauser's modification was backed financially by the Ideal Toy Co., which eventually marketed a toy version that made millions). The gun proved so popular with little boys that it received its own fan mail, and was the subject of more than one magazine article. And countless gadgets were created for the men from U.N.C.L.E. Rolfe envisioned the agents in continuous radio contact with HQ, and as these were the days before cell phones the prop men created concealed "communicators" disguised as cigarette cases and—most famously—a fountain pen. But all of this was yet to come.

Felton was delighted with Rolfe's work, and in the summer of 1963 he travelled to London and showed the prospectus to Ian Fleming. Fleming was also impressed—and he shocked Felton by asking if he could buy a couple of the plot outlines Rolfe had included with his prospectus! (Fleming's greatest difficulty in writing the Bond novels was coming up with plots.) One of these was a story that involved a secret organization, based under the ocean, firing rockets full of wheat-eating bacteria into Soviet crops. Their aim: to bring about a nuclear war between the U.S. and U.S.S.R. Once the two superpowers had decimated each other, *they* would rise from the ocean and take over. Although there's no way to be sure, this could have been one of the plots that interested Fleming. In any case, it bears an uncanny resemblance to the plot of the 1977 Bond film *The Spy Who Loved Me* (though *not* the Fleming novel from which it took its title, and only its title). (This plot outline was later developed into one of the early episodes of *U.N.C.L.E.*, "The Neptune Affair," broadcast December 8, 1964.)

Though their meeting had begun in this auspicious manner, Fleming then disappointed Felton by informing him that he was being pressured by Bond producers Broccoli and Saltzman not to have any involvement in the series. And, besides, he was spread a bit thin. Fleming then signed over all rights to "Napoleon Solo" to Felton for the token sum of £1. Eon Productions would later bring legal action against Felton, MGM, and NBC claiming the use of "Solo" was copyright infringement. Their case was a weak one. As noted earlier, the "Solo" of *Goldfinger* was a gangster (if you've seen the film, he's the one Goldfinger sends off on a "pressing engagement"). But Felton *et al.* were eager to make the whole thing go away, so while they held firm on the use of "Napoleon Solo," they agreed to change the title of the series. Felton wanted to call it *U.N.C.L.E.*, as it seemed mysterious, and was incensed when someone at NBC insisted on the title *The Man From U.N.C.L.E.*

The fact that Felton held firm on "Napoleon Solo," though he didn't even like the name, is an indication that he was in no hurry to dispel the idea that Fleming had something to do with the series. Indeed, the copy of Rolfe's prospectus that he showed to Fleming and others had a cover page that read "Ian Fleming's *SOLO*," and made no reference to Rolfe at all. Furthermore, instead of offering Rolfe the "created by" credit that he really deserved, MGM-Arena offered him "developed by." At the time, Rolfe didn't think it made much of a difference. He later discovered that it did — financially and otherwise.

ACT THREE: "THE MUSH FROM U.N.C.L.E."

Eventually someone pointed out that there is a state law in New York prohibiting the exploitation of "U.N." or "United Nations" for commercial purposes, so "U.N.C.L.E." had to be given a meaning. Thus "Unified Network Command for Law and Enforcement" was proposed, with "Unified" soon becoming "United."

As to why it's "Law *and* Enforcement," that is a bit of a mystery. But if you want to piss off an *U.N.C.L.E.* fan, just try leaving out the "and." It may have something to do with the fact that Rolfe wanted U.N.C.L.E. agents to be called "Enforcement Agents," a term used a few times in the subsequent series and then totally forgotten about. But what were they "enforcing"?

Sam Rolfe was a pretty apolitical chap, but Norman Felton was not. In college at the University of Iowa, he was a member of one of the student "John Reed Clubs," which were under the direction of the American Communist Party. While Felton was not, strictly speaking, a Marxist, his convictions were far to the Left of center, and remained so throughout his life. Felton was a life-long supporter of liberal causes. When he died in 2012 at the age of 99, his family suggested that in lieu of flowers donations could be made to the ACLU.

Felton was a one-worlder, a peacenik, an anti-violence-on-TV producer of violent TV, and so staunch a death penalty opponent that when his daughter, granddaughter, and son-in-law were brutally murdered in 1982 he plead for clemency at the sentencing of the killers (three blacks looking for money to buy drugs). Felton wrote in an article some years afterwards: "I later learned that one of the men who committed the murders had been taken from his mother when he was only seven months old and put into foster homes until at age 16 he was let go, having had no meaningful relationships."[1] The entire article depicts as sad a case of liberal delusion as I have ever encountered.

In fairness, I must point out that Felton was no Neiman Marxist or limousine liberal. Born in London, the child of a lithographer and a cleaning lady, he had left school to work at age 13. His family moved to the U.S. three years later, seeking a better life. Through talent and a lot of luck Felton wound up attending the University of Iowa, though he didn't have a penny. I would guess that he acquired his political convictions through his friends in the Teamsters, of which he was a member before he was 20. His surname will invite speculation about his ethnicity, but Felton seems to have been raised a Christian.

It is quite likely that Felton influenced Rolfe in having Solo work for an international organization, rather than a U.S. government agency. For Felton, this struck a blow against nationalism. And one detail from the Felton-Fleming notes that Rolfe did retain was Solo as Canadian (though this was quickly forgotten about and never mentioned in the series). This was important for Felton because of a chance conversation he had had in London in June 1961 with Joanna Spicer, BBC assistant controller of planning for television. She cornered Felton and asked him why the leads in American TV shows were always tall, two-fisted, well-built Americans. Felton gave her no answer. But internally, good liberal that he was, he had to admit that this was indeed a deucedly appalling state of affairs.

Hence, "Solo" is Canadian. And hence Robert Vaughn and

---

[1] http://heinonline.org/HOL/LandingPage?handle=hein.journals/blorij28&div=3&id=&page=

David McCallum—who were both nice looking (McCallum's appeal to young girls has already been discussed) but hardly physically imposing. In answer to Miss Spicer, Felton wanted to present what he called "a new kind of hero," and essentially this amounted to short and scrawny. Vaughn was about 5'9"; McCallum a mere 5'7." Both were cast by Norman Felton, as Sam Rolfe elected not to produce the pilot film, though he later decided to produce the first season. Rolfe originally envisioned Illya as physically massive.

And as to U.N.C.L.E. being an international organization, for Rolfe it was a plus simply because if Solo worked for the U.S. government, "we'd be doing anti-communist stuff every week," as he told *TV Guide* (October 24, 1964). It wasn't that Rolfe was pro-communism, it was that he was bored with thrillers that used the Russians as convenient villains. Even Fleming was bored: that's why he (co-)created S.P.E.C.T.R.E.

Nonetheless, later on this drew the ire of none other than Ayn Rand, who devoted a significant portion of a 1965 article to attacking *U.N.C.L.E.*[2] Remarkably, the famously rational Miss Rand—one of whose followers later claimed that she had "a mind like a computerized laser drill"—manages to miss the point of a great many things in the episodes she watched. For example, it's apparent from her descriptions that she couldn't follow several of the plots (plots that I followed when I saw the series as teenager), and so she declares "It is impossible to tell who is doing what or why." She also failed to discern when Robert Vaughn was playing Solo, and when he was playing Solo playing an undercover role. One of these episodes (unfortunately) involved Solo playing a buffoon in order to lull the bad guys into a false sense of security (the aforementioned "Neptune Affair"). So Rand got her wires crossed and thought Vaughn's Solo buffoonish. Nevertheless, she manages to raise some good questions.

First of all Rand, who was a refugee from Soviet Russia, asks

---

[2] The article was "Bootleg Romanticism," in the January 1965 issue of *The Objectivist Newsletter*. When this article was reprinted in *The Romantic Manifesto* (New York: New American Library, 1969), all the material on *U.N.C.L.E.* was deleted. The series had been canceled by this point, and so Rand considered discussion of it no longer topical.

"what would be wrong with 'doing anti-communist stuff every week'?" Good question. But from Rolfe's perspective, again, there was a legitimate answer: audiences were bored with it. The early episodes of U.N.C.L.E. include an explanatory sequence with voice-over stating that the organization "is involved in maintaining political and legal order anywhere in the world." Rolfe never meant those words to be analyzed too carefully. But then he'd never met Ayn Rand. She asks:

> If "U.N.C.L.E." is dedicated to international law enforcement, does this mean that it protects indiscriminately any sort of government? . . . If so, then would "U.N.C.L.E." have protected the Nazi government in Germany against the Jewish refugees? Would it protect Castro's government against the Cuban refugees? Would it protect the Soviet government against the refugees from one third of the globe? The presence of Illya Kuryakin among the knights of "U.N.C.L.E." would seem to indicate the affirmative, which is pretty sickening. Aw, it's not supposed to be taken seriously — the producers would probably answer — we're only kidding, it's all "tongue-in-cheek." But the question is: which cheek? Left or right? The answer is probably: the middle — that is, tongue stuck out at the audience in the name of nothing in particular.[3]

Ouch. But some of these are pretty fair questions. What is unfair is the imputation of cynicism to the show's producers. Many years later in an interview, Rolfe heaped scorn on "tongue-in-cheek" saying "tongue-in-cheek means 'I don't know what the hell I'm doing so I'm giving it a name.'" Like *Have Gun – Will Travel*, the Rolfe-produced first season of *U.N.C.L.E.* (1964-1965) was light hearted, but had solid plots and genuine suspense. After his departure, however, the producers really became what Rand saw them as: cynics with tongues stuck out at the audience.

---

[3] Ayn Rand, "Bootleg Romanticism," *The Objectivist Newsletter*, January 1965, p. 3.

But what really were the politics of the U.N.C.L.E. organization? What was meant by saying that it maintained "political and legal order anywhere in the world"? Well, the 105 episodes of the series make it plain that this "international organization" was not, as Rand seemed to think, a value-free agent of the political *status quo*. Instead, its mission was the spread of the Western model of the "open society." You see, Solo and company don't go around propping up dictators. In fact, they topple a few in the course of the series. Exactly how could such an organization enlist multi-national cooperation, including that of the Soviet Union? The writers and producers of the series were never really forced to deal with this question, because the villains on *U.N.C.L.E.* were almost always "Thrush," a fictitious nation devised by Rolfe. And this is where the plot thickens — or gets *really* confused, depending upon your perspective.

ACT FOUR: "OY! AGAIN WITH THRUSH!"

If you already know anything at all about this series, you probably think that Thrush is an organization, not a nation. And you may think that it's "T.H.R.U.S.H." But this was not Rolfe's original conception. He came up with the idea for the same sort of reason Fleming came up with Solo's pet bird: to get around plot problems. Faced with the prospect of coming up with new villains, with new motivations every week, Rolfe invented Thrush as a convenient fallback, to be used only now and then. And when it made an appearance the villain's motives would be instantly clear: he's doing it "for Thrush." (Though in the series' later years it would be seen again and again and again—in virtually every episode.) But what exactly was Thrush?

Early on, Rolfe conceived of Thrush as an organization of baddies "for hire" — sort of how S.P.E.C.T.R.E. was depicted in the film version of *You Only Live Twice* (which came four years later, of course). No one seems to know how the name "Thrush" was arrived at. But it was pointed out that it sounded a bit too much like "Smersh," the Soviet murder organization that shows up in several of Fleming's novels. This may have simply been a product of Rolfe's subconscious mind, as he certainly had imagination enough to come up with a name that didn't sound like

Smersh. But there was the fear that some might see Thrush as Smersh + S.P.E.C.T.R.E. Thus, anxious to avoid another volley of "cease and desists" from Broccoli and Saltzman, Rolfe was asked to make Thrush distinctively different.

In his notes on Thrush from April 1964 — written five months after production on the pilot wrapped — Rolfe notes that Thrush operates by means of a large number of semi-autonomous units called *satraps*, which are always disguised as something else:

> A satrap may take the form of a manufacturing complex . . . or a school . . . or a hospital . . . or a series of underground tunnels or caverns . . . or a department store, etc. They exist as functional parts of the society in which they have been set down . . . but they have a shadow existence all their own . . . a secret life in which they dedicate their fanatic loyalty to Thrush.

So far this sounds uncannily like a concept Norman Felton must have been very familiar with: the Communist "cell," answerable to the Comintern. But the notes actually begin this way:

> There is a nation named Thrush on this earth. If you were to examine the globe carefully, you would not find the name engraved anywhere. Yet time and again, as you passed your hand over country after country, you would have placed your fingers (unwittingly) on territory under the domination of Thrush.

The germ for this was actually established in the *U.N.C.L.E.* pilot: when Solo accuses one of the baddies of selling out his country the man replies "Thrush is my country." In his notes, Rolfe goes on to refer to Thrush as a "supra-nation." "There are no geographical boundaries to Thrush," he writes.

At the top of the organization is a Council, whose members meet periodically in a cemetery in Prague.

Just kidding! But that did seem like where this was going, didn't it? (It probably wouldn't have seemed that way to Rolfe;

I have no reason to think that the parallels I am drawing here were conscious or deliberate on his part.) Actually, Rolfe writes that "At regular intervals these members of the Council meet in the Capital City of the organization. The Capital City is called Thrush and the entire organization takes its name from this city."

In earlier versions, Rolfe had left things vague—saying that Thrush might even be a code name for a single individual. This was suggested in several episodes Rolfe produced, as he wanted to keep Thrush mysterious for as long as possible—even implying that U.N.C.L.E. itself did not know what "Thrush" meant. One thing is certain: it was definitely not intended to be an acronym. One of the authors of the Ace Books *U.N.C.L.E.* paperback series (David McDaniel) made the absurd suggestion that Thrush meant "Technological Hierarchy for the Removal of Undesirables and the Subjugation of Humanity." But this was never used in the series and is not considered "canonical."

McDaniel does nicely sum up what Thrush is about, however. Rolfe writes: "Thrush, like many a nation, has a national purpose. Thrush's purpose is to dominate the earth." Many of the members of Thrush, Rolfe tells us, hold positions of importance in the countries they (outwardly) claim as their own. "But no matter where they live," Rolfe writes, "they pledge their allegiance to Thrush." Contrary to what your suspicious minds may be thinking, the City of Thrush is not located in Israel. In fact, Rolfe specifies that it is mobile and regularly changing locations.

A misunderstood Austrian wrote the following when Rolfe was a toddler:

> The Jew's domination in the state seems so assured that now not only can he call himself a Jew again, but he ruthlessly admits his ultimate national and political designs. A section of his race openly owns itself to be a foreign people, yet even here they lie. For while the Zionists try to make the rest of the world believe that the national consciousness of the Jew finds its satisfaction in the creation of a Palestinian state, the Jews again slyly dupe the dumb

Goyim. It doesn't even enter their heads to build up a Jewish state in Palestine for the purpose of living there; all they want is a central organization for their international world swindle, endowed with its own sovereign rights and removed from the intervention of other states: a haven for convicted scoundrels and a university for budding crooks.[4]

The first part of this quote inspired in me the following reverie. Now, it's not clear if the upcoming *U.N.C.L.E.* movie will feature Thrush (or merely an organization that *could* be Thrush). But imagine a new *U.N.C.L.E.* series with the following premise. Instead of hiding in the dark, members of Thrush now openly proclaim their true national allegiance, proudly hanging the Thrush emblem over their manufacturing complexes, schools, hospitals, series of underground tunnels or caverns, and department stores. Further, they present themselves as aggrieved victims — victims of U.N.C.L.E.'s decades-long campaign of genocide.

You see, when Thrush's citizens developed their earthquake machine, brain killing machine, volcanic activator, and their army of beautiful-but-deadly-female-robots — when they threatened to unleash invisible killer bees and hiccup gas on the world, they were just trying to protect themselves. And their children. Just like in "The Children's Day Affair" (December 10, 1965), where Thrush really did open its own school. An elementary school, to be exact. (And, by the way, all the above are actual plot McGuffins from *U.N.C.L.E.* episodes.)

Perhaps the saddest chapter in this long history of persecution was depicted in the two-part "Concrete Overcoat Affair" (11/25/66 and 12/2/66 — released overseas theatrically as *The Spy in the Green Hat*). In this particular *shoah*, U.N.C.L.E. cruelly sabotages Thrush's plan to build a permanent homeland for itself by diverting the Gulf Stream and turning Greenland into a

---

[4] Adolf Hitler, *Mein Kampf*, vol. 1, ch. 11, "Nation and Race," trans. Ralph Manheim (New York: Houghton Mifflin, 1943), 324–25.

lush, tropical paradise (which will be renamed "Thrushland" — no, I'm not kidding, this was an actual plot!).

Thrush would flourish in today's society. They could do everything they did in the 1960s, but out in the open. And no one would dare say a word. U.N.C.L.E. would be driven out of business. Illya Kuryakin would be languishing in prison, charged with crimes against humanity. Napoleon Solo would be somewhere in Argentina, hounded by Thrush avengers. Every four years, U.S. presidential hopefuls would make the trip to lush, tropical Thrushland, appear before the Council swearing to protect America's "special relationship" with Thrush, and would cover their heads and pray before the Ultimate Computer. (Oh, yeah, I forgot to mention that according to Rolfe the Ultimate Computer — yes, that's a proper name — is housed in the City of Thrush, where it devises Thrush's plans.)

American television sitcoms would all have to feature at least one Thrush member, who would be the smartest person on the show and make the others look dopey. Mary's neighbor, or the dentist in Bob's office suite, or Rob's co-writer — all would show up wisecracking in Thrush berets and coveralls, carrying sniper scopes. Non-Thrush people dining in restaurants all over the world would have to stew silently while Thrush members monopolized the waiter's time, asking for multiple substitutions. Hotels in New Delhi would offer a special "Thrush rate."

And the Chinese would use U.N.C.L.E. to sell noodles. Wait, I think that's actually happening . . .

Tag

Is *The Man From U.N.C.L.E.* any good? I'm talking about the series. The word on the street is that the upcoming film is pretty fine — but then it's also been known for some time that it has virtually no real relation to the series (it's a "reimagining"). As to the TV show, it depends on how you look at it. Compared to other hour-long adventure series on 1960s American TV, about half the episodes hold up really well. The first season of *U.N.C.L.E.*, produced by Rolfe, is generally considered the best. The second season, the first in color, begins to get more hip and tongue-in-cheek. But when it's hip it's really hip, and the music is exquisite.

In the third season the show was taken over by one Boris Ingster, who had the looks of an NKVD interrogator and the artistic sensibilities of a Borscht Belt comedian. Under his guidance, *U.N.C.L.E.* became almost astonishingly bad (the nadir reached, by general consensus, in "The My Friend the Gorilla Affair," in which Robert Vaughn dances the Watusi with a man in an ape suit). Perhaps Ingster owed his real allegiance to Thrush. That was the same year *The Girl From U.N.C.L.E.* (starring Stefanie Powers and Noel Harrison) enjoyed its one and only season. Famed TV critic Cleveland Amory described this series as having "all the credibility of women's wrestling." This is actually an undeserved slur on women's wrestling. Trust me, no amount of marijuana will make *The Girl From U.N.C.L.E.* seem good.

When the ratings tanked, Felton did a creditable job of dragging *Man* back to reality in its fourth season. Under the guidance of producer Anthony Spinner, the series became almost too serious — and at the same time looked brighter, slicker, and more expensive that it ever had. But it was too late. *U.N.C.L.E.* was cancelled midway through its fourth year, and replaced by *Rowan and Martin's Laugh-In*, the biggest hit of the late '60s.

Compared to the British offerings of '60s TV, *U.N.C.L.E.* pales. It's not nearly as smart or slick as *The Avengers*, *The Prisoner*, or *Danger Man*. (Though oddly the British didn't think so — they went *U.N.C.L.E.* crazy and thought their own shows lacking.) Unless you have watched a good deal of TV and cinema of yesteryear, you are unlikely to be able to look past *U.N.C.L.E.*'s relatively slow pace (considered fast-paced at the time), mild action (considered ultra-violent then), and small budget (big for the time). (How times change.) I can't imagine a twenty-something or a teenager being able to sit through it.

Still, despite its silliness and other shortcomings, U.N.C.L.E. is a far more literate series than almost any today. It actually assumes that its viewers know something about history and geography, and that they know what words like *au courant* mean.

It's often witty. A perverse, mole-like Thrush villain says to his beautiful female subaltern "I like you. [Dramatic pause.] I've never said that to anyone before." The camera work is quite good, and the color is often stunning. Vaughn and McCallum have an undeniable chemistry — but as the series wore on both began to act like they were phoning it in. (Vaughn admitted years later that he seldom read a script all the way through — only the bits that he was in.) And there is virtually no real characterization: Solo and Kuryakin are just ciphers.

In the music department, as I have alluded to already, if you love cool '60s jazz scores you will feel like you have died and gone to heaven. And, in general when *U.N.C.L.E.* is good it is very, very cool. If you like '60s style, and retro this and that, you will probably flip over this show.

The foregoing account might suggest that the series is laden with Lefty sentiments. But that's all built into the foundations, so to speak. Never once does the series get preachy or deliver "message" shows. (These were the days before producers felt comfortable openly parading their political views before Mr. and Mrs. Middle America.) But the youngsters who thrilled to the adventures of Solo and Kuryakin got the subtext: almost all first generation *U.N.C.L.E.* fans are dyed-in-the-wool Democrats.

When the film is released, I promise you a review. And, by the way, now that you know that there were eight *U.N.C.L.E.* feature films released in the '60s (all cobbled together from the TV episodes), you can baffle your friends by saying "I can't believe they've made a ninth *U.N.C.L.E.* movie!"

Counter-Currents/*North American New Right*,
August 11 & 12, 2015

Guy Ritchie's
The Man From U.N.C.L.E.

As you know, I am an aficionado of the '60s superspy series *The Man From U.N.C.L.E.* But I awaited Guy Ritchie's "reimagining" of U.N.C.L.E. with some trepidation. A big screen adaptation of the series has been in the works for around 40 years. And an execrable TV movie was actually made in 1983. The theatrical film project has changed hands many times, and innumerable scripts have been written. After *Pulp Fiction*, Quentin Tarantino announced that *The Man From U.N.C.L.E.* would be his next project (I reacted to this news with mixed feelings). Then Steven Soderbergh almost made the film—before quitting due to disagreements over the budget. This was bad news, since Soderbergh had reportedly studied the series' first (and best) season carefully. Tom Cruise (barf!), George Clooney (yawn), and other major stars were cast as secret agent Napoleon Solo, then left the project for one reason or another.

The first reports about how Ritchie would approach the film immediately suggested to me that it would have little in common with the original series. And later reports explicitly confirmed this: there would be no actual U.N.C.L.E. organization in the film, no Thrush, and Napoleon Solo and Illya Kuryakin have only just met. In short, this would be an "origin story." I objected to this, but it was no use: Ritchie would not return my calls. And so when I went to see the film on its opening day, I took what I thought to be the only logical, and fair approach: I would judge the film on its own merits, without constantly comparing it to the original series. *U.N.C.L.E.* fan sites have been abuzz for the better part of the year complaining about Ritchie's approach, asserting that Robert Vaughn and David McCallum could "never be replaced," etc. This just seemed foolish to me.

So, judged on its own merits . . . . this film just isn't that great. And—yes, yes I just can't help it: it's not an improvement on the TV series, except in its production values and the technical skill with which it was carried off. But then it's hardly fair to compare the production values of a current feature film, which cost $75 million (cheap by today's standards!) to those of a TV series that premiered more than fifty years ago.

I was shocked when I read an account of the plot months ago: the forces of good must stop an evil organization from acquiring . . . *an atomic bomb*. But wait—isn't that *Thunderball*? And isn't it also the plot of the godawful TV movie *Return of the Man From U.N.C.L.E.*?

Any single episode of the original series has a better plot—or, let us just say, a better McGuffin—than this film. Yes, I must admit that the film has a more *complicated* plot than most episodes of the TV show. But that's actually not one of its virtues.

As to the stars, physically they are undeniably an improvement on Robert Vaughn and David McCallum—who would look like dwarfs standing next to Henry Cavill (Solo) and Armie Hammer (Illya). And they are far better looking. The trouble is that on the whole they are not as interesting. Cavill's face is so handsome it doesn't look real. But he is also very bland in this role. (I've not seen any of his other films, so I can't really make a judgment about his acting skills as a whole.)

Cavill is British, in case you don't know, and the American accent he affects in this film sounds like he is trying to imitate an American TV announcer. No, not that throaty, expressive one who used to say "The Loooooooooooooooooove Boat." No, I mean one of those really bland, flat nasally announcers like they had in . . . well, like they had in the 1960s. His Solo has been completely "reimagined" as a former thief blackmailed into working as a spy for the U.S. government. This has no relation to the Solo of the original series. Instead it is a rip off of the premise of another '60s spy show, *It Takes A Thief*.

By contrast, Armie Hammer as Illya Kuryakin is not half bad. And his Russian accent is far more believable than Cavill's American accent. And I will even venture the heresy that Hammer is more convincing as a Russian than McCallum. In one of the film's few parallels to the series, Illya is the more interesting and complex character, whereas Solo is portrayed as a one-dimensional womanizer. Illya is hard to get, whereas Solo is easy. Hammer's Illya actually seems like he might be a virgin.

Vaughn and McCallum had chemistry, whereas Cavill and Hammer have little to speak of. You can already guess exactly what happens, *vis-à-vis* their partnership. Working on opposite sides, Solo and Illya begin as enemies. They duke it out and fling barbs at each other—literally and figuratively—but then they begin to develop a grudging respect . . . Blah, blah, blah, blah. Respect and, yes, affection. Though I saw nothing at all "homoerotic" in their relationship, contrary to what other reviewers have asserted. This is basically a buddy film.

As I have mentioned, Thrush are not the villains here. Who is? Well, can you guess?

Yes—you got it right! It's the Nazis. Or former Nazis (the film is set in 1963). Or something like that. The main villains in the film are actually Italians with connections to Mussolini, who happen to be employing ex-Nazis. But, no matter: they're all called "Nazis" in this film. The most unpleasant moment comes when Solo is captured by a former Nazi torturer. The torture he then endures is nothing, however, compared to the fact that when the Nazi reveals his past Ritchie treats us to a brief montage of the Nazis and WWII complete with obligatory "Sieg Heil!" audio clip. Apparently this is there in case audience members are too stupid to know what the character is referring to when he mentions WWII.

Of course, I have argued elsewhere that Thrush and S.P.E.C.T.R.E. and B.I.G.O. and all the rest of them are really Nazis in disguise, and that U.N.C.L.E. and Bond and Matt Helm *et al.* are all fighting the Nazi/fascist menace, as viewed through the lens of Allied propaganda. (U.N.C.L.E. must stop Thrush from *taking over the world!* Etc. See "The Flash in the Pan.") The difference here is that at least the makers of these '60s products had the imagination to disguise their Nazis. Here they are just Nazis. Just like the villains in every other Hollywood film. The fight against Hitler really never ends . . .

There is absolutely nothing surprising, original, or innovative about the storyline of this film. It even employs the hackneyed "kidnapped scientist's beautiful daughter" plot device (used more than once in the original *U.N.C.L.E.*, and—once more—a plot device in 1983's *Return of the Man From U.N.C.L.E.*). Virtually any episode of the original series is more imaginative and less predictable than what we are offered here.

The best thing I can say about this film — aside from Hammer's surprisingly engaging performance — is that it's got plenty of style. The photography is gorgeous. The costumes — all retro, retro, retro — are a feast for the eyes. The editing is the right kind of "fast paced" — not the jerky, never-hold-on-anything-for-more-than-two-seconds style that plagued Daniel Craig's second Bond outing, *Quantum of Solace*, and many other recent films. And yet even on the issue of style I must qualify my compliments. For nothing is new here; all is derivative. Ritchie is trying to recreate the look and feel not just of the '60s, but of '60s cinema. He even throws in a split-screen sequence *à la* 1968's *The Thomas Crown Affair*.

I thought that Daniel Pemberton's score had its moments. At times it reminded me of Gerald Fried and Robert Drasnin's scores for the second season of *U.N.C.L.E.* But then it also manages to (literally) lift material from Ennio Morricone and a host of other composers. Indeed, the score reminded me of one of those albums by Nicola Conte that are deliberate attempts at a retro '60s style. You listen to them thinking "Now he's doing *U.N.C.L.E.* . . . Now he's doing *I Spy* . . . Now's he's doing *Seven Golden Men* . . ."

Come to think of it, this entire film is like a Nicola Conte album. It's kinda this, kinda that, kinda this, kinda that. Ironically it's hardly at all kinda like the original *U.N.C.L.E.* Is it kinda entertaining? Yeah. But I think I wouldn't have liked it that much even if I hadn't seen the original series. I found myself sighing with impatience at several points in the film. But that may be because I'm kinda old. Would younger folks (i.e., guys) like this movie? Yes, I think so. Actually, they might like it a lot. We shall see. As to women, they may like it less. Though I saw it with a woman, who actually liked it more than I did. (She was quite taken with Armie Hammer.)

Aside from Cavill and Hammer, the film features a so-so performance by Alicia Vikander as the scientist's beautiful daughter. Vikander is being overhyped. The real female standout of the cast is Elizabeth Debicki, who is very good as the villainess. She reminds me — in looks and wardrobe — of Camilla Sparv in the 1966 Matt Helm film *Murderers' Row*.

Die-hard *U.N.C.L.E.* fan that I am, I doubt I would see this film again except under pressure. But, to be honest, I am hoping there is a sequel. One that would introduce the U.N.C.L.E. organization, Thrush, and all the cool gadgets (the current film is pretty light on gadgets). This outing leaves the door open for that. But I am not getting my hopes up. Ritchie's *Man From U.N.C.L.E.*, sadly, is more a symptom of the times than anything else. Like *Mad Men*, it yearns for an earlier, more stylish, more honest time — with the virtue that unlike *Mad Men* it doesn't simultaneously spit at it. However much this yearning may seem (somehow) commendable and healthy, it simply has the effect of highlighting how empty are the souls of the men making this stuff. Ritchie and company have nothing of their own to say. You see, those who yearn are those who lack. Their hearts are tugging them in the right direction (kinda), but their hearts are still empty, yearning to be filled. And, ultimately, the fact that they yearn to be filled with the spirit of the '60s is pretty damned sad.

Counter-Currents/*North American New Right*,
August 14, 2015

Gangway for a *Führer*:
Proto-Fascist Cinema of
the Great Depression

1. "Brother, can you spare a *Duce*?"

Apparently, that was the question on the lips of many Americans during the early years of the Great Depression. They watched from afar as Mussolini, unburdened by political opposition, made tremendous strides in ridding Italy of unemployment and bringing back economic prosperity. Many Americans wondered if their problems could really be solved by democratic means, and whether a dictator might not be the most sensible solution.

But they didn't want a dictator of the Red variety. Despite the swelling ranks of the American Communist Party during the "Red decade," average Americans never got past their horror at Communism's atheism and totalitarianism. It was authoritarianism we needed, they said—not totalitarianism. What they wanted was a "third position"—something between the American crapitalist Scylla and the communist Charybdis.

Not surprisingly, Hollywood responded to this mood.

In 1933, Columbia released a 76-minute documentary, narrated by NBC journalist Lowell Thomas, entitled *Mussolini Speaks*. The film was a largely uncritical celebration of Italy's progress under fascism. At one point in his narration Thomas exclaims "This is a time when a dictator comes in handy!" In its first two weeks at New York's Palace Theater, *Mussolini Speaks* was seen by almost two hundred thousand patrons. (Hitler was just getting started, of course—but in time Germany's spectacular renewal would also be widely and openly admired.)

The American longing for a Führer was the subject of Hollywood fiction as well. The two most significant such films are, without question, Gregory La Cava's *Gabriel Over the White House* (1933) and King Vidor's *Our Daily Bread* (1934). These films were controversial in their time, with many critics and viewers denouncing them as "fascist."

They remain controversial today — among the tiny number of people who have even heard of them. As cinema, neither film holds up well. They are interesting entirely for the light they shed on their era — and for reminding us that, once upon a time, fascism was considered a live option by many Americans. Though chronologically it comes second, I will deal first with *Our Daily Bread* as it is in many ways the more interesting film.

2. *OUR DAILY BREAD*

This film would make a great triple-feature along with a couple of other King Vidor classics: *The Crowd* (1928) and *The Fountainhead* (1949) — which are two of the most misanthropic films ever made. *The Crowd* is now widely regarded as among the greatest American silents. It centers on a young married couple, John and Mary Sims, who struggle to make ends meet in a cold and cruel world. The film's downbeat conclusion (which threw Louis B. Mayer into a tizzy) has Sims reduced to wearing a clown costume and carrying a sandwich board that reads "I am happy because I always eat at Schneider's Grill."

The Crowd has often been seen as a critique of modernity and of urbanization. Indeed, Vidor's politics seem to have been vaguely Right-wing (with the accent being on "vaguely"). He was a member of the anti-Communist Motion Picture Alliance for the Preservation of American Ideals — as was Ayn Rand.

Leftist critics have always claimed to see something "fascist" in Rand's work, and Vidor's film of *The Fountainhead* was denounced by *The Daily Worker* as "an openly fascist movie." Rand's followers always angrily dismiss such accusations by pointing to explicitly anti-fascist and anti-collectivist statements in her non-fiction. But this is a little like claiming that because Christianity preaches chastity there can't be any sex in the Bible. The truth is that Rand's fiction — especially *The Fountainhead* and its film version — reeks of anti-democratic elitism and quasi-Nietzschean *Übermenschlichkeit*.

So, there is ample reason for us to polish our monocles and take a closer look at Mr. Vidor's *Our Daily Bread* — which may turn out to be about a little more than just living off the land.

The film centers on a young married couple named John and

Mary Sims. Yes, that's right: the very same names used in *The Crowd*, which makes it arguable that Vidor intended *Our Daily Bread* as a sequel to his greatest film. Indeed, Vidor confirmed this in an interview many years later: "I wanted to take my two protagonists out of *The Crowd* and follow them through the struggles of a typical young American couple in this most difficult period."

In fact, Vidor originally offered the role of John Sims of *Our Daily Bread* to the man who had played Sims in *The Crowd*: James Murray. By then, however, Murray was a hopeless drunk and panhandler who dismissed Vidor's offer as "charity" (he would die two years later, a drowning victim and possible suicide). Offering the part of Mary Sims to Eleanor Boardman, the actress who played her in *The Crowd*, would have been awkward, as Vidor had divorced Boardman in 1931. In *Our Daily Bread*, John is played by Tom Keene and Mary by Karen Morley.

When I first saw the film, my reaction was that their acting (especially Keene's) was about on the level of an Ed Wood movie. Imagine my surprise when I did a little research and found that Keene's final film was none other than *Plan Nine From Outer Space* (he plays Colonel Thomas Edwards, Chief of Saucer Operations). Virtually all the acting in *Our Daily Bread* is stilted and unconvincing. Indeed, there is a kind of awkwardness and cheapness about the whole production (alleviated now and then by some great moments and well-crafted sequences).

This is no accident. Vidor proposed the project to MGM, but according to him "they were afraid of it." So he mortgaged his house in order to finance the film. That was how strongly he believed in *Our Daily Bread*. Unfortunately, it must have been a very small house. Vidor could not afford top actors or expensive sets (or multiple retakes). One wishes, though, that he could have looked around a bit more before hiring Keene. The ideal actor would have been Jimmy Stewart (who would make his film debut a year later, in 1935).

In any case, John and Mary are depicted as a typical young American couple struggling to survive in the darkest days of the depression. They literally have to pawn their possessions in order to put food on the table (thankfully, they have no children).

Things look pretty bleak until an uncle offers John a disused farm that is about to be foreclosed on. Maybe John can get the place up and running and make it profitable. Eager to try anything, John and Mary relocate to the farm, which they find to be in a considerable state of ruin. Undaunted, they begin cleaning up the house and tilling the soil—though neither of them has any idea how to work the land (it's kind of like a depression-era *Green Acres*). In desperation, John puts up signs along the road asking for ten men with useful skills to come settle on the farm and help him work it. A large crowd shows up in response—men and their families desperate for any kind of employment, desperate just to eat.

We forget today just how calamitous the Great Depression was (and it doesn't help matters that the recent recession has been likened to it; there really is no comparison). By the time Vidor made *Our Daily Bread*, unemployment in the U.S. had hit 25%. More than 5,000 banks had failed. Hundreds of thousands of people had defaulted on loans and were driven from their homes, some gathering in shanty towns called "Hoovervilles" (in reference to President Herbert Hoover, whose policies did nothing to alleviate America's economic misery and in some cases worsened it). To make matters worse, a drought hit the American heartland, creating the infamous "Dust Bowl" and the great Okie migrations.

People were homeless and starving, but—in one of capitalism's many harsh ironies—it was not for lack of homes or food. As Greg Johnson puts it in his essay "Money for Nothing":

> In an economic depression, the land does not suddenly go sterile. The udders of cows do not go dry. Men do not suddenly become stupid and lazy. The sun keeps shining; the crops keep growing; the chickens keep laying; people keep working. Goods pile up in warehouses and stores. And on the demand side, people still need to eat. But silos are bursting and people are starving because, for some mysterious reason, there is suddenly "not enough money."

People have no money to spend, or they are afraid to

part with the money they do have, because of a climate of uncertainty. After all, half way around the world, a massive swindle has been discovered; a bank has collapsed; a speculative bubble has burst. So, naturally, back in Hooterville, stores are filled with sour milk and rotting vegetables and children are going to bed hungry.

It was precisely Vidor's indignation over this sort of perverse spectacle that led him to make *Our Daily Bread*, and to suggest an alternative.

That alternative soon presents itself in the film as the cooperative farm built by John and Mary Sims. John finds a way to use most of the men who come to him — even the "high class pants presser" and the violinist. One of them, a Swede named Chris Larsen is actually a farmer, and under his direction they begin to till the soil.

A meeting is held outdoors after dark, and John makes an inspirational speech about how they must all now work together as a community, in the spirit of the men who first settled the country. The question then comes up of what sort of government their little community should have, and what unfolds is the most fascinating sequence in the film. Sims scratches his head and says that he'll go along with whatever government most of the crowd wants. In a kind of exaggeratedly reverent tone, one man proclaims: "Then I suggest, my friends, that we bind ourselves together in sacred covenant and establish an immortal democracy!"

The response to this is astonishing. The crowd jeers, and one man cries: "It was that kind of talk that got us here in the first place!"

Another man, his voice sharp and strident, declares: "We must have a socialistic form of government! The government must control *everything*. Including the profits."

The crowd jeers this as well, and at this point Larsen, the sensible Swede, speaks up: "I don't know what them words mean. All I know is we got a big job. And we need a big boss! And John Sims is the boss!" (The word "leader" is carefully avoided here.)

The crowd roars its approval, and John Sims is essentially

made dictator of the farm. The scene is fascinating on several levels. First of all, it is amazing to hear democracy jeered (by the good guys) in an American film. More significant, however, is the way in which what is expressed is the need for a third position, in answer to the unacceptable alternatives of democracy (read here democratic-capitalism) and Soviet-style socialism. At one point, they agree to place all their valuables in a kind of storehouse from which each can draw, so long as he works (sound familiar?). Ironically, what they arrive at is a kind of anarcho-collectivism, with one tiny difference: there's a Führer.

In a recent article published on Counter-Currents, "The Color of Capitalism", Matt Parrott quotes Noam Chomsky on anarchism, then offers his own thoughts:

Chomsky claims that *"The consistent anarchist, then, should be a socialist, but a socialist of a particular sort. He will not only oppose alienated and specialized labor and look forward to the appropriation of capital by the whole body of workers, but he will also insist that this appropriation be direct, not exercised by some elite force acting in the name of the proletariat."* In summary, the workers of the world should sort of take back the wealth and power in a disorganized manner, trusting one another to equitably share whatever spoils they reap from the capitalists. If you're struggling to imagine how this would actually work in practice, you're not alone.

Vidor realized the naïveté of anarchist and utopian socialist theories. While they may present an economically viable — and just — scenario, their understanding of human nature is absurdly optimistic. There is an order of rank among men, and every time some egalitarian scheme has been tried, the alpha males always emerge and assert themselves — and are generally welcomed (especially by the women). Someone's got to be in charge, if only to save people from themselves.

Time passes, and we see that this gang of homeless men and their families has formed itself into a small society. They have even built makeshift houses for themselves out of odds and ends, even parts of old cars. The scene recalls the Hooverville shanty towns, only this is no longer a mob of disgruntled bums and hoboes. The inhabitants of John Sims's farm have learned to trade and barter with each other. The stonemason helps build a wall for the carpenter, and the carpenter erects the frame for the stonemason's house. The pants presser offers his services in trade. Even the violinist finds gainful employment, since someone wants their little boy to take violin lessons, and they are willing to trade this and that for so many hours of instruction.

It's all rather reminiscent of the first stages of Socrates's "city in speech" in *The Republic*. Only this is no "city of pigs": as we shall see, these people are united by a sense of obligation to the whole, and of the necessity of self-sacrifice. Vidor's little utopia is "diverse" in the sense that it includes several immigrant families. However, all of them are European. There are no blacks, Asians, or Hispanics. There is one Jewish family, the Cohens (Mr. Cohen is the pants presser).

There is no reason to think that Vidor was any sort of racialist. Indeed, Vidor's *Hallelujah!* (1929) was one of the first all-black films made by a major studio (MGM). In his autobiography, Vidor writes warmly of his black cast—but also not without a good deal of bemused condescension (especially when he recounts the story of the black man who carried around an old telephone on which he said he could call God). It is clear from *Our Daily Bread*, however, that Vidor understood that the sort of community he envisioned would be undermined if the racial and cultural differences between its members were too great.

One of the best scenes in the film has John and Mary discovering the very first sprouts emerging from the soil. "It really works, doesn't it?" says John, movingly. "It makes you feel safe, comforted. Like somebody was kinda watching over you. There's nothing for people to worry about. Not when they've got the earth."

It is fascinating to consider this film in relation to *The Crowd*. In the earlier film, John worked a demeaning and deadening desk job. He and his family lived in New York, which is depicted as a cold, ugly, and inhuman war of all against all. At one point, John's youngest child is run down in the street. (A scene which still reduces audiences to tears.) The response from his fellow

New Yorkers is indifference — or fleeting, mock concern. Their sentiments have been atrophied by the alienation and dehumanization of modern, urban, capitalist life. (An intertitle famously announces "The crowd will laugh with you always. But it will cry with you for only a day.") In *Our Daily Bread*, John and Mary have left all this behind. They have rediscovered the earth, and a genuine sense of human community and fellow-feeling.

For a while, everything seems copacetic. There is jubilation on the farm when word gets around that the earth is still delivering. But it doesn't last long. Soon the news comes that the farm has been foreclosed on and that the sheriff will soon arrive to auction it off. John and Mary are devastated, but their friends — who include a number of rather shady tough guys — are not about to let their dream be sold out from under them. At the auction, the men of the farm insert themselves into the crowd of elegantly-dressed investors and physically intimidate them into not bidding! The winning bid (of $1.85) is made by one of the scabbier-looking members of the collective, and the sheriff and his cohorts leave in disgust. Little Eden is saved!

But what's Eden without a serpent? She arrives one dark and stormy night in a convertible, seeking shelter for herself and her ailing father. She is Sally, a blonde bombshell, a doll, a flapper. A bit of a dumb Dora, but one thing's for sure: she ain't no bug-eyed Betty. Is she trouble? And how! We know she's trouble when we find out she's brought jazz records with her. These come to light when she plays them on the day the farmers bury her father's body on the hill. You see, when John and company went out to her car in the pouring rain, they found the father dead in the back seat. (Was it really her daddy, or just a sugar daddy? And how exactly did he die? We never find out.)

Critics have often objected that Sally is an unnecessary character, and the subsequent events surrounding her are something of an unwarranted intrusion on the main plot. In truth, the character essentially represents the amoral, selfish, degenerate elements of city life that Vidor so detested. Sally arrives to remind us of these things, and to set up a contrast to the emerging social ethics of the farm, which places the good of the whole above all else. This ethics is embodied by one of the men, who turns out to be an escaped convict. Without telling any of the others, he turns himself in so that Sims can collect the $500 reward for his capture, a tremendous boon for the farm. Sally finds his sacrifice inexplicable.

The community uneasily accepts Sally, though a number of them suspect that she has set her sights on John. Mary gives Sally the benefit of the doubt and tries to befriend her. Besides, they've all got bigger things to worry about: a drought has hit, and it is a humdinger.

The community looks to John for ideas, but John has run out. The corn is dangerously close to dying, and John grows more and more despondent. Finally, he simply loses his grip and runs off with Sally under cover of darkness in her convertible. They don't get very far, however, before John literally sees a vision of his self-sacrificing convict friend (wearing prison garb) looming over the highway and warning him to stop. John pulls the car over to the side of the road—and suddenly has an inspiration. There is a creek some distance from the farm. If they can dig a canal they might just be able to divert the creek and irrigate the crops! He runs off into the darkness, headed back to the farm. An enraged Sally zooms off in her car, and out of the story.

On his return, John finds the community reluctant to trust him again, but with the aid of Chris Larsen he manages to convince them of his scheme. It will not be easy, though. The creek is several miles away, over hills and through areas blocked by heavy boulders that will have to be cleared out. In a long and extremely effective sequence, Vidor shows the community triumphing against all odds, building its canal, and irrigating its parched crops. The End.

Since its premiere, critics and film historians have debated the politics of *Our Daily Bread*. Some have claimed it for the Left, while others have perceived that it veers dangerously close to fascism. (For my money, it veers and falls right in.) Vidor actually got the idea for the film from a *Readers' Digest* article by a leftist economics professor who recommended the formation of co-operative farms as a solution to unemployment. But this means nothing: political space is curved, and there are points at which the Right and Left meet and become virtually indistinguishable.

Reviews at the time were mostly very positive, though the film flopped at the box office. Surprisingly, *Our Daily Bread* won second prize at a film festival in Moscow. Vidor was told that the film would have won first prize, but it was perceived as "capitalist propaganda." There's just no winning with some people.

3. *GABRIEL OVER THE WHITE HOUSE*

Philosophically or ideologically, *Our Daily Bread* is the more interesting of the two films discussed here, but *Gabriel over the White House* is far more polished and entertaining. It is also far less politically ambiguous: *Gabriel over the White House* is openly, unapologetically, almost naïvely fascist. And it was perceived as such and denounced at the time.

Made by the studio that had refused to back *Our Daily Bread*, an internal MGM memo described the script of *Gabriel over the White House* as "wildly reactionary and radical to the *n*th degree." But there were powerful forces who wanted to see this film made — including William Randolph Hearst, who gave the production financial backing and promoted it in his newspapers. On *Gabriel*'s release, just a few weeks after Franklin Delano Roosevelt's inauguration, *The Nation* declared that the film's aim was to "convert innocent American movie audiences to a policy of fascist dictatorship in this country." *The New Republic* labeled it "a half-hearted plea for fascism."

Hearst supported the film because he supported Roosevelt. Essentially, he saw *Gabriel*'s protagonist, a dictatorial American president, as the sort of leader he was hoping he had bought with FDR.

For his part, Roosevelt loved the film. Apparently, he even read the screenplay during his campaign and suggested a few changes. After seeing an advance screening, he wrote to the film's producer (Walter Wanger), "I want to send you this line to tell you how pleased I am with the changes you made in *Gabriel over the White House*. I think it is an intensely interesting picture and should do much to help." Franklin and Eleanor are supposed to have seen the film several times and after one screening the First Lady wrote "if a million unemployed marched on Washington . . . I'd do what the President does in the picture!"

Americans today have forgotten not only the extent to which Roosevelt ruled as a dictator—but also the extent to which he was openly *asked* to do so, and often publicly praised for it. Journalist Walter Lippmann wrote in his column at the time: "The more one considers the scope and the variety of the measures that are needed for relief and reconstruction the more evident it is that an extraordinary procedure—'dictatorial powers,' if that is the name for it—is essential . . . ." Privately, he told Roosevelt, "The situation is critical, Franklin. You may have no alternative but to assume dictatorial powers." The *New York Herald Tribune* greeted Roosevelt's inauguration with the headline: "FOR DICTATORSHIP IF NECESSARY."

This is the context needed to understand *Gabriel over the White House*—the circumstances of its production, and why it struck a chord with many (though it was not a big hit). It may seem odd that a film both I and critics of the time have called "fascist" could have been enjoyed by Roosevelt, who was a man of the Left. But this is yet another instance of political extremes meeting. The President in the film is indeed much further to the Right than Roosevelt, abandoning even the semblance of democracy. (Or does that make him much further to the Left?)

The basis for *Gabriel over the White House* was a novel by Thomas Frederic Tweed called *Rinehard*. Tweed was an advisor to Lloyd George—considered the founder of the modern welfare state—from 1927 until Tweed's death in 1940. Curiously, *Rinehard* is not mentioned at all in the credits of *Gabriel*, and it is said to be based upon a novel by "anonymous."

The story opens with the inauguration of President Judson Hammond (Walter Huston, who delivers a really splendid performance). In a wise move, the screenplay never identifies Hammond's party, because it simply doesn't matter: the perspective of the filmmakers is clearly that the two major parties are corrupt, out of ideas, and virtually identical. (More than one recent commentator has noted that this film feels in some ways like it was written last week!) Hammond inherits the Depression. But he is positively the worst man for the job. He is a dolt, a cynic, a vulgarian, and a party hack. The opening scenes at the White House show the aftermath of Hammond's inaugural ball, where he exchanges jokes with his supporters, laughing about how he's going to break his promises to the people, and about all the votes that he had to buy.

We are introduced to Hammond's new secretary, an idealistic young man named Hartley Beekman (Franchot Tone), whom Hammond insists on addressing as "Beek." So overawed by the chance to serve as secretary to the President of the United States, Beek doesn't notice Hammond's foibles at first. But his eyes are opened later in the evening when Hammond's mistress shows up.

Her name in the film is Pendola "Pendy" Molloy, and her character is actually based on Lloyd George's secretary and mistress (with whom Thomas Frederic Tweed also had an affair). The part is played by none other than Karen Morley, "Mary Sims" of *Our Daily Bread* (in real life Morley was alleged to be a Communist, whose Hollywood career ended in 1947 after her refusal to answer questions before the House Un-American Activities Committee).

Pendy Molloy just walks through the front door of the White House and presents her calling card to Beek. This is not the first time such an event occurs in the film. (Even if it is not true that individuals had such easy access to the White House in 1933, it is certainly revealing that Americans were prepared to believe that they did.) The fact that the President (who is depicted as unmarried) would entertain his mistress in the White House is supposed to indicate to the audience that this is not only a man of questionable morals, but questionable judgment as well.

Pendy turns out to be not such a bad gal after all, and she and Beek soon form a friendship. Both wish that Hammond were a better man, and she tries to urge him to do something meaningful with the power he's been given. But Hammond won't hear of it. "The party has a plan," he says. "I'm just a member of the party." He reaches decisions at cabinet meetings with lines like "Well, if it's alright with you boys then . . ." He plays hide and seek with his little nephew while listening to a radio broadcast about the plight of the unemployed. And he spouts insufferable, dimwitted bromides to the press about "America's greatness." It is all too depressingly familiar.

And Hammond is reckless. He insists on driving his own car, and on one outing exceeds ninety miles per hour. Unfortunately, he doesn't negotiate one curve all that well and winds up in an accident — and in a coma. President Hammond lingers unconscious for weeks. Just when it looks like he is near death, he suddenly awakens. A strange light plays over his face, as the curtains in his bedroom are gently moved by a sudden afternoon breeze. Hammond looks around the room as if seeing it for the first time. And it as if we see him for the first time: some peculiar change has come over him. In fact, what has occurred is that he has been possessed by the Archangel Gabriel.

Hammond rises from his bed a changed man. Gone is his sloppy, informal, glad-handling manner. Gone is his cynicism and irreverence. He behaves as if he does not even know Pendy, calling her Miss Molloy. (I have to note here that Huston, the father of director John Huston, does a brilliant job in creating two distinct Hammonds — even his bone structure seems to have changed.)

At a cabinet meeting, the President is informed that a million unemployed men led by a rabble-rouser named John Bronson are about to march on Washington. He is urged to call out the Army. Instead, Hammond insists on the right of every citizen to a decent, living wage and proclaims his intention to meet with Bronson and his men. When his Secretary of State threatens resignation, Hammond sacks him on the spot. Later, when he discovers his cabinet is plotting against him, he sacks the lot of them.

And then he travels to Baltimore to meet with Bronson's "Army of the Unemployed." Hammond promises to turn them into a real army — an army of laborers who will be put to use across America, working various construction projects and stimulating trade and industry. This, of course, is precisely the sort of thing Roosevelt would soon create with his Civilian Conservation Corps — though Hammond's paramilitary conception is far closer to Hitler's *Reichsarbeitsdienst*.

(The "Army of the Unemployed" of the film is based on an actual situation that occurred during the Hoover administration, when Hoover sent the Army to disperse a large group of unemployed protesters with tear gas. Roosevelt responded to them in a manner not unlike Hammond—with the difference that he sent Eleanor to talk to them, rather than going himself.)

Meanwhile, Congress is debating whether the President should be impeached and removed from office. Throwing all protocol out the window, Hammond simply walks into the House of Representatives and addresses them. When he asks them for money to fund his new Labor Service, the Congressmen jeer him. So Hammond does exactly what I would do: he politely requests that Congress adjourn indefinitely and grant him special powers! Immediately, they accuse him of wanting to destroy democracy and set himself us as a dictator. Hammond's response is remarkable.

He defends himself by invoking a tactic often used by both fascists and communists. He argues that what he intends to bring about is *true* democracy, because he will be acting according to the will of the people. Congress, on the other hand, has failed to listen to the people. If this is dictatorship, Hammond declares, it is one based upon the original principle of Jeffersonian democracy: "the greatest good for the greatest number!" (Ahem, actually Jefferson never said this. I believe it was Jeremy Bentham who first coined the phrase, which is associated with the utilitarian philosophy.) When Congress refuses to adjourn, Hammond simply declares martial law. A newspaper headline declares: "Hammond Dictator."

Hammond's invocation of Jefferson is typical of the sanctimonious way the film often wraps itself in the flag. (John in *Our Daily Bread* also appeals to America's "glorious history" in order to motivate the collective.) *Gabriel* features frequent gag-inducing references to Lincoln, including lingering close-ups of a bust of Lincoln in Hammond's office. Huston had actually portrayed Lincoln three years earlier in a film directed by D. W. Griffith (one of only two sound films made by Griffith). And it is clear that director La Cava wants to portray Hammond as a latter-day

Lincoln. He even lights Huston so as to accentuate his cheekbones and give him a "gaunt," Lincolnesque appearance.

I suppose this is appropriate, given that Lincoln was also a tyrant—but of course that view is at odds with the naïve, unctuous twaddle Americans tend to secrete whenever they talk about Lincoln, and American history in general.

Neither *Our Daily Bread* nor *Gabriel over the White House* wants to argue that there is anything fundamentally wrong with the American founding philosophy. Instead, they draw on the American mythology in order to justify their complete negation of it. It's a shrewd way to try and win over ordinary Americans (who have never been the slightest bit interested in self-criticism).

Now Hammond decides to go after the racketeers who have profited from prohibition. Personally, I find prohibition extraordinarily hard to fathom. It is a good example of the senseless fanaticism Americans are often capable of (though a few other countries adopted similar measures during the same period). That it lasted in America from 1920 until December of 1933 is astonishing.

Still, it wasn't all that hard to get a drink during prohibition: organized crime kept the liquor flowing, just as organized crime keeps drugs on the streets today. And just like the drug lords of today, the criminals who brewed and distributed the booze during prohibition became extremely wealthy, and extremely brazen. When the Depression hit, American resentment against prohibition became particularly intense. Part of the reason was the knowledge that while so many were starving and homeless, bootlegging gangsters were sitting on easy street.

Hammond addresses the nation by radio, promising to put an end to the racketeers. This is followed by an astonishing scene: a drive by machine-gunning of the White House! As Hammond, Beek, and Pendy stand inside one of the entrances to the mansion, a car zooms by while one of its occupants sprays the building with bullets. A doorman is hit—as is Pendy. The scene is both ridiculous and shocking, as the violence is pretty graphic for its day (this was a "Pre-Code" film, after all).

This "drive by" has been instigated by the top hood in the

country, Nick Diamond (an immigrant whose real name is revealed as Antone Brilawski). Diamond is so arrogant he's ready to take on the President himself.

Though Pendy is seriously wounded, she lives. And love blossoms between her and Beek. (A completely gratuitous and unnecessary distraction from the film's main plot.) As Hammond is married to the Nation now, he gives his blessing to the relationship. While visiting Beek and Pendy, he asks Beek to head his new "Federal Police," a uniformed paramilitary force that will be charge with maintaining domestic law and order. It's sort of like . . . oh, I just can't recall the name. Starts with an S. And ends with an S . . .

Led by Beek, in his snazzy new uniform, the Federal Police barrel down on Nick Diamond's distillery with tanks and blow it to kingdom come. No warrant is ever proffered. Diamond and his subalterns are captured alive and tried by military tribunal (remember, the nation is still under martial law). In a rather blatant case of a conflict of interest, one of the members of the tribunal is Beek himself, the arresting officer. (Strangely, he seems disinclined to recuse himself.) Unsurprisingly, Diamond and his men are found guilty. In his closing remarks, Beek refers to how lucky America is to have a president who has cut through all the legal red tape and gotten back to "first principles." Diamond and his men are then stood against a wall and summarily executed by firing squad!

It was this series of events that made me start thinking of George W. Bush, and feeling a little uncomfortable about how much I was enjoying this film. After all, I was as scandalized as a libertarian by Bush's warrantless wiretaps, indefinite detention, military tribunals, waterboarding, and extraordinary rendition. (And anyone wishing to know my view of the Department of Homeland security need only read my essay "Guys."[1])

But I suppose that my indignation over these things is not because I find them *intrinsically* wrong. I don't object to them as such; I object to the particular set of interests they were intended to serve. Bush's "dictatorial" measures were not put in place to

---

[1] http://www.counter-currents.com/2012/01/guys/

protect "the homeland" or people like me. No, the US government is committed to screwing people like me, and allowing the unchecked invasion of the "homeland" by those who openly hate and wish to displace the descendants of the people who founded the country. No Arabs were waterboarded to protect the interests of John and Mary Sims. They were waterboarded to protect the interests of the Nick Diamonds of this New World Order, the fat cat globalist destroyers of our people, our culture, and our earth. I can get behind waterboarding—it all just depends on who's doing it, who it's being done to, and why.

So, to return to our story: As if all this weren't enough, Judson Hammond now achieves world peace. He tells the press that he will soon be meeting with representatives of the European powers to demand that they pay their debts to America (incurred during the Great War). Wearing top hat and tails, Hammond meets with the diplomats on board a ship. He surprises them by bringing along microphones, to broadcast their meeting to the entire world. When Hammond demands that they pay their debts, the diplomats are oily and condescending—but he patiently explains to them that he has a plan. If every debtor nation will simply stop sinking money into armaments, they can easily pay what they owe the US.

To make this argument stick, Hammond unveils America's newest secret weapon: an air force of biplanes! As the European diplomats watch in amazement, the American biplanes destroy two obsolete and decommissioned American warships. The message is clear: continuing to develop and stockpile armaments is futile, as America's air force can easily crush them. Instead, use the money for peaceful purposes, like repaying your debts. As to the security of your nation, fear not! America will protect you. America will secure the peace.

The scene shifts to a great hall where the diplomats are all poised to sign on the dotted line—pledging to place themselves in America's hands and to repay their debts. But then comes the sad and shocking news: President Hammond has died. Having solved America's and the world's problems, the Archangel Gabriel has headed home, leaving Hammond behind like a discarded skin. Beek and Pendy are devastated, but their grief is assuaged by the knowledge that Judson Hammond has left them with a bright and secure future. Here endeth *Gabriel over the White House*.

4. Conclusion

I wouldn't call either of these films "great." In fact, they're not even that good.

But they have good things about them. As I've already discussed, *Our Daily Bread* is marred by bad acting and a generally cheap, creaky quality. Still, that it has some bright moments should be unsurprising, given that it was helmed by one of America's greatest directors. Chiefly, it is interesting for its ideas, which are genuinely thought provoking.

Gabriel over the White House is a much sillier movie, but honestly it's a lot more fun. True enough, it is contrived, naïve, and often just plain dumb. It is also much too short a film (only 86 minutes). The events are sort of rushed on screen, barely giving us a chance to absorb and digest them. Nevertheless, the film has that same luminous platinum quality so many MGM films from the 1930s possess. And it has the kind of infectious effervescence that really shows itself in full flower only later in La Cava's greatest film, *My Man Godfrey* (1936). *Gabriel* is the sort of picture Frank Capra would have made, had he stayed in Italy and made movies for Mussolini. It is not a "film of ideas" like *Our Daily Bread*. Rather it is basically wish fulfillment for the fascistically inclined. It is the feel-good fascist movie of 1933.

Speaking of Frank Capra, no one ever accused him of being a fascist but his work is interesting for its populist, and often vaguely anti-capitalist elements. In 1941 Capra made a film which, in certain ways, can be seen as his "answer" to the fascist-inclined films of the preceding decade: *Meet John Doe*.

The plot concerns a fictitious letter to a newspaper, in which an unemployed "John Doe" threatens suicide. The letter sparks a nationwide movement of "John Does," focusing attention upon society's less fortunate and advocating a return to "neighborliness." (In this way it is very much a film of the Depression. Though by 1941 America's economic picture had greatly improved, unemployment was still fairly high.)

Fascism enters the picture in the form of a newspaper magnate (almost certainly based on Hearst) who wants to use the John Doe movement to form a third, vaguely fascist party. He even has his own paramilitary outfit who, in one amusing scene, engage in some precision drilling on motorcycles.

But *Meet John Doe* is a story for another time.

These films are not great cinema, but they are fascinating because they show us how close Americans once were to embracing fascism. Ah, the good old days . . .

Counter-Currents/*North American New Right*,
February 14, 2012

Disingenuous Genius:
A Tribute to Leni Riefenstahl

Leni Riefenstahl would be 109 today, had she lived. And if she had lived to such an advanced age, I would hardly have been surprised. For a while it seemed that she was indestructible. She released her final film (*Impressionen unter Wasser*) the year before her death, when she was 100. It consisted entirely of color footage she had shot while deep-sea diving over the course of many years. She was certified as a scuba diver at age 72 — but had to lie about her age (she claimed she was 52).

Leni never lived down the fact that she made *Triumph of the Will* and *Olympia* for Hitler, and she was hounded and harassed until the day she died. Shortly before her death there was even talk that the German government intended to put her on trial because she had denied (as she always did) that gypsy concentration camp inmates had figured as extras in her film *Tiefland* (released 1954). And *Impressionen unter Wasser* was, of course, the first film Leni had been able to make since *Tiefland*.

If one reads Leni's memoirs or watches her interviews (such as those included in the fascinating *The Wonderful, Horrible Life of Leni Riefenstahl* documentary), one will be struck by her almost childishly clumsy attempts to disassociate herself from Hitler. She claimed, for example, that she was completely ignorant of politics; that she was almost forced to make *Triumph of the Will*; that she barely knew anyone in Hitler's inner circle (even though we know that she saw them frequently); and that she abhorred the arch anti-Semite Julius Streicher (even though her friendship with him is well documented; they even addressed each other with the familiar *du*).[1]

---

[1] See Jürgen Trimborn, *Leni Riefenstahl: A Life*, trans. Edna McCown (Faber and Faber, 2007). Trimborn's book is highly critical of Riefenstahl, but there is no reason to believe that the evidence he cites is somehow fabricated. For Leni's own account of her life, see Leni Riefenstahl, *Leni Riefenstahl: A Memoir* (New York: St. Martin's Press, 1995).

If Leni wanted to exculpate herself (albeit disingenuously), why didn't she simply take the course others did and say "I supported Hitler at first because I thought he was good for Germany. I was also overwhelmed and flattered by his attention and his offers of patronage. And yes, I did move in those circles. But I now see that I was wrong, blah, blah, blah . . ."? Leni did say that meeting Hitler was the worst catastrophe of her life, but why did she lie about things so ineptly? Why did she put forth fabrications that could be so easily exposed? Earlier I used the adjective "childish" to describe her actions—and there is indeed something childishly egocentric about her. Leni seemed to lack any real self-consciousness about how she appeared to others and perhaps even about her own motivations.

But great men . . . Oops, I mean, great people usually have great flaws.

LENI & ARNOLD: A LOVE STORY?

Another of Leni's flaws was an inability to give credit to others who helped her or influenced her. And as a filmmaker, no one was a greater influence on Leni than Arnold Fanck. Derek Hawthorne has been writing a terrific series for Counter-Currents about the films Fanck made with Leni as star, and in his essay on *The Holy Mountain*, he tells us the story of how Leni and Arnold met in 1924.

Leni was 23 at the time and establishing a career for herself as a dancer. A knee injury threatened to cut that career short, however, and it was on her way to visit a specialist that she saw a poster for Fanck's *Der Berg des Schicksals* at the Nollendorfplatz U-bahn station. Transfixed by the poster's image of a mountain climber in a rather difficult spot, she immediately went to see the film. Then she travelled to the Dolomites to meet its star, Luis Trenker.

On meeting Trenker, Leni announced that she would be co-starring with him in his next film. This was typical of her—and when she set her mind on something she usually got her way. The egotistical Trenker, who probably feared being upstaged by Leni, was not encouraging.

On her return to Berlin, Leni's financial backer Harry Sokal arranged a meeting for her with Arnold Fanck. They met one afternoon at a café on the Kurfürstendamm. Fanck said little, and Leni assumed she had not made a good impression. In reality, Fanck was head over heels in love. He wrote to Trenker that Leni was "the most beautiful woman in Europe" and would soon be "the most famous woman in Germany."

Leni then went into the hospital to undergo (successful) knee surgery. While there she received a visit from Fanck, who brought her a film script inscribed with the words "The Holy Mountain: Written for the Dancer Leni Riefenstahl." He had written it in three days. Once Leni had fully recovered, she traveled to Freiburg to stay with Fanck. She herself said that he became her intellectual mentor.

Leni claimed that she rejected Fanck's advances (which, by her account, were constant). However, a recent biographer, Steven Bach, is not so sure.[2] Leni reports in her memoirs that love blossomed between her and Luis Trenker while making *The Holy Mountain* and that Fanck was insane with jealousy. She describes a fistfight breaking out between Trenker and Fanck, which only came to an end when she threatened to jump out a window. Leni even claims that Fanck made a (rather lame) suicide attempt.

It was from Fanck that Leni learned everything she knew about cinema. From the very beginning, on the set of *The Holy Mountain* (1926), Fanck expressed his love for Leni by proudly explaining to her all the facets of filmmaking. When she finally made her own film, *The Blue Light*, in 1932, Fanck re-edited the film for her. This enraged Leni, but she had to grudgingly admit that in many ways he had improved it.

If one studies the films of Arnold Fanck and Leni Riefenstahl, the influence of the former on the latter is obvious. *The Blue Light* is, of course, a mountain film in its own way. Leni worked on her films with crews that were virtually identical to Fanck's (e.g. cinematographers Hans Schneeberger and Sepp Allgeier). One need only view Fanck's skiing sequences in *The Holy Mountain*

---

[2] Steven Bach, *Leni: The Life and Work of Leni Riefenstahl (Vintage)* (New York: Alfred A. Knopf, 2007). Bach is also harshly critical of Riefenstahl, but like Trimborn he backs up his claims with documentary evidence.

to see how he influenced Leni's documentary style in *Olympia*. The quick-cut style of *Triumph of the Will*, where the camera is almost always in motion, is also heavily influenced by Fanck's technique. He was a master at capturing real events with an unsurpassed energy and immediacy. Fanck even mounted cameras on the ends of skis.

None of this is meant to take away credit from Leni—who was heavily influenced by Fanck, but never "copied" him. She was a brilliant filmmaker in her own right. And one of the most remarkable women of the twentieth century.

By the end of the Second World War, Fanck's love for Leni seemed to have soured into hate. When she was on the lam from the allies and looking for someone to harbor her, she called Fanck—who flatly refused to have anything more to do with her. In later years, they both had few kind words to say about each other. Steven Bach reports an incident many years later in which Leni exploded at an American doctoral student who told her she had interviewed Fanck:

> "Dr. Fanck will *never* tell you the truth even if he is speaking well about me. *Never*. He lies, *one hundred per cent*! You can't believe one word of what he says. He's a liar. *Very bad!*" Her voice rose in excoriation of Fanck's talent, his vanity, his politics, his finances, his romantic life, and his ingratitude, climaxing in outrage at his "telling people that my mother was Jewish!" Her agitation was strident enough to provoke [partner Horst Kettner's] alarm. "Is the [tape] machine still on?" he asked in panic, to which Leni shouted "I don't care!"[3]

In all, Leni made six films with Fanck. The last was *S.O.S. Iceberg* (1933). She traveled to Greenland to make that film, carrying with her a copy of *Mein Kampf* and a framed photograph of Hitler.[4] Who knows? Perhaps Hitler had just asked her to deliver them to some Eskimo.

---

[3] Bach, 279
[4] Trimborn, 60.

PLOTTING HER COMEBACK

Leni was briefly imprisoned after the war. She was subjected to a number of trials and threats of trials, accused of breaking various *ex post facto* laws. She tried and tried again to relaunch her career as a filmmaker. Leni scored a small triumph in 1954 with the belated premiere of *Tiefland* (filmed a decade prior). As mentioned earlier, *Impressionen unter Wasser*, released the year before Leni's death, was the only other film she managed to make.

No one wanted to be associated with her. When Ray Müller made *The Wonderful Horrible Life of Leni Riefenstahl*, he wanted to open the film with a series of brief interviews with major figures, all stating what the name "Riefenstahl" meant to them. All refused.

I have always wondered why Leni didn't simply pull up stakes and go to Japan. In the Far East, Hitler is used to sell noodles, and the holocaust sounds like a great idea for a theme restaurant. Arnold Fanck actually made a film in Japan: 1937's *Die Tochter des Samurai*. Leni could have made spectacular Japanese mountain films with huge casts of flag-bearing Samurai, à la Kurosawa. There are obvious difficulties with this, but it is still an appealing fantasy.

In later life, Leni tried to improve her reputation by photographing black people. This backfired on her, however, because they had fantastic bodies. To her credit, Leni never compromised her aesthetics; she never went in for the modern "ugly is the new beauty" aesthetic. Consequently, no one was fooled. The odious Susan Sontag certainly wasn't. In 1974 she reviewed Leni's *The Last of the Nuba* under the title "Fascinating Fascism." Sontag accused her of perpetuating the fascist "cult of beauty." It became apparent to everyone, including Leni, that there was simply no way to win the critics over.

In the last years of her life, however, more balanced treatments of Leni began to appear. The most significant of these was Ray Müller's documentary (released in Germany under the more dignified title *Die Macht der Bilder*). For those who have not seen it, this film is a real treat.

It is predominantly quite fair to Leni, though Müller includes revealing, raw footage of her arguing with him and others. At one point she flies into a rage, insisting that it is impossible for her to walk and talk at the same time! On another occasion, dissatisfied with the light in which Müller intends to shoot one scene, she grabs him and begins shaking him and shrieking. To me, these scenes are more amusing than anything else. To the flat-souled, the simpleminded, and the bourgeois, they are images of a nasty old woman. Actually, they merely depict the typical volatility and perfectionism of a great artist.

Predictably, Leni hated Müller's film when it was released in 1993. However, when the film met with acclaim and renewed interest in her work, Leni softened on Müller and they developed an uneasy friendship. Sometime later, Müller accompanied her and Horst Kettner to the Sudan for a reunion with the Nuba (now forced by their Muslim overlords to cover up). For Ray Müller the visit provided a memorable glimpse into Leni's soul. Steven Bach writes:

> Shortly after their arrival, as Müller took a break from filming and Leni was chatting up a cluster of aged Nuba, he heard an outcry. He looked up, alarmed to see Leni charging furiously toward him. She had just inquired after two of her oldest Nuba friends. Told they were dead, she began to weep, when she suddenly realized Müller's cameras were idle. He had missed the dramatic moment, her emotion, and the proper angle to capture tears running down her face. Her fury mounted as she berated him and then stalked away, shaking with rage and frustration . . . She relented, giving him one last chance to rectify his inexcusable ineptitude with his cameras. She returned to the cluster of old men and, missing not a beat, repeated her inquiry, her shock, and her tears as if the moment were spontaneity itself.[5]

Equally endearing is Müller's story about the helicopter crash

---

[5] Bach, 292.

that occurred shortly thereafter. Leni suffered broken ribs, an injured back, and various cuts and bruises. She was unconscious for several days. When she awakened, she asked Müller if he had photographed her being pulled from the wreckage. When she learned that he had not, she asked if it might be possible to recreate the incident using special effects.

You've just got to love her. An artist to the end.

WHY THEY COULDN'T FORGIVE LENI

Other artists who had worked for Hitler (like Arno Breker) fared much better than Leni did and continued to work. Why did Leni have it so hard in the post-war years?

Perhaps it's because *Triumph of the Will* was simply too good. It was not just a great propaganda film, it was a great film, period. A great work of cinematic art, which set a new standard in documentary filmmaking and has since been endlessly imitated. Leni could not be forgiven for producing a great work of art for the Nazis. But, of course, Breker's sculptures were also great works of art, and he continued to work until the day he died, producing portraits of Anwar Sadat and Konrad Adenauer, among others. So something more is involved, I think.

If I can be forgiven for a moment for sounding like a feminist, I think it has to do with the fact that Leni was a woman. Female film directors are a very rare breed, and for one to produce several genuinely great films (*The Blue Light*, *Triumph of the Will*, and *Olympia*) is an even greater rarity. By all rights, Leni ought to be a feminist goddess, but of course she had the wrong politics. That history's only great female filmmaker was a Nazi just doesn't sit well with the Left.

Since Leni's existence couldn't be denied, they simply had to make it as miserable as possible.

Counter-Currents/*North American New Right*,
August 22, 2011

WHY TIM BURTON'S *DARK SHADOWS* SUCKS

I was a very small child when the *Dark Shadows* serial was first airing on ABC at 4:00pm Monday through Friday. Some of my most vivid early memories are associated with it. *Dark Shadows* was originally conceived as a Gothic romance. Premiering on June 27, 1966, it centered on Victoria Winters, a young woman who takes the job of governess to the young scion of the wealthy Collins family, who reside in the spooky Collinwood mansion in spooky Collinsport, Maine. (Victoria was played by Alexandra Moltke, actually Countess Cornelia Alexandra Moltke, herself the scion of an aristocratic Swedish family. She later gained notoriety as the mistress of Claus von Bülow.)

The series floundered in the ratings for 209 episodes, until in desperation producer Dan Curtis decided to try something outrageous by the standards of daytime TV. Hunting for treasure, local loser Willie Loomis, finds a secret room inside the Collins family vault and unwittingly releases vampire Barnabas Collins. The earlier episodes had featured supernatural elements, but nothing as radical as this.

To appreciate part of the reason why *Dark Shadows* made such a big cultural impact in the mid to late '60s, one has to keep in mind that it was, after all, a daytime soap. These programs were designed primarily for stay-at-home moms and were sponsored by companies like Proctor and Gamble (who make soap, in case you don't know—hence, "soap opera"). They dealt with family problems and love affairs. Scenes took place at the breakfast table or in the living room and were mostly heart-to-heart chats (the kind that women like to have). Someone was always pouring someone else a cup of coffee. It was all very familiar, comforting terrain, albeit glamorized by perfect hair, makeup, and teeth. Female viewers identified with the characters and their problems. To add to the realism, soaps were shot on videotape, which always has a more immediate, direct quality to it (unlike the glossiness of film).

And into this homey, lace curtain and checked table cloth terrain, into this world of "Will Brad ever ask Janet to . . . ?" came the undead Barnabas Collins, crawling out of his moldering crypt, bent on sucking the life out of perky local waitress Maggie Evans (Kathryn Leigh Scott) and turning her into his vampire bride. Suddenly soap operas were scary.

Although people laugh at *Dark Shadows* today (for reasons I'll turn to in a moment) it was often genuinely creepy. The fact that Barnabas had been injected into that mundane afternoon world that female viewers so closely identified with made the program feel unaccountably weird. It almost felt like these events were really happening; like the uncanny and horrific *really had* suddenly pierced the sunny veil of suburban placidity. And the fact that it was videotaped, with a minimal budget added to the weird quality of "realness" that the whole thing had. (As any horror film fan can attest, low budgets often enhance creepiness.)

In the first few Barnabas episodes, viewers were left in suspense, wondering if he really is a vampire (or one of those "fake" vampires that you sometimes see on TV; like the haunted house that turns out, at the end of the hour, to be not really haunted after all). In a memorable scene at the close of one episode, he walks into Maggie's bedroom as she sleeps and proceeds to grin wide, revealing . . . a set of perfectly ordinary teeth. But audience members—at least some of them—were *sure* they had seen fangs. And so viewers were left in suspense over the weekend: were there fangs in Barnabas's mouth, or not? The mystery was resolved on Monday when, at the beginning of that day's episode, the scene was reshot. This time when Barnabas opened his mouth no one could fail to perceive that he was sporting a set of *very* realistic vampire fangs. And it was clear that he was up to no good.

But as the writers developed the Barnabas storyline, it emerged that he was a tortured soul, and anything but a simple villain. Back in the 1790s he had spurned the affections of a glamorous witch named Angelique. Her vengeance consisted in killing Barnabas's beloved fiancé Josette and turning him into a vampire. When Barnabas's grief-stricken father discovered his son's terrible fate, he sealed him in an iron coffin, wrapped it in chains, and hid it in the secret room in the family crypt. And so Barnabas lay in that coffin, mad with blood lust, until released by Willie Loomis in 1967. The reason Barnabas goes after Maggie, by the way, is that he believes she is the reincarnation of his dead Josette. Horrified by his condition, Barnabas allows Dr. Julia Hoffman (Grayson Hall, wife of series writer Sam Hall) to experiment on him in the hopes of curing his vampirism.

In short, it was all terribly tragic and romantic—and imaginative and engrossing. Barnabas was the first "tragic" vampire: before *Blacula* (yes, *Blacula* was a tragic vampire), *Interview with the Vampire*, the Coppola *Dracula* film, *Angel*, the *Twilight* films, and *True Blood*. (Did I miss one?) In 1973 Dan Curtis made a TV movie version of *Dracula* starring Jack Palance in the title role. Both Curtis and writer Richard Matheson felt that Stoker's character was one-dimensional; a thorough villain whose motives were often inexplicable. And so Curtis dipped back into the well of *Dark Shadows* and came up with an anguished Dracula obsessed with the woman he sees as the reincarnation of his long-dead wife. If this *Dracula* sounds very familiar, it's because Francis Ford Coppola stole the idea for his 1992 film *Bram Stoker's Dracula* (no, there is nothing like this in Stoker's novel!). And, if you've noticed, virtually all the vampires since then have been troubled, reluctant, and vulnerable. But it all started with Barnabas Collins.

In any case, to return to the 1960s: *Dark Shadows* became a major ratings hit—and Jonathan Frid, the actor who played Barnabas, became an unlikely heartthrob. Frid was 43 when he joined the cast, and not conventionally handsome. But there was something fascinating about both his physical appearance as Barnabas, and his performance—something that appealed to women (especially older women, I think).

As Barnabas, Frid could be alternately sinister and affecting. He was often undeniably stiff, but that actually helped because Barnabas was conceived as very much a gentleman of the 1790s: gallant, courtly, and flawlessly polite. Undoubtedly, this was one of the major aspects of the character that appealed to women. He was not a man of the present. He was a man out of a better, more genuine age. He *really loved* Josette. He was masterful. He could put women under his power. And he knew how to deal with ruffians like Willie. He knew what honor meant—and what it means to make a vow. And he *really* . . . sniff . . . *loved* Josette. (Trevor Lynch has given us a very perceptive analysis of why vampire stories appeal to women in his review of the first *Twilight* film.[1]) When Jonathan Frid made personal appearances he was inevitably mobbed by screaming and weeping female fans. The Barnabas cult of the late 1960s had a kind of creepy, necrophile quality to it. But then again, this was the era when Tiny Tim was a sex symbol.

Of course, *Dark Shadows* was not just a hit with housewives and their still-single, bespectacled older sisters. Go online and read around and you'll find countless people a little older than me talking about how they "ran home from school every day" to watch *Dark Shadows*. (Ironically, this was one of the reasons the series was cancelled when its ratings begin to slip: kids didn't make the buying decisions in households — not then anyway. And so *Dark Shadows* became less attractive to advertisers.) The response to the juvenile fans of the series came in the form of lunch boxes, posters, model kits, board games, coloring books, jigsaw puzzles, and comic books. Paperback Library published *thirty-two* (yes, thirty-two) novels based on the series, penned by Marilyn Ross (actually, Dan Ross — Marilyn was his wife's name).

This is where I come in. My mother only let me watch *Dark Shadows* now and then, because she thought it was too scary for a small child (and she was right: I still get chills when I remember the episode where the face of the evil Angelique appeared in the fireplace, laughing maniacally). What I knew about it I got mainly by word of mouth and by reading the comic book published by Gold Key. (Those *Dark Shadows* comic books, by the way, were published until 1976: *five years* after the series was cancelled.) Like Johnny Depp — I became utterly fascinated with Barnabas Collins.

I longed to own Barnabas's wolf's head walking stick. I even combed my hair like Barnabas. I would roam through the neighborhood at dusk (something you could do in the early '70s), watch the neighbors eat dinner through their dining room windows, and try to put them under my hypnotic spell. I owned a Barnabas model kit ("Barnabas's Vampire Van") which was sort of a hearse

---

[1] Trevor Lynch, *Trevor Lynch's White Nationalist Guide to the Movies*, ed. Greg Johnson (San Francisco: Counter-Currents, 2012).

with Barnabas inside. One day it disappeared from my room. My mother told me she had accidentally broken it while dusting. I learned much later she had thrown it away — concerned at the effect such a macabre toy might have on my young mind. Needless to say, this did no good, and I just got weirder and weirder. She was shutting the garage door after the hearse had already gone.

It was in the 1980s, I believe, that I got to finally sit down and really watch a lot of *Dark Shadows*, because that's when it came to our area in syndication. I was disappointed, because it seemed really bad. The actors flubbed their lines a lot, parts of sets would fall over, props would malfunction, and you could see the shadow of the boom (the microphone that hangs over the soundstage) *practically all the time*. (This is how the series earned the industry nickname "Mic Shadows.") But I had to admit that the story was *great*. It crossed my mind that somebody ought to take that story and do it over again — but this time rehearse the actors a little, spend more money on sets, and take a little more care with the lighting.

Producer Dan Curtis, it turns out, was thinking the same thing. In 1970 he made the feature film *House of Dark Shadows*, starring the original cast. It was Curtis's first major credit as director and holds up quite well today. The film followed the basic Barnabas Collins story (only in the end he gets staked!) and demonstrated the great potential of the *Dark Shadows* saga — when accompanied by rehearsals, a bigger budget, and better lighting. (This film was followed, unfortunately, by a very weak sequel called *Night of Dark Shadows*, which should be avoided at all costs.)

In 1991, Curtis brought *Dark Shadows* back to television as a big-budget prime time series on NBC. The cast was entirely new — and terrific. Ben Cross played Barnabas Collins and the great horror actress Barbara Steele played Dr. Hoffman. The writers again followed the basic storyline of the original serial, right down to the sequence of events wherein Victoria travels back in time to the 1790s so that we can see how Barnabas becomes a vampire. It was an excellent series, and demonstrated once more that whatever the faults of the soap opera may have been, at its core was a timelessly classic romantic tale. Alas, the series was preempted so many times by coverage of Operation Desert Storm that it lost its audience, and was cancelled after one season.

But Curtis did not give up! In 2004 he filmed a *Dark Shadows* pilot for the WB network, with Alec Newman as Barnabas, but it was not picked up. And two years later Curtis died of a brain tumor. *Dark Shadows* fandom was far from dead, however. Fans have kept the memory of the series alive, luring the surviving cast back to *Dark Shadows* conventions (yes, it's big enough for conventions), and even persuading them to appear in newly-penned *Dark Shadows* audio plays. I suppose I have to admit that I'm a fan (in case you haven't already figured that out). And so I was delighted when I heard that Tim Burton was making a $150 million feature film version starring Johnny Depp.

It didn't bother me that Burton was the director, as I've enjoyed several of his films (especially *Ed Wood*). I thought he would bring an interesting, quirky approach to the material—and I had heard that both he and Johnny Depp were fans. The news reports about the film bothered me slightly. Almost every single one described the original series as "campy," which is simply not accurate. Yes, *Dark Shadows* is often unintentionally funny: when the actors flub their lines or fake trees fall over, etc. But "camp" is something from which we derive a kind of delicious ironic enjoyment because it's unoriginal, naïve, or in bad taste (and the greater the pretensions of the makers, the funnier it is).

Camp can be produced unintentionally or intentionally. Ed Wood's films are campy because he thought they were good, while in fact they are terrible. By contrast, the *Batman* TV series of the 1960s was deliberately campy. But *Dark Shadows* doesn't fall into either category. It's actually quite original and it features, as I've said, a clever, imaginative, and absorbing plotline. And it was always in good taste. To paraphrase what Brigitte Bardot once said about sex, when *Dark Shadows* is good it's really good, and when it's bad it's still pretty good. So good, in fact, that one overlooks the flubbed lines and mic shadows.

So I found it troubling when I heard that the film promised to be a "campy" reinvention of the "campy" series. However, I often enjoy deliberate camp, so I was prepared to accept Burton's film. Once I saw the trailer, in fact, I was prepared to love it. It seemed riotously funny, imaginative, and visually arresting. And so last

Thursday I queued up and saw the film in a cinema in Manhattan. I deliberately avoided seeing it on its opening day, as I assumed cinemas would be packed. I assumed wrong, however, as *Dark Shadows* has done disappointing business so far. When I saw it there were only about 15 people in the theater with me—though admittedly it was four o'clock on a Thursday afternoon.

I was disappointed that the film did not open with Robert Cobert's classic theme (re-used in the 1991 series), but my disappointment quickly turned to delight. As others have pointed out, Burton has done a masterful job of re-creating 1972: the year in which the film is set (the original series ended in 1971). Right down to lava lamps, door beads, bean bag chairs, and Donovan. The film re-tells the basic story of Barnabas—how he becomes a vampire (in flashback), how he returns to Collinsport, his love for Josette, his occult war with Angelique—though a great deal has been truncated and otherwise altered. And it is uproariously funny. I literally laughed so hard parts of me hurt—though I often seemed to be the only one in the theater getting the humor.

Indeed, the humor is this film's greatest asset. And its greatest flaw.

Although I have to say that I enjoyed this film, by the time I was about thirty minutes away from its conclusion it began to give me a kind of empty feeling. It was funny, but it wasn't amounting to anything. There was no suspense. I never felt afraid, or awed, or moved. And, most importantly, I didn't care about anyone. I didn't care about Barnabas or his family (portrayed in this film as dysfunctional, unlikeable weirdoes), or his love for the new Josette. The last fifteen minutes of the film turned into a depressingly predictable, over-the-top special effects fest, and I was glad when it was over. I have no plans to see it again. I laughed, but it meant nothing to me.

In short, *Dark Shadows* has gotten the predictable postmodern treatment. The original series was deadly serious (as was the 1991 remake). There was nothing ironic about it. Barnabas Collins was not a figure of fun; he was a tragic hero, for whom we felt sympathy, admiration—and who sometimes genuinely frightened us. And the story of his undying love for Josette was truly moving. In the Tim Burton film, all of this is treated with ironic distance.

Barnabas becomes an Edward Scissorhandish oddball who thinks little people live inside the TV set, and that the M in the McDonalds sign stands for "Mephistopheles."

Barnabas's belief that Victoria Winters is the reincarnated Josette is handled in a kind of a smirky, ironic, offhand manner. It's as if Burton and screenwriter Seth Grahame-Smith are so convinced the audience will find this plot element all-too-familiar they do not even attempt to handle it in a fresh, dramatic, or interesting manner. If you blink you'll miss the scene where Barnabas "recognizes" Victoria as Josette. And the actress who plays Victoria (Bella Heathcote) has that flat, bland, unrefined quality that so many young actresses have today.

The rest of the cast is interesting, but they have little to do. The one who probably comes off the best is Eva Green as Angelique (Green was the girl in the Bond film with Daniel Craig, *Casino Royale*). Burton's girlfriend Helena Bonham Carter plays Dr. Hoffman, and both the actress and the character are wasted in this film. In the original series, it was clear that Dr. Hoffman loved Barnabas, while he did not return her feelings. In the film version, this translates into Dr. Hoffman getting on her knees and giving Barnabas a blowjob.

Quite a lot happens in *Dark Shadows*. There are actually several subplots going simultaneously, but none of them is developed or resolved adequately. In the last ten minutes of the film we discover that little Carolyn Collins is actually a werewolf. This is thrown in apparently because . . . well, apparently because they wanted to throw in a werewolf (the original series featured one, though he was Quentin Collins).

Jonathan Frid and three of the original cast members from the series appear in the film, briefly seen as guests at a ball Barnabas organizes (with Alice Cooper as musical entertainment—one of the film's funnier sequences). This was apparently included for the *Dark Shadows* fans, and in a sense so that the original cast could be seen as giving their imprimatur to the film. Frid died at the age of 87 a little less than a month before the premiere of *Dark Shadows* on May 11th. A number of writers have suggested that it is a good thing he didn't live to see this film. I can't disagree with them.

I wouldn't brand this film as a "travesty" of the original series, because it's clear that Burton and Depp had their hearts in the right place. It is meant to be a kind of affectionate parody. The problem is that Burton simply was not up to the task of dealing with this story. It's a case of a very postmodern, ironic director attempting to translate to the screen a story brimming with very unpostmodern romance, and genuine horror. The characters in *Dark Shadows* (the series, that is), really *felt things*. They felt true passion, obsession, and terror. They were open to the possibility of true love. They felt the weight of history, and the presence of the uncanny. I don't think Tim Burton has ever felt any of those things.

In the end, as I rode home on the subway, the chief thought on my mind was: *what a wasted opportunity*. *Dark Shadows* is such a wonderful story—probably the best vampire story of all. And vampires are really hot right now. Had Burton (or, preferably, a different director) made this film totally straight—no camp, just real horror and romance—they could have launched another *Twilight* series (only *much* better) and made a bajillion dollars. But reviews of this film have been bad, and the box office has been very disappointing. There will almost certainly be no sequel, no new television series. Hollywood will conclude that there's no money in *Dark Shadows*. For years, fans hoped to see the story that had so fascinated them translated to the big screen and finally given the treatment it deserves. But Tim Burton has buried *Dark Shadows* for all time. It's as good as stuffed in a coffin, wrapped with chains, and sealed in the Curtis family crypt.

Like Barnabas Collins himself, *Dark Shadows* now truly belongs to the past.

Counter-Currents/*North American New Right*,
May 21, 2012

THE KING'S SPEECH IS C-C-CRAP

I suppose I'm just about the last person to see this film, which won Oscars in all major categories (Best Picture, Best Director, Best Actor, Best Original Screenplay). This is odd considering my fascination with the British Monarchy. However, film audiences today annoy me so much I usually wait for things to come out on DVD. So it was with great anticipation that I awaited the arrival of *The King's Speech* from Netflix. And I do love a good film about the British Royal Family. I thoroughly enjoyed 2006's *The Queen* with Helen Mirren.

The plot, as just about everybody knows by now, concerns the efforts of Prince Albert, Duke of York (later King George VI) to overcome his pronounced stammer. In the 1930s, he meets a speech therapist (a man, in fact, with no formal training) with whom he works—reluctantly at first, owing to the man's unorthodox methods and insistence on calling him "Bertie." Matters become more pressing when George V dies and Albert's brother Edward ascends the throne. Edward is hell-bent on marrying an American divorcée, Mrs. Wallis Simpson. Eleven months later, he winds up abdicating and Albert succeeds him. After much work, and friction, Logue manages to make a great deal of progress with the King. The real test comes just after Britain declares war on Germany, and the new monarch must address the nation. In the film's climax, Logue stands by the King, who, after a halting start, delivers an almost flawless radio address.

It sounds like a recipe for a wonderful film . . . but about ten or fifteen minutes into it I noticed I was becoming more and more uncomfortable. Something seemed a bit . . . off. It was in the dialogue. Something simply did not ring true. And a thought occurred to me: Could this film have been written by an American? I initially dismissed the idea. The cast is British (mostly), the locations are authentic, the director is British, and the subject ever-so-British. Surely the Brits would not allow an American to script their dialogue for them.

But it turns out I was right. The screenwriter is one David Seidler, a playwright and film and television writer (notable for having scripted the 1999 TV movie *Come On, Get Happy: The Partridge Family Story*). In press for *The King's Speech* Seidler is always described as "British born." In fact his family emigrated to the United States when he was three years old, and he was raised on (gasp) Long Island. Bloody hell!

The King's Speech, in truth, is pretentious middle-brow junk—almost as bad as 1998's *Elizabeth*, a film about Queen Elizabeth I (and my stock example of pretentious middle-brow junk). As is typical of Americans, Mr. Seidler sees the English as pompous, uptight windbags, undersexed and out of touch with their "feelings." And Mr. Seidler seems to have only the most superficial knowledge of British Royalty, and (as we shall see) British history.

When the Duke of York (played by Colin Firth) first meets Lionel Logue (Geoffrey Rush), Logue insists that they address each other by their first names. Logue's grandson Robert flatly denied it ever happened. Instead, what we have here is something born of the egalitarian American mind, which always wants to tear down anything that has height (except skyscrapers). Poor, poor Bertie: stammering helplessly in his frosty world of manners and protocol and deep, dark repression. If only he could let his hair down, and allow himself to be treated like a regular bloke. Then he'd be cured!

Poor Bertie is also full of prejudices. Tsk, tsk. Several times he makes snide references to the fact that dear Mr. Logue is Australian. Needless to say, in order to be *fully* cured our Bertie will have to overcome his prejudices as well . . . (Jesus, this movie is just by-the-numbers!)

As if all this weren't bad enough, Seidler treats us to scenes of the future monarch chortling, waving his arms, and hopping about like a nancy boy in a high school drama warmup. It's all part of the therapy, you see. But you haven't heard the worst of it, gentle reader. Logue decides that "Bertie" needs to sample the liberating effects of cursing. And so we are subjected to a protracted scene in which the father of the present Queen shouts "Shit! Shit! Shit! Shit! Fuck! Fuck! Fuck! Fuck! Bollocks! Bollocks!

Bollocks! Bollocks!" (Logue's grandson disputes this as highly unlikely.) *The Sun*, a British paper with less credibility than *The New York Post*, reported that the Queen watched this shitty, fucked-up, bollocky film at Sandringham House around Christmas 2010 and found it "moving" and "enjoyable." I sincerely doubt this, unless what she saw was a heavily-edited version.

Helena Bonham Carter plays the Duchess of York (later Queen Elizabeth, the Queen Mother). I've always liked Bonham Carter quite a lot, primarily because of her terrific performance in *Fight Club*. But here she is miscast. Though she gives it a good effort, she simply does not have the dignity to portray Elizabeth. In one scene, Logue's wife comes home early and finds Queen Elizabeth seated at the dining room table. The Queen calmly says to her "It's 'Your Majesty' the first time, after that it's 'ma'am' as in 'ham,' not 'ma'am' as in palm." Funny, eh? Trouble is the line is lifted from *The Queen*, where an equerry says to Tony Blair "It's 'ma'am' as in 'ham,' not 'ma'am' as in 'farm.'" Like a shifty college freshman, Seidler changes one word to disguise his plagiarism. As is the case with most Americans, Mr. Seidler's knowledge of the world has been primarily mediated by film and television.

I've always found Edward VIII, later Duke of Windsor, rather fascinating, and Mrs. Simpson even more so (not because I think they were exemplary people—far from it). However, the portrayal of them in this film practically turns them into Warner Bros. cartoon characters. It is true that Edward was besotted with Wallis, but he was not the idiot he is portrayed as here. Nor is there any reason to believe that he was cruel to his brother. Up until the abdication, in fact, the two men were quite close. Wallis is on screen for about half a minute, played by an even uglier woman than the real thing. But the half minute shows Wallis and Edward nuzzling in front of their guests at Balmoral Castle—something that would *never* have taken place. Mr. Seidler also peppers his dialogue with rumors about Wallis Simpson that have long since been dismissed by competent historians (e.g. she was trained in exotic sexual techniques in a brothel in Shanghai).

However, this just scratches the surface of the film's historical revisionism. Churchill (presented here as a cigar-chomping cartoon facsimile) is depicted as critical of Edward and looking forward to his departure. In fact, the real Churchill was Edward's staunchest supporter. (This has been pointed out in an editorial by Christopher Hitchens, taking *The King's Speech* to task for its historical inaccuracies.) Churchill stood by Edward right up until the abdication, showing up in the House of Commons drunk and making rambling speeches in support of a man who was manifestly unworthy of being King.

And then there's Hitler. You *knew* Hitler was coming, didn't you? In today's Hollywood, all roads eventually lead to him. It is a notorious fact that many of the Royal Family, including Edward and very probably George VI, were sympathetic to the Nazis. As Hitchens points out, when Chamberlain returned from Munich (after handing over to Hitler a large portion of Czechoslovakia) he was immediately whisked to Buckingham Palace and led out onto the balcony before throngs of cheering Britons. This was a gross violation of custom, whereby the actions of Prime Ministers receive Royal assent only *after* they have been submitted to Parliament. George VI and his family (who are, of course, German) were quite anxious to avoid a war with Hitler.

In this film, however, we see George VI and family watching a newsreel of Hitler speaking. As is the custom in American films (today and at the time), we are treated to a few seconds of Hitler "ranting," without any subtitles explaining what he is saying. Little Elizabeth (later Elizabeth II) asks, "What's he saying, Daddy?" The King says he does not know, but seems awfully disturbed by Mr. Hitler. (In actual fact, he probably spoke German quite well, as did his brother Edward.) But, of course, we don't *need* to know what Hitler is saying. He is just obviously crazy!

Mr. Seidler quite deliberately leaves us with the idea that it's a damned good thing that that crypto-Nazi Edward left the throne, so that the good anti-Nazi Albert could guide his nation to victory over Hitler. And this makes the whole issue of stammering all the more important, doesn't it? God, what suspense! Suppose Logue can't cure the King. Will Britain succumb to the brownshirt hordes? If the King can't get over that stammer, all of Europe might well be blanketed in gas chambers.

Oh, and all of the above is accompanied by Mozart's *Marriage of Figaro*, his clarinet concerto, Beethoven's Seventh Symphony, Brahms's *German Requiem*, etc. In short, oft-heard classical standards familiar to middlebrow audiences, who will no doubt feel quite pleased with themselves that they can recognize them. What a curious mess this film is, and what a sign of the times it is that so many could think this so good. Let's take stock. It's egalitarian, anti-WASP, anti-Establishment, anti-xenophobia. It's scatological ("Shit! Shit! Shit!"). It steals shamelessly from other films. And it all comes down to saving the world from Hitler. What could explain such a strange combination of elements?

Incidentally, did I mention that Mr. Seidler is not an Anglican?

Counter-Currents/*North American New Right*,
July 20, 2011

Rage Against the Machine:
A Very American *Ring* Cycle

It heaves and groans. It shimmies and clicks. One holds one's breath during the best parts, hoping it will not malfunction and ruin the whole evening. One fears for the performers, halfway expecting it to devour them.

I am speaking of the gigantic Wagner Machine, built for the Metropolitan Opera's most recent production of *Der Ring des Nibelungen*.

At first glance, it looks like an enormous keyboard. There are 24 "keys" in all, connected by a central axis. Controlled by a computer, the giant steel segments can move individually, creating different shapes. And each has been equipped with some kind of rear-projection technology that is quite beyond my ability to explain. Suffice it to say that this enables images to be projected onto the Machine, in 24 segments. It's like the Wagner production Ernst Stavro Blofeld would have designed.

I saw the thing in action at the beginning of this month, sitting through all four operas in some very choice seats.

The Met's previous Otto Schenk Ring production was very "traditional" (i.e., true to Wagner's intentions) and lasted for about two decades. This new mechanized version is the brain child of Peter Gelb, the Met's general manager, a post he has occupied since 2006. Mr. Gelb has established a reputation as the P. T. Barnum of opera. Under his supervision, the Met has tended toward vulgar, flashy productions employing Broadway-like effects: laser shows, computer graphics, and acrobatics. Think *Spiderman* and Cirque du Soleil, if you want a good idea of what Mr. Gelb seems to be shooting for. All in a desperate effort to attract attention and, especially, to attract a younger crowd. Going to the opera, you see, is a lot like going to church. Too many gray heads.

The new *Ring* was staged by Mr. Robert Lepage, who actually has worked with Cirque du Soleil. I don't know whether he designed the Machine himself, but I will blame him for it anyway (though ultimately it is Gelb who is truly responsible for this tasteless fiasco).

Das Rheingold opens with the segments of the Machine set at a steep angle and glowing blue (with bubbles!), to signify the waters of the Rhine. Suspended on cables, the Rhine Maidens scoot up and down the Machine (receiving, one imagines, an abrasion or two). At least the angle of the thing makes it genuinely difficult for Alberich to catch them.

Das Rheingold is not divided into acts at all, but consists instead of several distinct scenes—with relatively little pause between them. As soon as scene one ends we hear Wagner's lovely music bridging the two scenes—and along with the music we hear CREAK! CLICK! THONK! as the segments of the Machine swivel into place to form the setting of scene two.

I chatted with some of the patrons during intermissions on the following three nights. "It made more noise last year," an older women told me. Her accent seemed to be French. "It's ghastly. Just ghastly," she said. New York's Eurocrowd was out in full force for the *Ring*. During *Die Walküre* I was entirely surrounded by Germans. Whenever the Machine would CLICK! or GROAN! they would begin giggling. During the final act of *Götterdämmerung* one woman behind me was chortling and guffawing so loudly I finally turned around and told her to shut up. Quite honestly, my reaction was the same as hers—but I kept it on the inside, which is what polite people do.

Fortunately, I wasn't there on the night when, during a performance of *Die Walküre*, the Windows logo appeared on the Machine for a few seconds, sending the audience into hysterics (at one of the opera's most dramatic moments). Another performance of *Die Walküre* had to be delayed for about 45 minutes when something on the Machine went wrong. I was also absent on the evening when something else went awry and the Machine refused to form the rainbow bridge at the climax of *Das Rheingold*. I was told that "they worked a lot of the bugs out." Thank God I waited a year!

To return to *Das Rheingold*: once the heaving of the Machine has finished distracting us from Wagner's music, we find ourselves in scene two. But surely there must have been some mistake, we think. The Machine has simply swiveled a few of its segments into new positions, some up and some down. With a little red glow in the background. And this is supposed to be the setting for scene two? The old Otto Schenk Met production had the gods on a kind of precipice with a gigantic, barbaric-looking Valhalla looming in the background. It looked like something out of Fritz Lang. The present production's scene two looks like something hauled out of Ground Zero. (No wonder they're searching everyone's bags at the Met now.)

At the end of scene two, Wotan and Loge resolve to descend into Nibelheim to steal the ring from Alberich, and Wagner's music bridging the transition from this scene to the next is among his most memorable. Normally, the curtain simply closes, or some smoke appears, while the scenery changes. But not at Cirque du Wagner! Before my wide eyes, the Machine heaved and lifted itself up into the rafters of the stage, forming into a kind of Escher-like staircase. From the upper wings, two stunt doubles (standing in for Mark Delavan as Wotan and Stefan Margita as Loge) climbed across the staircase suspended on cables, descending into "Nibelheim." Gee whiz! It was such a spectacle, I forgot there was any music that went with it.

But the real low point came at the end of *Das Rheingold*, when the gods cross the rainbow bridge into the newly-built Valhalla. Again, this is one of the musical highlights. The segments of the Machine stood erect, but then several of the central keys swiveled downwards to form a steep incline. The gods disappeared off stage, and then reappeared attached to cables, climbing up the steep "bridge." (Several did so, incidentally, with evident trepidation). And, by the way, to complete the picture: onto the "bridge" was projected a "rainbow pattern" that was just a little too . . . well . . . *gay*. I was so preoccupied by the idea that someone might hurt himself, or something might go wrong, I once more forgot to notice Wagner's music.

And for some reason I kept thinking of the huge "Moloch Machine" from Fritz Lang's *Metropolis*. You know the scene. Freder Fredersen descends into his city's version of Nibelheim and finds an army of alienated laborers serving a great "heart Machine." Suddenly, he sees it as a temple to Moloch, and the workers as sacrifices being herded into its great flaming jaws.

Just as suddenly, I saw the performers being devoured by the great Wagner Machine. And indeed they were devoured, as was Wagner himself. Because the Machine is the real star of this production. As the critics have unanimously and correctly proclaimed, the Machine is a distraction. It heaves like a three-masted schooner, and I haven't even mentioned the worst part: it not only moves between acts and between scenes, it actually moves about *during* scenes.

I have nothing to complain about where the music and singing are concerned. Fabio Luisi's conducting was masterful. Katarina Dalayman was an excellent Brünnhilde, and Jay Hunter Morris was a simply stellar Siegfried. But it was the Machine that—quite literally—occupied center stage. My attention was continually drawn away from Dalayman and Morris whenever the Machine made an ominous noise. Every time it began to move I held my breath, waiting for something to go wrong.

During my favorite parts—like the "Wotan's farewell" scene at the end of *Die Walküre*—I sat with my hands tensed around the armrests, praying that the Machine wouldn't spoil everything. After a while, like that over-electrocuted mouse we all heard about in Psychology 101, I just sat there numb, reminding myself that if something goes wrong there will always be other *Ring* cycles, other productions. It's not like Wagner will be ruined forever. The whole thing became an experience to be endured, and I felt like a weight had been lifted from me when the curtain came down at the end of *Götterdämmerung*.

I also noticed early on that I couldn't shake a certain morbid preoccupation: I continually imagined the performers' limbs getting caught up in the Machine. In my mind's eye I saw Peter Gelb as a Caribbean slave master, standing in the wings wielding a machete, waiting to hack off the foot of some unlucky soprano. Back to the whole "Moloch Machine" business, I suppose. Back to man serving the Machine.

But that's exactly what this is. The Machine has taken over. The Machine become diva. We no longer notice the music, or the singers. We notice the tech. In other words, going to the opera has become like going to the movies. It's not the story that matters, it's the special effects.

But, of course, what the Met has done to poor Wagner is part of much larger cultural trends. It's just what Spengler warned us about: eventually technics take over. What had been built to serve man, man now serves. The god Wotan is nothing beside the God of the Machine, who could easily crush his head like a walnut between two of its great pincers.

And there is, of course, something terribly American about the whole thing. Why is it Americans always have this attitude that if something *can* be done then it *should* be done? "Yes, by God, we can spend $17 million building a 45 ton computerized Wagner Machine that will strike terror into the hearts of audiences and make them completely forget about the music! We can do it! We have the technology! We can make Wagner better, stronger, faster."

But why stop there? Why not introduce bionic singers — or, better yet, completely robotic ones. Instead of Deborah Voigt we'll see on stage a kind of chrome piggy bank with spears and helmets stuck all over it. Though maybe I am underestimating the current state of robotics. Maybe more lifelike androids could be created, turning the Met into a kind of Disney-like Hall of Presidents spectacle. There's a lot of standing around in Wagner, so it doesn't really matter if the robots can't move that much. Oh, but perhaps I'm dating myself. Why not an entirely CGI *Ring*?

The truth, of course, is that Wagner is bigger than all this, and when that Machine has been sold for scrap he'll still be going strong. And, incidentally, it has just been announced that the Machine will be . . . uh . . . "retired" for a few years. This certainly isn't the first time Wagner has been desecrated by a bad production. Just recently the Deutsche Oper am Rhein in Dusseldorf mounted a new production of *Tannhäuser* with the cast decked out in SS uniforms. (Now this I would like to have seen! Though in the clips I've watched on German TV I've noticed some errors in the insignia.) Amid an enormous public outcry, the production was cancelled after only a few performances.

Why do they do this sort of thing to Wagner and, not, say, to

Puccini? Wait. Don't tell me. I think I know why. And I think it goes without saying.

But if Wagner was such a really, really bad German (enjoyed by a really, really bad Austrian), why do they keep performing his work? The answer, of course, is that like the Machine he's simply too big to hide away somewhere. And, of course, he sells too many tickets. So, they keep on performing Wagner—but they just can't restrain themselves from spitting at him at the same time. The Dusseldorf production, of course, is trying to "deconstruct" Wagner (HEAVE, GROAN). The American production has, in typical American fashion, no such intellectual pretensions.

I imagine something like the following dialogue must surely have taken place, somewhere in an office backstage at the Met:

> *Gelb*: Wagner is like, you know, soooooo boring we have to do something to liven this thing up, or the kids are just gonna, you know, stay away.
> *Lepage*: What about a gigantic Machine that would dwarf the performers and distract the audience from how dull the story is?
> *Gelb*: Yes. And if it made a lot of noise, maybe people wouldn't notice how much Wagner sounds like John Williams.
> *Lepage*: I think we've got something here.

In truth, all these "modern" Wagner productions simply have no faith in Wagner—neither in his words, nor in his music. (So why exactly do these producers think performances keep selling out? Because of the crappy productions they put on?) The cardinal rule of any opera production—of any work by any composer—ought to be that the settings, costume, and acting complement the music and the story. Instead, these *Ring* productions distract one from the music and the story. They are just enormous ego trips for directors and designers. What they have done to Wagner is really not much different from painting a moustache on the Mona Lisa. And ought to be greeted with complete outrage. To the credit of the Met's audience, and its critics, this production has in fact prompted outrage. Every audience member I spoke to was disgusted by it. Even the stage hands I chatted with said that they think it stinks.

This won't be the last Wagner desecration, of course—but audiences keep turning up. (The Met was packed every night that I was there—with nary an unoccupied seat in the house.) You see, in one way Wagner isn't like the Mona Lisa. If we paint a moustache on her, you can't see her anymore—she's been destroyed. But because music dwells in the eternal realm of ideas, it can never actually be touched or destroyed. And so no matter what kind of crap they heap up on stage, Wagner's glorious music will still shine through.

Smash the Machine!

Counter-Currents/*North American New Right*,
May 21, 2013

Dystopia is Now!

Whatever happened to the Age of Anxiety? In the post-war years, intellectuals left and right were constantly telling us—left and right—that we were living in an age of breakdown and decay. The pre-war gee-whiz futurists (who'd taken a few too many trips to the World's Fair) had told us that in just a few years we'd be commuting to work in flying cars. The Cassandras didn't really doubt that, but they foresaw that the people flying those cars would have no souls. We'd be men at the End of History, they told us; Last Men devoted only to the pursuit of pleasure—and quite possibly under the thumb of some totalitarian Nanny State that wanted to keep us that way. Where the futurists had seen utopia, the anti-futurists saw only dystopia. And they wrote novels, lots of them, and made films—and even one television show (*The Prisoner*).

But those days are over now. The market for dystopias has diminished considerably. The sense that something is *very, very wrong*, and getting worse—something felt forty, fifty years ago even by ordinary people—has been replaced with a kind of bland, flat affect complacency. Why? Is it because the anxiety went away? Is it because things got better? Of course not. *It's because all those dire predictions came true.* (Well, most of them anyway.)

Dystopia is now, my friends! *The future* is where we are going to spend the rest of our lives. The Cassandras were right, after all. I am aware that you probably already think this. Why else would you be reading websites like Counter-Currents? But I'll bet there's a tiny part of you that resists what I'm saying—a tiny part that wants to say "Well, it's not *quite* as bad as what they predicated. Not *yet*, anyway. We've got a few years to go before . . . uh . . . Maybe not in my lifetime . . ."

Here is the reason you think this: you believe that if it all really *had* come true and we really *were* living in dystopia, voices would be raised proclaiming this. The "intellectuals" who saw it coming decades ago would be shouting about it. If the worlds of

Brave New World, Nineteen Eighty-Four, Fahrenheit 451, and *Atlas Shrugged* really had converged and been made flesh, everyone would know it, and the horror and indignation would bring it all tumbling down!

Well, I hate to disappoint you. Unfortunately, there's this little thing called "human nature" that makes your expectations a tad unrealistic. When I was very young I discovered that there are two kinds of people. You see, I used to (and still do) spend a lot of time decrying "the way people are," or "how people are today." If I was talking to someone *simpatico* they would grin and nod in recognition of the truth I was uttering. Those are the people who (like me) didn't think that "people" referred to them. But to my utterly naïve horror I discovered that plenty of people took umbrage at my disparaging remarks about "people." They thought that "people" meant them. And, as it turns out, they were right. They were self-selecting sheep. In fact, this turned out to be my way of telling whether or not I was dealing with somebody "in the Matrix."

Shockingly, people in the Matrix take a lot of pride in being in the Matrix. They don't like negative remarks about "how things are today," "today's society," or "America." They are fully invested in "how things are"; fully identified with it. And they actually do (trust me on this) believe that how things are now is better than they've ever been. (Who do you think writes *Mad Men*?)

And that's why nobody cares that they're living in the Village. That's why nobody cares that dystopia is now. Most of those old guys warning about the "age of anxiety" are dead. Their children and grandchildren were born and raised in dystopia, and it's all that they know.

In the following remarks I will revisit some classic dystopian novels, and invite you to consider that we are now living in them.

1. *BRAVE NEW WORLD* BY ALDOUS HUXLEY (1932)

This is, hands down, the best dystopian novel of all. It is set in a future age, after a great cataclysmic war between East and West, when Communism and assembly-line capitalism have fused into one holistic system. Characters are named "Marx" and "Lenina," but they all revere "Our Ford." Here we have Huxley anticipating Heidegger's famous thesis of the "metaphysical identity" of capitalism and communism: both, in fact, are utterly materialistic; both have a "leveling effect."

When people discuss *Brave New World*, they tend to emphasize the "technological" aspects to the story: human beings hatched in test tubes, pre-sorted into "castes"; soma, Huxley's answer to Zoloft and ecstasy all rolled into one; brainwashing people in their sleep through "hypnopedia"; visits to "the feelies" instead of the movies, where you "feel" everything happening on the screen, etc.

These things get emphasized for two reasons. First, some of them enable us to distance ourselves from the novel. I mean, after all, we can't hatch people in test tubes (yet). We are not biologically designed to fit caste roles (yet). We don't have "feelies" (virtual reality isn't quite there—yet). So, we're not living in *Brave New World*. Right? On the other hand, since we really have *almost* developed these things (and since we *really do* have soma), these facets of the novel can also allow us to admire Huxley's prescience, and marvel a tad at how far we've come. The fantasies of yesteryear made reality! (Some sick souls feel rather proud of themselves when they read *Brave New World*.) But these responses are both defense mechanisms; strategies to evade the ways in which the novel *really* comes close to home. Without further ado, here they are:

The suppression of *thumos*: *Thumos* is "spiritedness." According to Plato (in *The Republic*) it's that aspect of us that responds to a challenge against our values. *Thumos* is what makes us want to beat up those TSA screeners who pat us down and put us through that machine that allows them to view our naughty bits. It's an affront to our dignity, and makes us want to fight. Anyone who does not feel affronted in this situation is not really a human being. This is because it is really *thumos* that makes us human; that separates us from the beasts. (It's not just that we're smarter than them; our possession of *thumos* makes us different in kind from other animals.) *Thumos* is the thing in us that responds to ideals: it motivates us to fight for principles, and to strive to be more than we are. In *Brave New World*, all expressions of *thumos* have been ruthlessly suppressed. The world has been completely pacified. Healthy male expressions of spiritedness are considered pathological (boy, was Huxley a prophet!). (For more information on *thumos* read my essay on *Fight Club*, and Francis Fukuyama's *The End of History and the Last Man* — a much-misunderstood book, chiefly because most readers never get to its fifth and final part.)

Denigration of "transcendence." "Transcendence" is my convenient term for what many would call the "religious impulse" in us. This part of the soul is a close cousin to *thumos*. In *Brave New World*, the desire for transcendence is considered pathological and addressed through the application of heavy doses of soma. Anyone feeling a bit religious simply pops a few pills and goes on a "trip." (Sort of like the "trips" Huxley himself took — only without the Vedanta that allowed him to contextualize and interpret them.) In the novel, a white boy named John is rescued from one of the "Savage Reservations," where the primitives are kept, and brought to "civilization." His values and virtues are Traditional and he is horrified by the modern world. In one particularly memorable scene, he is placed in a classroom with other young people where they watch a film about penitents crawling on their knees to church and flagellating themselves. To John's horror, the other kids all begin laughing hysterically. Religion is for losers, you see. How could anyone's concerns rise above shopping? Which brings me to . . .

Consumerism. The citizens of *Brave New World* are inundated with consumer goods and encouraged to acquire as many as possible. Hypnopedia teaches them various slogans that are supposed to guide them through life, amongst which is "ending is better than mending." In other words, if something breaks or tears, don't fix it — just go out and buy a new one! (Sound familiar?) Happiness and contentment are linked to acquisition, and to . . .

Distractions: Drugs, Sex, Sports, Media. These people's lives are so empty they have to be constantly distracted lest they actually reflect on this fact and become blue. Soma comes in very handy here. So does sex. *Brave New World* was a controversial book in its time, and was actually banned in some countries, because of its treatment of sex. In Huxley's world of the future, promiscuity is encouraged. And it begins very early in life—*very* early (this was probably what shocked readers the most). Between orgasms, citizens are also encouraged to avail themselves of any number of popular sports, whether as participants or as spectators. (Huxley tantalizes us with references to such mysterious activities as "obstacle golf," which he never really describes.) Evenings (prior to copulation) can be spent going to the aforementioned "feelies."

The desacralization of sex and the denigration of the family. As implied by the above, in *Brave New World* sex is stripped of any sense of sacredness (and transcendence) and treated as meaningless recreation. Feelings of love and the desire for monogamy are considered perversions. Families have been abolished and words such as "mother" are considered obscene. Now, before you optimists point out that we haven't "abolished" the family, consider what the vector is of all the Left-wing attacks on it (it takes a village, comrades). And consider the fact that in the West the family has all but abolished itself. Marriage is now consciously seen by many as a temporary arrangement (even as a convenient merging of bank accounts), and so few couples are having children that, as Pat Buchanan will tell you, we are ceasing to exist. Why? Because children require too much sacrifice; too much time spent away from careering, boinking, tripping, and playing obstacle golf.

The cult of youth. Apparently, much of the inspiration for *Brave New World* came from a trip Huxley took to the United States, where aging is essentially regarded as a disease. In *Brave New World*, everyone is kept artificially young—pumped full of hormones and nipped and tucked periodically. When they reach about 60 their systems just can't take it anymore, and they collapse and die. Whereas John is treated as a celebrity, his mother is hidden from public view simply because she has grown old on the savage reservation, without the benefit of the artificial interventions the "moderns" undergo. Having never seen a naturally old person before, the citizens of *Brave New World* regard her with horror. But I'm guessing she probably didn't look any worse than Brigitte Bardot does today. (Miss Bardot has never had plastic surgery.)

The novel's climax is a marvelous dialogue between John and the "World Controller." The latter defends the world he has helped create by arguing that it is free of war, competition, and disease. John argues that as bad as these things often are, they also bring out the best in people. Virtue and greatness are only produced through struggle.

As a piece of writing, *Brave New World* is not that impressive. But as a prophecy of things to come, it is utterly uncanny—and disturbingly on target. So much so that it had to be, in effect, suppressed by over-praising our next novel . . .

2. *NINETEEN EIGHTY-FOUR* BY GEORGE ORWELL (1948)

This is the most famous of all dystopian novels, and also the one that is least prescient. Like *Brave New World*, its literary qualities are not very impressive. It is chiefly remembered for its horrifying and bizarrely over-the-top portrayal of a future totalitarian society.

As just about everyone knows, in *Nineteen Eighty-Four* every aspect of society is controlled by "Big Brother" and his minions. All homes feature "telescreens" which cannot be shut off, and which contain cameras that observe one's every move. The Ministry of Peace concerns itself with war, the Ministry of Love with terror, etc. Orwell includes slogans meant to parody Hegelian-Marxist dialectics: "war is peace," "freedom is slavery," "ignorance is strength." The language has been deliberately debased by "Newspeak," dumbed-down and made politically correct. Those who commit "thoughtcrime" are taken to Room 101, where, in the end, they wind up loving Big Brother. And whatever you do, don't do it to Julia, because the Women's Anti-Sex League may get you. In short, things are double-plus bad. And downright Orwellian.

Let's start with what Orwell got right. Yes, Newspeak reminds me of political correctness. (And Orwell's analysis of how controlling language is a means to control thought is wonderfully insightful.) Then there is "doublethink," which Orwell describes in the following way:

> To know and not to know, to be conscious of complete truthfulness while telling carefully constructed lies, to hold simultaneously two opinions which cancelled out, knowing them to be contradictory and believing in both of them, to use logic against logic, to repudiate morality while laying claim to it, to believe that democracy was impossible and that the Party was the guardian of democracy, to forget, whatever it was necessary to forget, then to draw it back into memory again at the moment when it was needed, and then promptly to forget it again, and above all, to apply the same process to the process itself — that was the ultimate subtlety; consciously to induce unconsciousness, and then, once again, to become unconscious of the act of hypnosis you had just performed.

This, of course, reminds me of the state of mind most people are in today when it comes to such matters as race, "diversity," and sex differences.

The Women's Anti-Sex League reminds me — you guessed it — of feminism. Then there is "thoughtcrime," which is now a reality in Europe and Canada, and will soon be coming to America. (Speaking of Brigitte Bardot, did you know that she has been convicted five times of "inciting racial hatred," simply for objecting to the Islamic invasion of France?) And yes, when I get searched at the airport, when I see all those security cameras on the streets, when I think of the Patriot Act and of "indefinite detention," I do think of Orwell.

But, for my money, Orwell was more wrong than right. Oceania was more or less a parody of Stalin's U.S.S.R. (Come to think of it, North Korea is sort of a parody of Stalin's U.S.S.R., isn't it? It's as if Kim Il-Sung read *Nineteen Eight-Four* and thought "You know, this could work . . .") But Orwell would never have believed it if you'd told him that the U.S.S.R. would be history a mere four decades or so after his book was published. *Soft* totalitarianism, not hard, was the wave of the future. Rapacious, unbridled capitalism was the future, not central planning. Mindless self-indulgence and phony "individualism" were our destiny, not party discipline and self-sacrifice. The future, it turned out, was dressed in Prada, not Carhartt. And this is really why *Brave New World* is so superior to *Nineteen Eighty-Four*. We are controlled primarily through our vices, not through terror.

The best description I have encountered of the differences between the two novels comes from Neil Postman's book *Amusing Ourselves to Death*:

> What Orwell feared were those who would ban books. What Huxley feared was that there would be no reason to ban a book, for there would be no one who wanted to read one. Orwell feared those who would deprive us of information. Huxley feared those who would give us so much that we would be reduced to passivity and egotism. Orwell feared that the truth would be concealed from us. Huxley feared the truth would be drowned in a sea of irrelevance. Orwell feared we would become a captive culture. Huxley feared we would become a trivial culture, preoccupied with some equivalent of the feelies, the orgy porgy, and the centrifugal bumblepuppy. As Huxley remarked in *Brave New World Revisited*, the civil libertarians and rationalists who are ever on the alert to oppose tyranny "failed to take into account man's almost infinite appetite for distractions." In *1984*, Orwell added, people are controlled by inflicting pain. In *Brave New World*, they are controlled by inflicting pleasure. In short, Orwell feared that what we fear will ruin us. Huxley feared that our desire will ruin us.

And here is Christopher Hitchens (in his essay "Why Americans are not Taught History") on the differences between the two novels:

> We dwell in a present-tense culture that somehow, significantly, decided to employ the telling expression "You're history" as a choice reprobation or insult, and thus elected to speak forgotten volumes about itself. By that standard,

the forbidding dystopia of George Orwell's *Nineteen Eighty-Four* already belongs, both as a text and as a date, with Ur and Mycenae, while the hedonist nihilism of Huxley still beckons toward a painless, amusement-sodden, and stress-free consensus. Orwell's was a house of horrors. He seemed to strain credulity because he posited a regime that would go to any lengths to own and possess history, to rewrite and construct it, and to inculcate it by means of coercion. Whereas Huxley . . . rightly foresaw that any such regime could break but could not bend. In 1988, four years after 1984, the Soviet Union scrapped its official history curriculum and announced that a newly authorized version was somewhere in the works. This was the precise moment when the regime conceded its own extinction. For true blissed-out and vacant servitude, though, you need an otherwise sophisticated society where no serious history is taught.

I believe this just about says it all.

3. *FAHRENHEIT 451* BY RAY BRADBURY (1953)

This one is much simpler. A future society in which books have been banned. Now that all the houses are fireproof, firemen go around ferreting out contraband books from backward "book people" and burning them. So, what do the majority of the people do with themselves if they aren't allowed to read? Why, *exactly* what they do today. They watch television. A lot of television.

I read *Fahrenheit 451* after seeing the film version by Francois Truffaut. I have to admit that after seeing the film I was a bit disappointed by the book. (This would be regarded as heresy by Bradbury fans, who all see the film as far inferior.) I only dimly recall the book, as the film manages to be more immediately relevant to current pathologies than the book does (perhaps because the film was made fourteen years later, in 1967).

I vividly remember the scene in the film in which Linda, Montag the fireman's wife, asks for a second "wallscreen" (obviously an Orwell influence). "They say that when you get your second wallscreen it's like having your family grow out around you," she gushes. Then there's the scene where a neighbor explains to Montag why his new friend Clarisse (actually, one of the "book people") is so different. "Look there," the neighbor says, pointing to the television antenna on top of one of the houses. "And there . . . and there," she says, pointing out other antennae. Then she indicates Clarisse's house, where there is no antenna (she and her uncle don't watch TV). "But look there . . . there's . . . nothing," says the neighbor, with a blank, bovine quality.

Equally memorable was a scene on board a monorail (accompanied by haunting music from Bernard Herrmann). Montag watches as the passengers touch themselves gently, as if exploring their own sensations for the very first time, while staring off into space with a kind of melancholy absence in their eyes. Truffaut goes Bradbury one better, by portraying this future as one in which people are numb; insensitive not just to emotions but even to physical sensations. In an even more striking scene, Montag reduces one of Linda's friends to tears, simply by reading aloud an emotionally powerful passage from *David Copperfield*. The response from her concerned friends? "Novels are sick. All those idiotic words. Evil words that hurt people. Why disturb people with that sort of filth? Poor Doris."

What Bradbury didn't foresee was a future where there would be no *need* for the government to ban books, because people would just voluntarily stop reading them. Again, Huxley was more prescient. Lightly paraphrasing Neil Postman (from the earlier quotation), "What Bradbury feared were those who would ban books. What Huxley feared was that there would be no reason to ban a book, for there would be no one who wanted to read one." Still, you've got to hand it to Bradbury. Although books still exist and nobody (at least not in America) is banning them, otherwise the world of today is pretty much the world of *Fahrenheit 451*.

No one reads books anymore. Many of our college graduates can barely read, even if they wanted to. Everywhere bookstores are closing up. Explore the few that still exist, and you'll see that the garbage they sell hardly passes as literature. (Today's bestsellers are so badly written it's astonishing.) It's always been the case in America that most people don't read a lot, and only read good books when forced to. But it used to be that people felt just a little bit ashamed of that. Things are very different today. A kind of militant proletarian philistinism reigns. The booboisie now openly flaunt their ignorance and vulgarity as if these were virtues. It used to be that average Americans paid lip service to the importance of high culture, but secretly thought it a waste of time. Now they openly proclaim this, and regard those with cultivated tastes as a rather curious species of useless loser.

Nobody needs to ban books. We've made ourselves too stupid to deserve them.

4. *ATLAS SHRUGGED* BY AYN RAND (1957)

Atlas Shrugged changed my life.

You've heard that before, right? But it's true. I read this novel when I was twenty years old, and it was a revelation to me. I've since moved far away from Rand's philosophy, but there's a part of me that still loves and admires this book, and its author. And now I'll commit an even worse heresy than saying I liked the film of *Fahrenheit 451* more than the book: I think that, purely as a piece of prose fiction, *Atlas Shrugged* is the best of the four novels I'm considering here. I don't mean that it's more prescient or philosophically richer. I just mean that it's a better piece of writing. True, it's not as good a book as *The Fountainhead*, and it's deformed by excesses of all kinds (including a speech by one character that lasts for . . . gulp . . . sixty pages). Nevertheless, Rand could be a truly great writer, when she wasn't surrounded by sycophants who burbled affirmatively over every phrase she jotted (even when it was something like "hamburger sandwich" or "Brothers, you asked for it!").

Atlas Shrugged depicts an America in the not-so-distant future. Collectivism has run rampant, and government regulation is driving the economy into the ground. The recent godawful film version of the novel (do yourself a big favor and don't see it) emphasizes this issue of government regulation at the expense of Rand's other, more important messages. (Rand was not simply a female Milton Friedman.) Rand's analysis of the roots of socialism is fundamentally Nietzschean, though she would not admit this. It is "hatred of the good for being the good" that drives people in the world of *Atlas Shrugged* to redistribute wealth, nationalize industries, and subsidize lavish homes for subnormal children. And at the root of this slave morality (which Rand somewhat superficially dubs "altruism") is a kind of primal, life-denying irrationalism. Rand's solution? A morality of reason, where recognition that A is A, that facts are facts, is the primary commandment. This morality is preached by Rand's prophet, John Galt, who is the leader of a secret band of producers and innovators who have "gone on strike," refusing to let the world's parasites feed off of them.

Despite all her errors (too many to mention here) there's actually a great deal of truth in Rand's analysis of what's wrong with the world. Simply put, Rand was right because Nietzsche was right. And yes, we are living in the world of *Atlas Shrugged*. But the real key to seeing why this novel is relevant to today lies in a single concept that is never explored in *Atlas Shrugged* or in any of the other novels discussed here: *race*.

Virtually everything Rand warned about in *Atlas Shrugged* has come to pass, but it's even worse than she thought it was going to be. For our purveyors of slave morality are not just out to pillage the productive people, they're out to destroy the entire white race and western culture as such. Rand was an opponent of "racism," which she attacked in an essay as "barnyard collectivism." Like the leftists, she apparently saw human beings as interchangeable units, each with infinite potential. Yes, she was a great elitist—but she believed that people became moochers and looters and parasites because they had "bad premises," and had made bad choices. Whatever character flaws they might have were changeable, she thought. Rand was adamantly opposed to any form of biological determinism.

Miss Rand (born Alyssa Rosenbaum) failed to see that all the qualities she admired in the productive "men of the mind"— their Apollonian reason, their spirit of adventure, their benevolent sense of life, their chiseled Gary Cooperish features—were all qualities chiefly of white Europeans. There simply are no black or Chinese or Hispanic John Galts. The real way to "stop the motor of the world" is to dispossess all the white people, and this is exactly what the real-life Ellsworth Tooheys and Bertram Scudders are up to today.

Atlas Shrugged, Brave New World, Nineteen Eighty-Four, and *Fahrenheit 451* all depict white, racially homogeneous societies. Non-whites simply do not figure at all. Okay, yes, there might be a reference somewhere in *Atlas Shrugged* to a "Negro porter," and perhaps something similar in the other books. But none of the characters in these novels is non-white, and non-whites are so far in the background they may as well not exist for these authors. Huxley thought that if we wanted epsilon semi-morons to do our dirty work the government would have to hatch them in test tubes. Obviously, he had just never visited Detroit or Atlanta. Epsilon semi-morons are reproducing themselves every day, and at a rate that far outstrips that of the alphas.

These authors foresaw much of today's dystopian world: its spiritual and moral emptiness, its culture of consumerism, its flat-souled Last Manishness, its debasement of language, its doublethink, its illiteracy, and its bovine tolerance of authoritarian indignities. But they did not foresee the most serious and catastrophic of today's problems: the eminent destruction of whites, and western culture.

None of them thought to deal with race at all. Why is this? Probably for the simple reason that it never occurred to any of them that whites might take slave morality so far as to actually will their own destruction. As always, the truth is stranger than fiction.

The dystopian novel most relevant to our situation is also—surprise!—the one that practically no one has heard of: Jean Raspail's *The Camp of the Saints*. But that is a subject (perhaps) for another essay . . .

Counter-Currents/*North American New Right*,
January 4, 2012

Tito Perdue's *Lee*

Tito Perdue
Lee
New York: The Overlook Press, 2007

Lee bothered me for days. That's not a bad thing, though. Because I saw myself in this book. Lee, the title character, is me. Right down to the hemorrhoids. Or, at least, he's what I might be in thirty years.

Lee Pefley—or *Dr.* Lee Pefley, as he styles himself—is perhaps the most misanthropic character in all literature. He's an old man in his seventies who has sold some property and moved back to his hometown in Alabama. But he finds the place rather changed. Gone is the imperfect little hamlet he grew up in, and in its place the modern world has plopped down. A weird, Southern-gothic take on it, but the modern world nonetheless, with all its soullessness and gutlessness.

Lee rents a room at a local boarding house, his only possessions a few articles of clothing and a large quantity of books. Exclusively the Western classics. He sleeps little, as old men do, and spends the days roaming the town, mentally annihilating everyone and everything he encounters. He and I have the same mission, you see: the destruction of the modern world. But in Lee's case his hate soon expresses itself, mostly with the aid of his cane, in acts of violence and mayhem. Or does it? It's not clear from the novel if these things actually happen, or are only imagined by Lee.

You see, Lee does have a vivid imagination. His move back home has been occasioned by the death of his beloved wife, Judy. But throughout the story he conjures her up and converses with her. One gets the feeling that Judy was the one source of joy in Lee's life, the one thing in this world he did not hate. And with her loss, the hate is all he has left. Our enemies, of course, say that hate will destroy us. There is some truth to this, actually. Even a stopped clock . . .

As I have argued elsewhere it's easy for our kind to become embittered by all that's wrong with the world. If we don't hold on to something that gives us joy, we could all become festering, nihilating old prunes like Lee. I fear I may be well on my way, as time and again reading this book I found myself identifying with him. As when the author tells us that "Deep was his hatred for the modern age, so deep and rich, a rich feast. How he envied the times to come, the world made clear" (p. 110).

And: "He now thought of himself as the unacknowledged prophet of the crumbling of the West. *This* was the good of books: for toying with Time. Old drawings in old books — he preferred this so much more than anything that was happening in the outside world. To his thinking, it were far more laudable to have been alive than to be alive, or than to be scheduled for the future" (p. 15). Do you see yourself in this too?

Lee's reactions to things are uncannily like my own, and yours I'll wager. Lee encounters a child: "He could see in this snot-nosed infant that taxpayer and sports fan of the future who was to be given as much voting power as he himself had ever had" (p. 12). And: "There was a crowd of gesticulating sixteen- and seventeen-year-olds all talking at the same time — he wanted to puke. They simply could *not* sit still. All his life he had wanted to identify what it was the masses most loathed, and then to see that they got it in spades. What he craved now was to *force* these children into utter motionlessness, days and days and days. To his thinking, nothing proved the weakness of this class of people more than their everlasting need for action, and for each other" (p. 12). The book is filled with such stuff, wherein Mr. Perdue seems to be reading my mind — *our* mind.

As I read further, however, and got to know Dr. Pefley better, a strange feeling took hold of me. I began by recognizing myself in him, and felt pleasure. But after a while this became displeasure, and just a tad bit of this was shame. I had the same feeling I got years earlier reading Flannery O'Connor and seeing myself in some of the snotty "intellectual" characters that she skewered so accurately and mercilessly.

"He felt a spasm at the base of his neck, followed by a headache that began spreading in a slow way, like a blotter in ink. It was his hatred. Never had he achieved that toleration said to be the final result of wisdom; in fact, he wanted nothing to do with it. What he did want was an advanced torture machine with the whole world attached" (pp. 25-26). That's me all right. But that's not good, and I know it. It's not healthy to set one's expectations of other people so high that one winds up hating all of humanity.

And aren't we supposed to be all about loving our own? This is the contradiction so many Right Wingers find themselves stuck in. I've known people who've actually given up on the Cause, saying "Why should I work to save the White Race when they're too damned stupid to see that they need saving? When they'd sooner spit in my face than thank me?" But the truth is that almost all people, in all races, are sheep. We just have the whitest, most promising sheep of all. Properly led, they're glorious. Otherwise, yes, they're so annoying one wants to hook them up to a torture machine. But this is where we really do have to learn toleration, which is where wisdom — and love of our own — should, in fact, lead us.

Lee does not love his own. He cannot connect. He returns to his hometown but feels no kinship with these people, only with his books. (Why does he go home? Is there something in himself, deep down, that yearns for connection, some part his conscious mind might deny?) For him the world divides into those that read and those that do not. And the books also have to be of the right kind. Lee likes to get in staring contests. He does so with one man early in the novel and Perdue tells us "The man was weak. Lee's gaze had ten thousand books behind it" (p. 13). And: "Who read the most books, and read well, it seemed to him, to that person belonged the world. As for the little people, those who did things, carrying out activities, they were good only for doing things and should be disqualified from reproducing" (p. 77).

For me, the heart of the novel was a long episode in which Lee, roving the countryside, winds up tarrying a while with an old farmer. The man is a good soul, a real salt of the earth. But of course Lee looks down on him. "Where are your books?" Lee asks him repeatedly. The old farmer senses his condescension and tells Lee that he has, after all, been to school. "Oh, yes, but you don't take it seriously," Lee shoots back. "I mean for you it's simply a measure of getting ready for life, isn't it so?" (p. 60). But what else should it be? The irony of Lee is that all his book-reading has not done him any good. He cannot relate to others, cannot take joy in life, cannot — for all intents and purposes — live.

And he has the gall to tell the farmer, who's raised six children, that "life is a getting ready for books." When the man speaks of what a good woman his late wife was, Lee responds "Look, *my* wife had four degrees. From four different universities too" (p. 63). It was about then — on page sixty-three — that I parted company with Lee. I'd like to think that whatever sense of superiority I have *vis-à-vis* others has to do with my knowledge and my insight — not with how many books I've read, or how many degrees I have. But there's a bit of that in me as well, and I'm not proud of it.

I don't know Tito Perdue, but I suspect Lee is his bad side too — and what he thinks he could become, given the wrong set of circumstances. I'm not going to reveal to you what happens to Lee. You'll just have to read the book. But I think you can guess that he's not moving toward a bright and rosy future.

The lesson I learned from *Lee* is kind of like the one I learned from my parents. My mother and father bequeathed to me two shining examples of exactly the sort of person I *don't* want to be, but could nevertheless become. My parents are like the bad parts of my character personified by some crafty novelist. And I do kind of look at life as if it's a text, wherein everyone and everything is a symbol or a lesson of some kind, directed at me.

Still, *Lee* was more to me than just a cautionary tale; a kind of "there but for the grace of God . . ." thing. What it communicated to me more than anything else was the need for what Confucius called *ren*, which often gets translated as "human-heartedness." There's none of that in Lee Pefley. But we need human-heartedness to save the race, not just book learning and a lofty sense of superiority.

Too many of our set are into all that "might is right" crap. They yearn for the re-establishment of "natural hierarchy" — in which they would, but of course, rise to the top (like curdled cream) and lord it over all the taxpayers and sports fans who picked on them in school. Our race needs hierarchy, all right. But not so that those on top can lord it over those below, but rather so that those on top can do the others the *kindness* of ruling them. That's what most people truly need, in order to lead happy, healthy, noble lives. And the quality our elite must possess above all else, if it expects to remain the elite, is a sense of *noblesse oblige*.

Aside from whatever message may be conveyed in *Lee*, it is a brilliant piece of writing. Mr. Perdue has a real gift for crafting some of the quirkiest metaphors I have ever read, and he can truly tell a tale. Do yourself a kindness and read *Lee*. You may just find yourself in it — as I did — and find much else as well.

Counter-Currents/*North American New Right*,
October 22, 2013

The Vermont Teddy Bear is a Giant Phallus

Last night I was so bored I actually turned on Fox News. I do this now and then, with the same sort of feeling I get when I pass a roadside accident and, against my better judgment, turn briefly to glimpse the carnage. It was around 10:30, so the execrable Sean Hannity was on. After a minute or so of the usual Obamacare coverage they went to a commercial. It was then that I received the revelation, and my life changed forever.

The commercial began with a tarty-looking young woman holding a ruler in a suggestive fashion and grinning lasciviously at the camera. Then a male voice intones: "Guys, this Valentine's Day *size really does matter*." The camera pulls back to reveal a four-and-a-half foot tall teddy bear. The Vermont Teddy Bear — specifically the "Big Hunka Love Bear" model. Available for Valentine's Day at the very reasonable price of ninety-nine dollars. "Score big," the announcer advises male viewers.

We see a tall, hunky guy entering what is presumably his house, handing the Big Hunka Love Bear to what is presumably his wife. "This guy is a four-and-a-half foot pile of awesomeness," the announcer proclaims. (I'm not kidding you.) Presumably, he means the stuffed bear, because the guy looks like he's about six feet tall. But maybe something else about him measures only 4 ½ (more about this later). By the way, at this point in the commercial a big, pink, upward-thrusting, fat arrow appears on the screen, over which is superimposed "4 ½ FEET TALL."

The hunky guy's pretty, redheaded wife embraces him and the bear. Over his shoulder, we see her grin in a peculiarly self-satisfied way — as if she and the bear share some secret to which the husband is not privy. We are then informed that the Big Hunka Love Bear is a much better Valentine's gift than flowers or chocolates. And in one shot, we see a brunette dumping out her box of chocolates. The suggestion is that they will make her feel fat. But something else is going on here. We've all heard that women crave chocolate because there's some sort of hormonal thing involved, right? The message we are getting, in fact, is that the Big Hunka Love Bear is better than chocolate as a sex substitute. He is like a great, big, cuddly dildo for a woman's heart.

This analysis is confirmed moments later when we see what appears to be the same brunette leaping onto her sofa and into the warm, hairy arms of her Big Hunka Love Bear, where she no doubt feels safe, secure, and affirmed. And this bear is not going to leave her, no matter what. Because the ad informs us that it is "GUARANTEED FOR LIFE." As she lies in the arms of her prodigiously-endowed bear watching the Lifetime channel, she can enjoy the fact it gives every outward indication of wanting to be there just for her. It will not try to initiate sex when she's not in the mood. It will not change the channel when she gets up to make herself a cup of soothing chamomile tea.

We next see a blonde executrix entering her tastefully-appointed office only to find, to her squealing delight, the Big Hunka Love Bear sitting at the desk. This bear, you see, is for powerful women too, not just housewives. He is big, strong-looking, and dependable. He will make her feel safe—while never actually displaying any genuine masculine assertiveness. The best of both worlds, in short. The Big Hunka Love Bear is actually empowering, because although it is like a big pacifier, the woman is in control of the bear at all times.

Then we glimpse the same blonde, now wearing a sexy, slinky red dress, jumping into bed with the bear and giving us a "come hither" look. The voice-over promises us that the bear will "keep her thinking about you." But I'm not so sure about this. Another scene shows a different husband surprising his wife in the kitchen with the Big Hunka Love Bear. Again, she hugs him and the bear ecstatically. He grins at the camera with a look that can only mean one thing: "Oh boy, I'm going to get some tonight." To confirm this, the announcer now tells us "It's a great gift for her. *It's sure to pay off for you.*" But, again, I'm not so sure.

In case it's not already obvious, this commercial suggests very deliberately that the Vermont Teddy Bear is a giant phallus—in a way that's so sick and weird it's actually tough to describe. In a different Vermont Teddy Bear commercial, a woman working in an office is thrilled when her bear is delivered by special courier. "He's *much* bigger than I thought!" she exclaims. "I could just kiss it and kiss it!" Meanwhile, the guy who (it seems) sent the gift is in the next cubicle watching the scene furtively, like an impotent voyeur spying on his wife's sex tryst with another man. This is then followed by a succession of really dumb guys practically drooling over the (very probably mistaken) idea that this stupid bear is going to get them laid.

But they are all living in a fool's paradise—for this stuffed bear spells their doom, their obsolescence.

Several years ago I watched the Coen brothers film *Burn After Reading* with my parents. Everything was going well, until we got to the scene where George Clooney presents his wife with a present he's been building for her in his spare time: a peddle-driven dildo machine. I wanted to crawl under my seat. My parents had no reaction—either because they didn't understand what was happening, or they were too embarrassed to acknowledge that they did.

The scene was funny on multiple levels. It was a perfect, and perfectly extreme parody of men's often shocking ineptitude and insensitivity when it comes to selecting gifts for their wives and girlfriends. It was also a hilarious sendup of that semi-autistic, Aspergerish quality in most men: their fascination with machines and with tinkering. But one also has to ask, what self-respecting man would give his woman a penis substitute as a gift? I'm reminded of the scene in *Fight Club* where Tyler notices the dildo on Marla's dresser and she says "Don't worry. It's not a threat to you." But only Tyler Durden would accept an answer like that.

Giving your wife or girlfriend a dildo as a gift would be a stunning admission of inadequacy—of not being up to the job, so to speak. But I don't see how giving her the Big Hunka Love Bear is fundamentally different. It's like you're saying "I know I'm not big enough, strong enough, stable enough, mature enough, or dependable enough. I know I'm just a weak, modern, emotionally-stunted, overgrown boy. I know I can't make you feel safe when I hold you in my arms. Sorry, but it's time for us both to admit I'm just not man enough. So, here, I'm giving you this giant stuffed bear as a man-substitute. And he's hairier than me, too." These commercials very deliberately play on men's anxiety that perhaps they just don't "measure up" — in all sorts of ways. Whispered, nay *shouted* solution: *buy her the bear, buy her the bear, buy her the bear* . . . In a perfect world, these Vermont Teddy Bear spots would be followed by ads for Enzyte.

Of course, the real solution is to be a man. And this, gentlemen, is what you should give your wives and girlfriends for Valentine's Day. Yes, give the traditional flowers and chocolate — and give her the gift of male strength. (But for God's sake *don't tell her* you are doing this! Just do it.) Don't create a vacuum that she needs a stuffed bear — or, uh, anything else — to fill.

I feel I should end this essay here, but I know many of you will be curious about the cynical, twisted minds behind the Vermont Teddy Bear. This company is indeed based in Vermont — in Burlington, to be exact. They are one of the world's largest manufacturers of teddy bears, around 500,000 a year. If you go on their site, you will find they even offer magical, Wonka-like tours of their factory. But, given what I now know, I think it would be best if you left the kids at home.

In another example of the company's good taste, a few years ago they marketed a "Crazy For You" bear wearing a strait jacket. It even came with its own "commitment papers." Mental health advocacy groups and even the governor of Vermont protested, but the company kept selling the item until they ran out of stock (it's not been offered again). As a result of the controversy, company head Elizabeth Robert was forced to resign from the board of Vermont's largest hospital.

It's no accident that these ads appear on the Fox News Channel, by the way. The Vermont Teddy Bear Company's radio ads have been carried by Premiere Radio Networks, which syndicates the Rush Limbaugh, Sean Hannity, and Glenn Beck shows. I've even heard that the Vermont Teddy Bear people marketed a "Rush Limbaugh for President" bear, but I've not been able to confirm this. What is it with the taste of these Republicans? Imagine: once you've gifted your special lady a Big Hunka Love

Bear you can curl up with her in your Snuggies and watch Fox News, or listen to Rush on your Bose Wave Radio. While drinking Snapple, of course — or, better yet, smoking cigars.

Do you need further proof that we are living in the Kali Yuga? Okay, how about the fact that when I typed "awesomeness" above, my computer recognized this as an actual word.

Counter-Currents/*North American New Right*,
February 5, 2014

BI-COASTAL ADVENTURES IN MODERN ART

September 29th: My friend Anastasia (not her real name) hits town. She's staying with some friends in Brooklyn and invites me to meet her at the Participant Gallery, on Manhattan's Lower East Side. Anastasia's old friend Clytemnestra (not her real name) is going to perform what is described to me as a "cat dance." I arrive on time to find the place quickly filling up with the most appalling collection of artsy-fartsy New York hipsters and self-conscious "individualists" that I have yet seen.

Anastasia and I sit on the floor alongside the stage. She used to be part of this whole scene. Her parents were both artists, and she grew up in Manhattan. But she has a healthy critical distance from it all. The show is supposed to begin at 7, but the appointed hour arrives and the stage still stands empty. Time creeps by and my empty stomach is rumbling. 7:30 and still no cat dance. All I can think about is getting out of there and finding something to eat. Anastasia is a few feet away from me talking to another old friend, this one of indeterminate sex. She keeps glancing at me and smiling, aware that I'm acutely uncomfortable.

At last around 7:45 there's a bit of a hubbub around the door to the gallery, then some gasps and a good deal of laughter. I can't see anything through the crowd, but I hear a human voice crying "Meow! Meow!" And then Clytemnestra appears: stark naked and covered in gray body paint, with pasteboard cat ears, whiskers, and tail affixed to her body. She slinks and claws the air in a sort of Julie Newmar fashion. "Meow! Meow!" She is then followed by two other identically-clad (and unclad), buxom young catwomen, all meowing and menacing the audience with their glued-on plastic claws.

Everyone is tittering and videoing the whole thing with their iPhones. Predictably, I can't get the camera on mine to work. Stagehands in the inevitable black turtlenecks and leotards bring out a huge litter box. The catwomen get in it and begin scratching imaginary litter. "Please don't . . . Please don't, umm . . . *go*," I think. My friend John Morgan of Arktos Publishing told me about some performance art in Sweden in which a naked women peed on stage and a man tasted it and said "Ummm. Tastes like art." But contrary to its reputation, this New York stuff is pretty tame, and the litter box segment is, thankfully, pure pantomime.

The box is removed and then a giant cat toy is produced from backstage and held out before the catwomen: a long pole with some strands of fabric dangling from it. The catwomen circle it frenetically, clawing at the strands, cat boobs jiggling. Then the toy is whisked away by some po-faced stage hands, and our performers begin banging drums with cat faces painted on them. They chant something or other, but I can't remember what it was. No matter. It made no sense anyway. And then the performance is suddenly over—ending just as enigmatically as it had begun. The question on everyone's lips: "Why?"

Much applause, followed by a short intermission which is then to be followed by someone doing a monologue about being a hermit. But I have had enough. And blessedly so has Anastasia. We step outside so that she can talk to some of her old chums. Inevitably, I am asked what I thought of the performance. "I've lived with a cat for thirteen years," I say. "I was not convinced by that." One of Anastasia's friends raises an eyebrow. "I doooooon't think that was the point," she responds, her voice dripping with condescension.

Anastasia is an attractive, beguiling woman. One of those people who seem to be able to fit in just about anywhere, and to charm any crowd. But I desperately want to ditch these artsy people and go have some dinner. Miraculously, I succeed in extricating Anastasia from her friends, and a few minutes later the two of us are sipping drinks at a Thai restaurant on 1st Avenue. "People think it's supposed to be funny," Anastasia says to me of Clytemnestra's performance. "But to her it's all about the fact that she doesn't know who she is or why she's here. It's an expression of existential *angst*."

And I just thought she was expressing hairballs.

Flash forward to October 15th: I am bumming around San Francisco with the artist Charles Krafft and the aforementioned John Morgan of Arktos. We take a bus to North Beach with the intention of visiting City Lights Books and pouring scorn upon their inventory. But first Charlie wants to have lunch at the San Francisco Art Institute. Their food isn't very good, but the café has a great view of the bay. I tell Charlie and John about my introduction to cat dancing two weeks earlier. The tale makes us all hunger to experience more contemporary art, and fortunately the San Francisco Art Institute is lousy with it.

This place is a school, in case you don't know. Filled with young, wan, entitled brats with "raised consciousness," sipping fair trade coffee and debating which local sushi joint serves the most ethical tuna, rolled-up yoga mats protruding from their North Face backpacks, lovingly assembled by barefoot Guatemalan peasants for pennies an hour. "Trustafarians," Herr Krafft declares. Grungy stoners with trust funds. Trust funds and no talent, as we soon discover.

The Diego Rivera gallery contains an interesting mural by Rivera, but its purpose is not to house the mural but to serve as a space for the petite larcenies that these kids call art. In the center of the room is a small group of mechanical plastic daisies, their stems swaying back and forth to battery power. In order to better understand the artist's intention we lie flat on the floor and study the daisies up close, as another friend (who must remain nameless) snaps a picture of us. Other visitors come and go, perhaps thinking we're just part of the art.

On one of the walls someone has taped a small square of human hair. "What's that?" one of us asks. "It's Hitler's moustache!" I proclaim, feeling suddenly inspired. And we are photographed with this exhibit as well. We visit other galleries at the Institute, and they are no better. It's all bollocks. Only one instance where I looked at a piece and thought, "It's crap, but I can see that the guy does have *some* talent . . ." I told Charlie that I have one hard and fast rule in judging art: if I look at it and think "I could do that," then it can't be any good. My being *unable* to do what the artist has done is a necessary, though not a sufficient condition of the piece being any good. And a five-year-old could do most of this.

But he would have to be a pretty malevolent five-year-old; a bad seed. Because this stuff is just a sneering fraud. A revenge against beauty and talent by a group I'd like to label "envious mediocrities"—but that would be paying them an undeserved compliment. Pardon me if I'm sounding like Ayn Rand. But for all her faults Rand had much of modern art nailed:

> "Something made by an artist" is not a definition of art. . .
> "Something in a frame hung on a wall" is not a definition of painting. . .
> "Something piled together" is not a definition of sculpture. . . ("Art and Cognition," in *The Romantic Manifesto*, 2nd paperback ed.)

And so on.

Most reactionaries dismiss modern art as bullshit. I don't think that is necessarily so. Attacking "modern art" is kind of like attacking "modern medicine." These categories comprise quite a lot—both good and bad. And there are modern artists I appreciate—like Paul Klee, Edward Hopper, Thomas Hart Benton, and, of course, Charles Krafft. But what we think of when the term "modern art" is invoked is "non-representational art" and "conceptual art." Some spots flung on a canvas; some stuff piled together; some human hair glued to a wall; some plastic mechanical daisies lined up.

But, ironically, a lot of modern artists seem to agree with the reactionaries, which is why most of today's "serious art" is just a cynical bullshit industry. There are no "concepts" behind "conceptual art." There are no "meanings" here for pretentious critics to expatiate upon. It means nothing. These narcissistic hipsters admitted to places like the San Francisco Art Institute might actually have some latent talent, but they quickly get the message: their job is simply to come up with something—anything—that's less meaningful than what the last guy did. Maybe this is all they really *can* do, because there's just no meaning inside them to come out.

The real, sorry truth is that the Nietzschean-Randian analysis—according to which the "modern" artist is moved by envy—probably gives most of these people too much credit. It's not that they want to spit at great art: they really just don't want to do anything of significance at all.

As we walked up Columbus Avenue, headed for City Lights, I thought: "Take heart, one day every last bit of it will wind up in our new exhibit of *Entartete Kunst*." Cat dance and all. But the Germans were too generous: they actually sold off all the stuff once the exhibit was over. Let's demolish it, and redirect these "artists" to their true calling: waiting tables.

Counter-Currents/*North American New Right*,
October 18, 2013

WHY I LIVE IN THE PAST

I don't like the present very much. So I live in the past.

Just about everything about this day and age depresses and angers me. The ignorance, the lies, the vulgarity, the hypocrisy, the bad manners. The witless movies aimed at those with IQs of 85 and under. "Diversity." Feminism. Having to press "1" to hear the menu in English. Having to hear a menu at all. The TSA (the last time I flew they removed the cheese from my backpack and X-rayed it separately). The relentless focus on money and "practicality." The inescapable ugliness of this concrete, advertisement-bedecked wasteland (which most ordinary people don't even notice anymore). The brassy, shrill, F-word besprinkled speech of today's slatternly young women. The use of "disrespect" as a verb. And I could go on.

One way I deal with all of this is by means of a kind of dark, detached, withering humor—which I direct at things from my throne high atop Olympus. When I get together with like-minded friends we spend most of our time observing others and rubbishing them. The other way I deal with the rot of the day is by entering into the past. For me, the past is like another world I can escape to. There are many doorways back into the past. Reading history is one of them, of course.

Another—perhaps my favorite way—is old movies. I like watching films from the '40s, '50s, and even the '60s—just because everyone dresses so much better in those films than they do today. (This is a large part of the secret to the success of *Mad Men*.) Everything I know about how to dress I learned from watching Hitchcock films, and James Bond. I like corny old movies, and I like them on principle. This is because I feel that the ability to enjoy them and be moved by them is a mark of purity and simple virtue. That most of us are unable to watch such films today without laughing is a sign of our corruption. Yes, I even watch silent films. To me they are to the cinema what Greek drama is to theater.

People seem more real in old movies. Men are men and

women are women. They have real emotions and let them out, without having to go through an ideological screening process. They seem *closer to nature* — even when they are shown living in urban environments. I get the same feeling when I look at very old photographs — such as the family photos we still have from the 19th century. As everybody always notices in these old pictures, the people aren't smiling. They have a harder, tougher quality. But what always fascinates me is the eyes. They have a faraway look, like every single one of them is a bit touched (as they say in the South). You feel like you can see history in those eyes. And a connection to something that we've lost. It's like they were all hooked up to the great pitiless, primal life-generator, whereas we are mere bloodless simulacra.

I like films from the past and films *about* the past — especially the distant past. Films set in the '40s or '50s do display a nice contrast to today, and make me feel wistful. But if you're clever you can perceive the rot beginning to set in, even back then. You can recognize the patterns of decay; the things that just kept on getting worse until we got saddled with now. (And, of course, these things will keep on getting worse.) Which is why I love films that take me back a few centuries — so long as there's some credibility to them. And so long as they don't fall into the "When things were rotten" mold. Reading a history of Rome is a way to enter into the past. But a film like *Quo Vadis?*, for all its flaws, makes that past come alive.

I also like films that are *preoccupied* with the past. A good example would be the very appropriately-named *Out of the Past* (1947) with Robert Mitchum. This is one of my favorite films, and it is the best *film noir* of them all.

But let's not forget television shows. A few months ago I reviewed the misguided Tim Burton *Dark Shadows* film, and it became an excuse for me to reminisce about the original TV series. And my own review then prompted me to start watching *Dark Shadows* on Netflix — and getting hooked on it all over again. *Dark Shadows* starts off as the story of Victoria Winters, a young woman who grew up in an orphanage with no knowledge of her parents at all. She goes to work as governess for the aristocratic

Collins family in Maine, a clan with a rich past. A woman without a past goes to work for a family that thinks about almost nothing other than the past.

Inevitably, Victoria becomes obsessed by the Collins family history and fantasizes about being one of them. Late in the show's first year the main character then becomes a figure literally *of* the past: Barnabas Collins, a 200-year-old vampire obsessed with his own past and with reliving his great romance with long-dead Josette. At a certain point, Victoria is transported back in time to the 1790s, where the ancestors of the present-day Collins family are played by the same set of actors. (This storyline lasted for many weeks, and these are considered *Dark Shadows*' "classic" episodes.)

This series was very accurately described as a "Gothic romance," and preoccupation with the past — old mansions and abbeys, family curses, hauntings, etc. — is a staple of Gothic fiction. Why? And why is Gothic fiction "Gothic"? What is it about the northern European soul that causes it to be so moved by dark and stormy nights, secret passages, and old family secrets? Other peoples value the past, and preserve tradition, but somehow with us it's different. The past is an uncanny thing for us. It really is like a different world, that sometimes has the capacity to cross over into this one.

In a sense, the past is more real than the present. It is more real because it is complete. My life is ongoing. I have no idea where it will lead, or what it will be defined by. In this sense, it is indefinite. A single act, a single spoken or written sentence can define an entire life and give it meaning. Think of any historical figure. Always in their biography there is some major deed or event that defines the whole life. Reading their story — knowing where their life is headed — we understand everything before the event as leading up to it, as preparing the way. If the historical figure survives this event, we understand everything after it as its result — or as anticlimax.

Historical lives are therefore like works of fiction. We only recognize that there's a plot once the life is over. Then we see it in terms of acts and story arcs. Fictional characters are "larger than life." They seem more real to us. Sherlock Holmes is far more real to me than my UPS man, and I know far more about him. But the same is true of historical figures. (I'm almost tempted to ask, given how fascinating the past is, who needs fiction when we have history?) Our lives, as we are living them, are like stories that keep going and going, making us wonder if there really is a point to it all. What's the plot? Or is there a plot? This is the same thing as wondering if there's any meaning or purpose to our lives.

But it is only once a life is over that we can truly know what its meaning and purpose was. Every completed life is like a completed story, and, like fiction, has much to teach us. This is true even of seemingly insignificant lives. The lives of great men are like classic, sprawling novels (or epic poems). The lives of little men are like short stories (or, in the case of *very* little men, limericks).

This perspective has taught me a great deal about how life should be led. Essentially, you really have to choose whether you want to be the author of your own story—your own life—or let circumstances (or fate) do the authoring for you. I have learned to adopt the perspective of a third party looking over my life and assessing it, discerning the patterns in it, seeing where it seems to be headed. I have learned that I must keep squarely in mind that every choice, every action on my part is *irrevocable*. All form part of my past—*instantly*, as soon as the choice is made or the action undertaken. All form part of the story that is my life. At every step, I must ask of my decisions and my actions whether I want *this* to be part of that story. I am, in a sense, actively seeking to create the past—at least where I am concerned.

Certainly, part of my concern is with what will be said about me after I am gone—with how I will be remembered. This will be dismissed as narcissism. However, as my readers know I owned (and defended) the narcissist label some time ago.[1] In fact, I don't think that my concern with my pastness is any different from that of my barbarian ancestors, who lived lives they hoped might be set down in sagas and sung about. Perhaps it is

---

[1] http://www.counter-currents.com/2012/04/i-am-an-off-the-chart-narcissist/

this that sets us apart from other people, where history and the past are concerned. We are the people who do not just remember the past, but seek to create a past for ourselves.

Or, at least, that's how we used to be. But Americans and (increasingly) Europeans are shockingly ignorant of history. It is to the future that we moderns now consistently orient ourselves. But the future is indefinite. It offers us no guidance. Only the past is definite; only in the past do we find lessons (really, myths) to live by. The result for our people today is that they are as indefinite as their future: devoid of a center, wishy-washy, changeable, malleable.

Fundamentally, the conflict between Left and Right is the conflict between the future focus and the past focus. Conservatives (real conservatives) are not seeking to go back, which is impossible. They are seeking to go forward, looking to the past for guidance. Finding in the past some evidence for unchangeable human truths. But the Left (and the phony "neo-cons") go forward blindly, sure in the belief that the past has nothing to reveal *because there are no unchangeable human truths.*

As a movement, the New Right seeks to move forward by looking to the past and learning from it. This is the essence of what some of us call Traditionalism. But some of us are also haunted by the thought that our efforts are in vain; that the forces arrayed against us are too strong. Perhaps all the reading, writing, activism, poverty, and self-denial are for nothing.

To such people, I recommend living in the past as I do. And I ask them to imagine that, after death, they could look upon their completed life and take in the whole story. Or to imagine that their life belongs to another, whose biography they happen to be perusing. At a certain point in the story, the life of the New Rightist comes to a crucial juncture: to give in to the doubts and give up; to "get a real job," and join the mainstream. Or to continue the fight and have faith — even if, in fact, it leads to naught. Which is the story that is more admirable? Which sort of man would you be more proud to be? Which is the sort of man that makes history? Only one answer is possible here. The detached focus one needs to see one's life this way is difficult to maintain. Still more difficult, however, is to exercise the will and *compel* yourself to take those actions that you know will make your life the proud story of a great man.

To save the future, we must look to the past—and act. In doing so, we create a glorious past for ourselves. A past that will, I promise you, be the stuff of new sagas. Think about this, when the doubt begins to nag.

Counter-Currents/*North American New Right*,
August 2, 2012

INDEX

A
ABC (TV network), 159
Abolition of Man, The, 9
ACLU, 118
Adenauer, Konrad, 158
Advocate, The, 63, 66
Age of Anxiety, 180, 181
Alberich, 93, 174-75
Allah, 62
Allen, Irving, 95
Allgeier, Sepp, 154
Alpha males, 67, 138; see also Males
Amazon.com, 4
AMC (cable network), 83
American Communist Party, 117, 133
Amis, Kingsley, 26
Amory, Cleveland, 126
Amusing Ourselves to Death, 187
Anarcho-primitivism, 72
Angel, 161
Angst (existential), 204
Anti-Communism, 119-20
Anti-Semitism, 23, 107, 152
Arabs, 24, 149
Arena Productions, 109, 117
Aristotle, 61
Arktos Publishing, 204
Arm and Hammer, 43
Armie Hammer, 129-31
Army of the Unemployed, 145-46
Arnold, David, 30
Art, conceptual, 207
Art, nonrepresentational, 207
Arthurian romance, 113
Asatru, 83
Asians, 139
Asperger's Syndrome, 200
Aston Martin DB5, 10, 15, 33, 35
Atheism, 61, 133
Atlas Shrugged, 17, 180-81, 190-92

Avengers, The (UK TV), 18, 99, 109-110, 126

B
Bach, Steven 154
Balmoral Castle, 170
Banks, Jonathan, 94
Bardem, Javier, 30
Bardot, Brigit, 164, 184, 186
Barnum, P. T., 173
Barry, John, 30
Barthes, Roland, 47
Batman (TV series), 164
Battle for Bond, The, 108
BBC, 118
Beck, Glenn, 201
Beethoven's *Seventh Symphony*, 172
Belle de Jour, 31
Bentham, Jeremy, 146
Benton, Thomas Hart, 207
Berry, Halle, 27
Better Call Saul!, 88, 89-93
Beverly Hillbillies, The, 76
Bible, The, 134
B.I.G.O. (Bureau of International Government and Order), 96-100, 104-05, 130
Big Valley, The, 110
Binder, Maurice, 96
Blacula, 161
Blair, Tony, 24, 170
Blofeld, Ernst Stavro, 14, 17-21, 24-25, 36, 36-45, 96-7, 99, 110, 173
Bloom, Harold Jack, 113
Blue Light, The, 154-55, 158
Blue Velvet, 81
Boardman, Eleanor, 135
Bonanza, 110
Bond, James, 1-45, 47, 95, 100, 108-10, 209
Bonobos, 54
Boone, Richard, 113

Boot camp, 56-57
Bradbury, Ray, 188-89
Brady Bunch, The, 76
Bram Stoker's Dracula (Francis Ford Coppola film), 161
Branden, Barbara, 102n2
Brave New World, 58, 180-87, 192
Brave New World Revisited, 187
Brazilian jiu-jitsu, 46
Breaking Bad, 76-82, 83-88, 89-94
Breker, Arno, 158
British Board of Film Classification, 55
British Communist Party, 23
British Empire, 8, 26
British Royal Family, 168, 171
British Union of Fascists, 97-98
Broccoli, Albert R. "Cubby," 39-40, 95, 116, 122
Bronson, John, 145
Brosnan, John, 10, 14, 17
Brosnan, Pierce, 24, 27-28, 32
Buddha, 54, 62
Buddhism, 54
B.U.F. (British Union of Fascists), 97-98
Buñuel, Luis, 31
Burn After Reading, 200
Burton, Peter, 9n3
Burton, Tim, 159-67, 210
Bush, George W., 148

C
Camp, 164
Camp of the Saints, The, 192
Canadian Highland Regiment, 111
Canadian Union of Fascists, 98
Capitalism, 72, 138, 181-82, 186
Capra, Frank, 150
Carroll, Leo G., 115
Carter, Helen Bonham, 66, 166, 170
Casino Royale (1967 film), 108
Casino Royale (2006 film), 3, 5, 28-29, 166
Casino Royale (CBS TV episode), 108
Casino Royale (novel), 1, 3-4, 7, 25, 108
Cavill, Henry, 129-31
Chayefsky, Paddy, 52
Chomsky, Noam, 138
Christianity, 15, 20, 118, 134
Churchill, Sir Winston, 34, 171
Cirque du Soleil, 173
City Lights (bookstore), 205, 208
Civilian Conservation Corps, 145
Clooney, George, 128, 200
Cobert, Robert, 165
Coen Brothers, 200
Collins, Barnabas, 159-167, 211
Columbia Pictures, 133
Communism, 181-82
Confederate flag, 73
Confucius, 196
Connelly, Cyril, 2
Connery, Sean, 5, 29-30, 39, 95
Consumerism, 183, 192
Conte, Nicola, 131
Cooper, Alice, 166
Cooper, Gary, 191
Coppola, Francis Ford, 161
Craig, Daniel, 28-29, 31, 34, 38, 108, 131, 166
Cranston, Bryan, 81
Crosby, Bing, 95
Cross, Ben, 163
Crowd, The, 134
Cruise, Tom, 128
Cruz, Raymond, 91
Curtis, Dan, 159, 161, 163

D
Dalayman, Katarina, 176
Dalton, Timothy, 28
Danger Man, 109, 126
Dark Shadows (TV series and films), 159-67, 210
Das Rheingold, 174
David Copperfield, 189
Dawson, Anthony, 42
De Tocqueville, Alexis, 105
DEA (U.S. Drug Enforcement Agency), 76, 80
Deakins, Roger, 29

Dean, Jimmy, 44
"Death of the author," 47
Death rays, 99, 104
Debicki, Elizabeth, 131-32
Deighton, Len, 39
Delavan, Mark, 175
Dench, Judy, 27, 30
Depp, Johnny, 162, 164, 166
Der Berg des Schicksals, 153
Der Ring des Nibelungen, 173-79
Deutsche Oper am Rhein, 177
Diamonds are Forever, 25, 39, 43, 45
Dictator, dictatorship, 133, 138, 142-43, 146
Die Tochter des Samurai, 156
Die Walküre, 174, 176
Disney Company, 177
Diversity, 139, 186, 209
DKNY, 48
Donovan, Jack, 63, 79, 83
Doublespeak, 185-86
Dr. No (novel or film), 2, 4, 6, 9-10n3, 13, 17n10, 27, 31, 39, 42, 95, 109
Dracula (Dan Curtis TV film), 161
Dragons and St. George, The, (proposed TV series), 113
Drasnin, Robert, 131
Durden, Tyler, 52-56, 59, 69-70, 200
Dystopia, 180-92

E
Edward VIII (later Duke of Windsor), 168, 170
Ed Wood (film), 164; see also Edward D. Wood, Jr.
Eleventh Hour, The, 112
Elizabeth (a film about Queen Elizabeth I), 169
Elizabeth I, 169
Elizabeth II, 22, 170, 171
Elizabeth, the Queen Mother, 170
End of History and the Last Man, The, 182
End of History, 52, 55, 180
Englehard, Charles W., Jr., 24
Enter the Dragon, 41

Entertainment Weekly, 63
Eon Productions, 1, 28, 39-40, 116
Ethnomasochism, 24
Evola, Baron Julius, 5

F
Fahrenheit 451, 180, 188-90, 192
Fanck, Arnold, 153-56
Fantasia of the Unconscious, 86
Fascism, 55, 71-72, 95, 100, 133-34, 141-42, 150-51, 156; see also New Right; the Right
Fascist Insignia, 95-105
Felton, Norman, 108-19, 122, 126
Femininity, 53, 61-62
Feminism, 186, 209
Fields, Peter Allen, 104
Fiennes, Ralph, 36
Fight Club, 32, 46-75, 86, 89, 170, 182, 200
Film noir, 30
Fincher, David, 47, 75
Finney, Albert, 33
First World War; see Great War
Firth, Colin, 169
"Flash and Circle," 99
Fleming, Ian, 1-8, 17-18, 21-26, 31, 33, 38-41, 47, 95-6, 108-22
Flint, Derek, 6, 99-104
For Your Eyes Only (film), 3, 40, 45, 97
Fountainhead, The, 92, 134, 190
Fox News, 198, 201-2
Frankfurt School, 65
Freudianism, 36, 65
Frid, Jonathan, 161-62, 164
Fried, Gerald, 131
Friedman, Milton, 190
From Russia With Love (film), 2, 9, 11, 17, 21, 25, 39, 42, 97, 109
From Russia With Love (novel), 39
Führer, 133, 138; see also Führer-Prinzip
Führer-Prinzip, 101; see also Führer

G
Gabriel, Archangel, 145, 149

Gabriel Over the White House, 133, 142-43, 147, 149
Gay (sexual identity), 25, 44, 51, 61-66, 175
Gayson, Eunice, 6
Gelb, Peter, 173-74, 176, 178
George VI, 168-69, 171
German Requiem, 172
Germany, 21, 83, 120, 154, 156, 166
Gilbert, Lewis, 43
Gilligan, Vince, 80, 87, 89
Gilligan's Island, 76
Girl From U.N.C.L.E., The, 107, 112, 124
God, 1, 20, 60-62, 64, 74, 139, 171, 177, 196
Gold Key Comics, 162
Goldeneye, 24, 27, 31, 36
Goldfinger (novel or film), 10, 15, 24, 31, 33-34, 109, 116-17
Goldfinger, Ernö, 23-24
Gone with the Wind, 47
Gothic romance, 159, 211
Götterdämmerung, 174, 176
Grahame-Smith, Seth, 166
Gray, Charles, 44
Great Depression, 136, 144, 150
Great Souled Man, 74
Great War (World War I), 149
Greek drama, 209
Green Acres, 136
Green, Eva, 166
Griffith, D. W., 146
Ground Zero, 175
Guardian, The, 2
Gunsmoke, 110

H
Hagakure: The Book of the Samurai, 7
Hall of Presidents, 177
Hall, Grayson, 161
Hall, Sam, 161
Hallelujah!, 139
Hamburger sandwich, 190
Hamilton, Donald, 95
Hannity, Sean, 198, 201
Harris, Naomie, 31

Harrison, Noel, 126
Have Gun – Will Travel, 110, 112-13, 120
Hawthorne, Derek, 53, 68, 86, 153
Hearst, William Randolph, 142, 151
Heart *chakra*, 57
Heathcote, Bella, 166
Hedonism, 2, 5, 7-8, 100-102, 197
Hefner, Hugh, 101
Hegel, G. W. F., 54, 61
Heidegger, Martin, 18, 182
Helm, Matt, 6, 95-102, 104, 130, 132
Hemingway, Ernest, 62
Hermann, Bernard, 189
Hermeneutic of suspicion, 65
Herostratus, 74
Hitchcock, Alfred, 115, 209
Hitchens, Christopher, 171, 187-88
Hitler, Adolf, 18, 124n4, 130, 133, 146, 152, 153, 155, 156, 158, 171, 172, 207
Holmes, Sherlock, 8, 211
Holy Mountain, The, 153-54
Homeland Security, 148
Homoeroticism, 65, 130
Homogenization, 18, 38
Honor, 50, 54, 80, 110, 161
Hoover, Herbert, 136, 146
Hoovervilles, 136, 138
Hopper, Edward, 207
House of Commons, 34
House of Dark Shadows, 163
House Un-American Activities Committee, 44
Huston, John, 145
Huston, Walter, 143, 145, 146-47
Huxley, Aldous, 181-92

I
I Spy, 131
IBM, 49
Ideal Toy Co., 116
IKEA, 48, 55
Iliad, the, 52
Implicit Whiteness, 71
Impressionen unter Wasser, 152, 156

In Like Flint, 100
Indefinite detention, 148
Indiana Jones and the Kingdom of the Crystal Skull, 36
Individualists, 203
Ingster, Boris, 126
Interview with the Vampire, 161
It Takes a Thief, 129

J
Jägermeister, 46
James Bond Dossier, The, 26
Jefferson, Thomas, 146
Jesus, 21, 62
John Reed Clubs, 117
Johnson, Greg, 74, 136
Johnson, Paul, 2-3
Jurgens, Curt, 40

K
Kali Yuga, 202
Karma yoga, 57
Keene, Tom, 135
Kennedy, John F., 2
Kettner, Horst, 155, 157
Kim Il-Sung, 186
King's Speech, The, 168-72
Kiss the Girls and Make Them Die, 99
Klebb, Rosa, 1, 25
Klee, Paul, 207
Kojak, 16
Krafft, Charles, 204-07
Kuluva, Will, 115
Kurosawa, Akira, 156
Kuryakin, Illya, 104, 113, 115, 119-20, 125, 128-30

L
La Cava, Gregory, 133, 146, 150
Labour Party, 24
Lacanianism, 65
Land of the Giants, 101
Lang, Fritz, 175-76
Larsen, Chris, 137, 141
Last Man or Men, the, 48, 55, 104, 180, 192
Last of the Nuba, The, 156

Laverne and Shirley, 90
Lawrence, D. H., 86
Lazenby, George, 36
Lee (novel), 193-97
Lee, Bruce, 41
Left, the, 1, 101, 103, 117, 141-43, 158, 184, 191, 213
Leni Riefenstahl: A Life, 152n1, 154n2
Leni: The Life and Work of Leni Riefenstahl, 154n2
Lepage, Robert, 173-74, 178
Lewis, C., S., 9
Liberalism, 15, 20
Licence To Kill (film), 3, 27, 30, 34
Lightning bolt, 97, 99-101, 105-06
Limbaugh, Rush, 201, 202
Lincoln, Abraham, 65, 146-47
Lippmann, Walter, 143
Live and Let Die (film), 20, 25, 29, 32
Live and Let Die (novel), 3, 22,
Lloyd George, David, 143
Logue, Lionel, 168-69, 171
Logue, Robert, 169-70
Lookism, 1
L'Osservatore Romano, 2
Louvre (musem), 74
Luisi, Fabio, 176
Lynch, David, 81
Lynch, Trevor, 162

M
Mad Men, 132, 181, 209
Maibaum, Richard, 109
Males, 32, 53; see also Alpha males
Man From U.N.C.L.E, The (TV), 99, 103-5, 107-27, 128-132
Man From U.N.C.L.E., The (film), 128-32
Man with the Golden Gun, The, 7, 15, 20, 25, 29, 30, 31
Männerbund, 57, 59, 65, 68
Manosphere, 83
Martin, Dean, 95
Marxism, 107, 117, 181, 185
Masculinity, 6, 50-51, 53, 54, 60-62, 64, 67, 79, 84

Master-Slave dialectic, 54-55
Materialism, 54
Matheson, Richard, 161
Matrix, The, 181
Maverick, 110
McCallum, David, 107, 119, 127-30
McClory, Kevin, 40-45, 96, 108
McDaniel, David, 104
McDonald's, 165
McGoohan, Patrick, 115
McKean, Michael, 90
Meet John Doe, 150
Mein Kampf, 124n4, 155
Mendes, Sam, 29
Mephistopheles, 166
Metropolis, 175-76
Metropolitan Opera ("The Met"), 173, 175
MGM (Metro-Goldwyn-Mayer), 109, 112, 116-17, 135, 139, 142, 150
MI6, 27, 30-31, 34, 36
Microsoft, 49
Mirren, Helen, 168
Mishima, Yukio, 74
Mission: Impossible (TV series), 99
MIT (Massachusetts Institute of Technology), 74
Mitchum, Robert, 210
Mithras, 62
MMA (mixed martial arts), 65
Modern art, 203-07
Modern civilization, 84-85
Moltke, Alexandra (Countess Cornelia Alexandra Moltke), 159
Mona Lisa, 74, 178-79
Moneypenny, Miss, 12, 36
Moore, Roger, 30
Morgan, John, 204
Morley, Karen, 135, 144
Morricone, Ennio, 131
Morris, Jay Hunter, 176
Mosley, Sir Oswald, 97-99
Mozart's *Marriage of Figaro*, 172
Müller, Ray, 156-58
Murderers' Row, 98, 132

Murray, James, 135
Mussolini Speaks, 133
Mussolini, Benito, 99, 130, 133, 150
My Man Godfrey, 150
Mythology, Germanic, 15, 61

N

Naked Spur, The, 113
Narcissism, 212
Nation, The, 142, 148
National Socialism (i.e. "Nazism"), 71, 130, 158
NBC, 107, 112, 116-17, 133
Neo-cons, 213
Netflix, 168, 210
Network, 46, 52
Never Say Never Again, 39, 45
New Right, 107, 203; see also The Right; Fascism
Newman, Alec, 164
Newman, Thomas, 30
Newmar, Julie, 203
Newspeak, 185-86
Nietzsche, Friedrich, 61, 74, 104, 190-91, 208
Night of Dark Shadows, 163
Nihilism, 57-58, 61, 69, 74-75, 187
Nine Inch Nails, 74
Nineteen Eighty-Four, 180, 185-88, 192
North by Northwest, 115
Norton, Edward, 32, 47, 66
Notorious, 115
NVKD, 126

O

O'Connor, Flannery, 194
Objectivist Newsletter, The, 119n2
Objectivist, The, 101
"Octopussy" (short story), 22
Octopussy (film), 23, 27
Odenkirk, Bob, 89
Odin, 15, 61
Olympia, 152, 158
On Her Majesty's Secret Service (film), 11, 20, 35-36, 43
On Her Majesty's Secret Service

(novel), 8, 38
Operation Desert Storm, 163
Orwell, George, 185-88
Oswald, Lee Harvey, 2
Our Daily Bread, 133-44, 146-47, 150
Our Man Flint, 100-102
Out of the Past, 210
Overman, 26; see also Superman; Übermensch

P
Palahniuk, Chuck, 47, 51, 56, 64, 66, 69, 71, 72, 74-75
Palance, Jack, 161
Parrott, Matt, 138
Parzival, 16
Patriot Act, 186
Paul, Aaron, 81
Pemberton, Daniel, 131
Percy, Eric Hamilton, 98
Perdue, Tito, 193-97
Phenomenology of Spirit, 54
Pitt, Brad, 46, 53, 55-56, 64, 66
Plan Nine from Outer Space, 135
Plato, 49, 182
Pleasance, Donald, 40, 43
Pohlmann, Eric, 42
Political correctness, 185-86
Pornography, 48, 51, 58, 74
Postman, Neil, 187, 189
Prisoner, The, 115, 126, 180
Proctor & Gamble, 159
Prohibition, 147
Puccini, Giacomo, 178
Pulp Fiction, 128
Purvis, Neal, 30

Q
Quantum of Solace, 29, 34, 131
Queen, The (film), 168
Quo Vadis? (film), 210

R
Race, 24, 63, 65, 123, 186, 191-92, 195-97
Racialism, 1, 21-26, 71, 139, 191
Racism, 1, 21, 191

Radical Faeries, 66
Rand, Ayn, 17, 40, 102, 119-20, 134, 190-91, 207
Raspail, Jean, 192
Rawhide, 110
Readers' Digest, 141
Realism, 16-17, 159
Reichsarbeitsdienst, 146
Ren (human-heartedness), 196
Republic, the (Plato), 49, 139, 182
Return of The Man From U.N.C.L.E.: The Fifteen Years Later Affair, The, 105, 129, 130
Riefenstahl, Leni, 152-58
Right, the, 2, 103, 142-43; see also Fascism; New Right
Rinehard, 143
Ring Cycle, 173, 177
Rivera, Diego, 206
Rockefeller Center, 72
Roddenberry, Gene, 115
Rolfe, Sam, 103-04, 112-25
Romantic Manifesto, The, 119n2
Romantic realism, 17
Romper Stomper, 57
Roosevelt, Eleanor, 143, 146
Roosevelt, Franklin Delano, 142-43, 145-46
Ross, Dan (a.k.a. Marilyn Ross), 162
Rowan and Martin's Laugh-In, 126
Rush, Geoffrey, 169

S
Sadat, Anwar, 158
Sadism, 2-3
Sagas, 16, 21, 212, 214
Saltzman, Harry, 39, 95, 116, 122
Samurai, 7, 66, 156
San Francisco Art Institute, 205-8
Savage, Doc, 8, 100
Savalas, Telly, 43
Savitri Devi, 38
Schenk, Otto, 173, 175
Schneeberger, Hans, 154
Schopenhauer, Arthur, 61
Science fiction, 16, 17

Scott, Kathryn Leigh, 160
Second World War, 34, 88-100, 155
Seehorn, Rhea, 92
Seidler, David, 169-72
Sermon on the Mount, 19
Seven Golden Men, 131
Shiva, 62
Siegfried, 176
Silencers, The, 95-98
Simpson, Wallis (later Duchess of Windsor), 168, 170
Skyfall, 1, 2, 27-37, 38, 42, 45
Slave morality, 191, 192
Smersh, 122
Soap operas, 159-60, 163
Socialism, 137-38
Socrates, 139
Soderbergh, Steven, 129
Soft totalitarianism, 186
Sokal, Harry, 153
Solo (proposed TV series), 112, 117
Solo, Napoleon, 103-04, 110-22
Sontag, Susan, 156
Sony Pictures, 40
S.O.S. Iceberg, 155
Southern gothic, 193
Soviets, 17-18, 102
Sparv, Camilla, 132
S.P.E.C.T.R.E., 17-18, 38-42, 96-98, 119, 121-22, 130
Spectre (film), 38-45
Spengler, Oswald, 177
Spicer, Joanna, 118-19
Spiderman (film or musical), 173
Spinner, Anthony, 126
Spy in the Green Hat, The, 124-25
Spy Spoofs, 95, 98-100, 105, 108-09
Spy Who Loved Me, The (film), 116
Spy Who Loved Me, The (novel), 15-16, 18, 20, 25, 40, 116
St. John, Jill, 44
Stagecoach, 110
Stalin, Joseph, 99, 186
Star Trek, 115
Star Wars, 15-16, 29
Starbucks, 49

Starsky and Hutch, 16
Steele, Barbara, 163
Stella Natura festival, 87
Stepin Fetchit, 113
Stewart, James, 113, 135
Stoker, Bram, 161
Storm over Mont Blanc, 68
Streicher, Julius, 152
Superman (archetype), 15; see also Overman; Übermensch
S.W.A.T., 16

T

Tannhäuser, 177
Tarantino, Quentin, 128
Television, 15-16, 52, 76, 83, 95-99, 108, 112, 114, 125, 163, 167-70, 180, 188-89, 210
Temple of Diana at Ephesus, 74
Tennyson, Alfred, Lord, 34
Thomas Crown Affair, The, 131
Thomas, Lowell, 133
Thoughtcrime, 185-86
Three Stooges, the, 47
Thrush, 100-106, 121-32
Thumos, 48-53, 61, 71, 182, 183
Thunderball (film), 39-40, 42, 97-98, 114, 129
Thunderball (novel), 17, 38-39, 96, 108
Thunderbirds, 11
Tiefland, 152, 156
Tiny Tim (Herbert Khaury), 162
Tomorrow Never Dies, 27
Tone, Franchot, 144
Traditionalism, 43, 72, 76, 213
Trenker, Luis, 153, 154
Triumph of the Will, 71, 152, 155, 158
True Blood, 161
Truffaut, Francois, 188
Trustafarians, 206
TSA (U.S. Transportation Safety Authority), 49, 209
Tsunetomo, Yamamoto, 7n2
Tuna (ethical), 205
Tweed, Thomas Frederic, 143
Twentieth-Century Fox, 101

Index

Twilight Saga (films), 161, 162, 167
Übermensch, 55, 134; see also Superman; Overman

U

UFC (Ultimate Fighting Championship), 46, 65, 77
Uhls, Jim, 47, 75
"Ulysses" (poem), 35
Uncanny, the, 160, 167
U.N.C.L.E. (United Network Command for Law and Enforcement), 103-04, 114-15, 117, 119, 128, 130, 132
Union Movement (post-War Mosley organization), 98
Untermenschen, 50
Ur, 187

V

Valentine's Day, 198, 205
Valentino, Rudolph, 53
Valhalla, 175
Vaughn, Robert, 107, 119-20, 126-30
Vedanta, 183
Venus, 12
Vermont Teddy Bear Co., 198-201
Vidor, King, 133-42
View To A Kill, A, 7, 23, 30
Vikander, Alicia, 131
Virility (Spiritual), 5-8, 96

Volsung Saga, 16
von Bülow, Claus, 159
von Sydow, Max. 45

W

Wade, Robert, 30
Wagner, Richard, 176-79
Waltz, Christophe, 41, 43
Wanger, Walter, 142
Warhead, 39-40
Way of Men, The, 79, 83
WB network, 164
Werick, Jan, 43
White Nationalism, 83
Whittingham, Jack, 38, 96, 108
Wonderful, Horrible Life of Leni Riefenstahl, The, 152, 156-58
Wood, Edward D. "Ed" Jr., 135; see also *Ed Wood* (film)
World Is Not Enough, The, 7, 8, 25
Wotan, 175-77

Y

Yes, Minister, 27
YMCA, 51
You Only Live Twice (film), 11, 20, 38, 40, 42-43, 97, 113, 121
You Only Live Twice (novel), 2

Z

Zen, 56

ABOUT THE AUTHOR

Jef Costello is the penname of a high-functioning bipolar narcissist with a touch of Asperger's who resides in a palatial, book-lined apartment in an unfashionable area of New York City. His many essays and reviews have appeared online at *North American New Right*, the webzine of Counter-Currents Publishing (www.counter-currents.com). He is the author of the novel *Heidegger in Chicago: A Comedy of Errors* (San Francisco: Counter-Currents, 2015). His writings have been translated into French, German, Russian, and Swedish.

www.ingramcontent.com/pod-product-compliance
Lightning Source LLC
Chambersburg PA
CBHW030336131224
18858CB00001B/53

9 781940 933085